Robert Cox is a former journalist and 'Eurocrat', with a professional profile ranging from diplomacy to management of EU humanitarian affairs. He is currently active with a policy think-tank in Brussels and divides his time between there, South-west France and travel.

Roger Sherwin spent his working life holding senior executive positions in a wide variety of engineering sectors, ranging from power stations to hospitals, and prisons to the mining industry. Now retired, he is pursuing his interests in photography, golf and wood carving, and continues to enjoy tastes and cultures around the world.

Tony Thompson is a former director of International House – an international chain of English as a Foreign Language schools – in London and Rome and subsequently set up his own EFL organization. Whilst at Cambridge University, he ran against Oxford University and played rugby for Middlesex. He enjoys walking and travel.

THE KOMBI TRAIL

Across Three Continents in a VW Van

Robert Cox
Roger Sherwin
Tony Thompson

I.B. TAURIS
LONDON · NEW YORK

Published in 2013 by I.B.Tauris & Co Ltd
6 Salem Road, London W2 4BU
175 Fifth Avenue, New York NY 10010
www.ibtauris.com

Distributed in the United States and Canada
Exclusively by Palgrave Macmillan
175 Fifth Avenue, New York NY 10010

ISBN: 978 1 78076 376 7

A full CIP record for this book is available from the British Library
A full CIP record is available from the Library of Congress

Library of Congress Catalog Card Number: available

Designed by Anne Sørensen

Typeset by Paul Tompsett at freerangeproduction.com

Printed in China

CONTENTS

Foreword – VW Kombi Phenomenon   vii

List of Photographs   ix

Preface – Bridging a Half-Century   xv

Prologue – Thumbing One's Way Through Africa   xix

An Idea Comes to Life   xxi

Maps   xxix

MOSCOW CALLING

1. Hiccups and Rumbles   2
2. Into Russia's Realm   5
3. Summer in Moscow   13
4. How to Get Out of Russia   31
5. Yugoslavia's Zenith   40

FROM ASIA'S EDGE

6. Anatolia – Eurasia's Crucible   50
7. A Bit Too Far East   62
8. Iranian Dynasties   67
9. Children of Abraham   83

TO ASIA'S HEARTLAND

10. Turkish Connections   102
11. Testing Afghan Patience   118
12. Kabul Before the Winter   127
13. To the Oxus – How Mehmed Pushed His Luck   143

SOUTH TO SERENDIPITY

14. Beyond the Indus   164
15. The Long, High Valleys of Nepal   188
16. A Would-Be Paradise – Ceylon   199

TASTING INDEPENDENCE

17. Into Africa   212
18. North to the Nile   229
19. Stand-Off in Cyprus   251

Epilogue   256

Kombi Z1235 – In Memoriam of a Faithful Chariot   264

Appendix: Distances Travelled by Kombis Between Major Cities   265

Index   267

FOREWORD

VW Kombi Phenomenon

On a fine June morning one of the authors of this book met a number of Volkswagen Transporter Kombi vans and Beetles of all ages streaming along a road in South West France. It turned out they were heading for the town of Rocamadour, perched high above a gorge, and a celebrated pilgrimage site for a over thousand years. This was a modern, motorised pilgrimage. Kombi owners do indeed get fervent about their vehicles.

The young men who undertook the Cambridge Afro-Asian Expedition fifty years ago still turn their heads today as one passes on the road. The modern version is still recognisably the same versatile and durable Kombi they knew then despite all the modern conveniences that equip those vehicles today. Fifty years ago Kombis were just fitted with basics – wheels, gears, steering, brakes – no bad thing given the challenges they faced during the Expedition.

Volkswagen Commercial Vehicles is proud to be associated with this book for several reasons. The Volkswagen Transporter Kombi has indeed become something of an icon and cult vehicle. And, more to the point, this is an unusual book spanning two generations of a fast changing world in three dynamic and often tormented continents. At one point the book says the Expedition experience of the Kombis was '… certainly better than carting vegetables around grocery stores, builders' materials or school kids anywhere from Bremen to Barcelona as so many of her lowly sisters did …'. Wherever they are, whatever they do, these are work-horses, treated unsparingly by generations of drivers.

As Europe's – indeed the world's – leading manufacturer of motor vehicles, Volkswagen is conscious of being a company with a European and global, not just a national, culture. The Cambridge Afro-Asian Expedition was run by British students but throughout the tale that their book tells we are constantly reminded of young Europeans, conscious of their emerging European identity, in empathy with the wider world of peoples, countries and cultures that are increasingly, in a globalising world, Europe's own close neighbourhood.

THE KOMBI TRAIL

The current model of Kombi
from VW (2012). The looks
have changed, but the heart is
still there.

This book is a landmark on how Europe and the wider world evolves and faces up
to the enormous challenges of the twenty-first century. Much patience and effort
went into producing it. Volkswagen Commercial Vehicles also joins the authors in
acknowledging a particular debt to the publishers, I.B.Tauris, and particularly to
Jo Godfrey, for her painstaking, imaginative and frequently patient encouragement
and guidance to all concerned through its preparation and publication.

LIST OF PHOTOGRAPHS

St Catharine's College Cambridge in 1960, where it all began. xiv

Bob transferred supplies from College to the British Rail container. xxii

Tim supervised the loading of supplies at the railway station in Ostend. 3

Traffic was light through Prague, Czechoslovakia, the first country visited behind the 'Iron Curtain'. 7

Tony and Traicho talking with a local in Prague. 8

Young Pioneers in distinctive uniform in the centre of Prague; they were the Soviet Bloc replacement for our scouting movement. 8

Farmer's transport, east of Warsaw, Poland – market day. 10

The friendly face of a local farmer. 10

Ostankino campsite, Moscow. Tim was repacking the extraordinary weight of food and supplies that was carried in each 1200cc Kombi. 14

Dominating the Moscow skyline at the time, the Ministry of Foreign Affairs. 14

The queue to visit the mausoleum containing the embalmed bodies of Lenin and Stalin. St Basil's is in the background, at the far end of Red Square. 15

Part of the mausoleum queue. The frocks were typical of the time. 16

The local petrol station. 18

The Chairman of the students' Komsomol Committee in his office. 20

The dinner hosted for the Komsomol Committee. 21

The classic symbol of Communism – officially entitled 'Worker and Collective-Farm Woman'; it is now dismantled, and the pieces stored in a lock-up on the outskirts of Moscow. 23

Traicho and Mehmed outside a Moscow hospital; Mehmed was recovering after 'nuclear' treatment. 28

Women hand-painting white lines in the middle of a busy Moscow street. 29

THE KOMBI TRAIL

The centre of Kiev was pleasantly tree-lined, and had a mature feel and style, in contrast to Moscow. 32

This small delivery vehicle was on the outskirts of Orel, and normally used for luggage, but apparently occasionally used to take away dissidents! 32

In Romania, the Kombi, flying the Union Jack and the Bulgarian flag, attracted a lot of curiosity from the locals. 36

The traditional white costume worn by the northern Romanian peasant farmers was distinctive and set them apart from the Russian peasants with their rather drab clothes. 36

Harvest time in the Ukraine, with mainly women in the fields, little mechanization, and men driving the horse and trailer! 45

The vast wheat lands of the Ukraine. 45

An abundance of fresh food outside the Iron Curtain – fish sellers by the side of the Bosphorus, Istanbul. 51

There were many spiralling roads, of uncertain surface quality, in the mountainous areas of central Turkey. 56

A typical mountain village with flat-roofed, stone-built houses, in eastern Turkey. 56

The end of the day – sunset on the two Kombis by the Black Sea coast, northern Turkey. 57

Driving – or leading – a herd of goats, in eastern Turkey. 60

Market stall in Tashkent. 64

Tea break, northern Iran. Left to right – Peter, Tony, Bob, Tim, Roger. 68

Typical village spring in northern Iran, forming the centre of village activity. 68

Darius' palace at Persepolis, which had been excavated only 30 years previously. 73

The size was breathtaking. This shows one of the four flights of stairs forming the Grand Staircase. 74

Seventeenth-century Lutfullah Mosque, originally a ladies' mosque, on Maidan Square. 77

Uniquely decorated cream tilework and lattice windows on the dome of Lutfullah Mosque. 78

Islamic decoration. 78

Food vendor, Kombi and mix of clothing on a typical Teheran street. 80

The long drive westwards from Hamadan to the Iran/Iraq border. 84

Shepherd's accommodation, western Iran. 84

A relatively minor hazard for the fully laden Kombi *en route*. 85

Bedouin encampment near the Roman city of Jerash in Jordan. 88

Jordanian children off to school, smartly dressed, on the eastern outskirts of Jerusalem. 91

Going through the Mandelbaum Gate, accompanied by the British Consul – the only way to go from Jordan to Israel in 1961. 91

First sight of modern, westernized Israel. 93

The UN post at the Gaza Strip. Visitors could stand with one foot in Israel and one in Egypt. 95

The Kombi being loaded onto a boat at Haifa, destined for Turkey. 96

Crossing the Bosphorus at Istanbul, this boat looked in imminent danger of sinking. 97

Accommodation at the British Embassy's summer cottage, on the outskirts of Istanbul, overlooking the Bosphorus. Bob was never photographed without a cigarette drooping from his mouth! 98

Last tea break on the way home after four months. The Colman two-burner petrol stove performed dutifully throughout the trip. 98

'Doctor' Thompson administering to the local tribal chief who had wrenched his hand driving the first tractor to come to his village. 105

Male-dominated group posing for the wedding party. Westerners were seldom seen in the Turkmen Sahra. 110

Preparing *pilau* for the all-day wedding feast. 111

The men did prepare some food. 112

As part of the wedding celebrations, there were horse races for 'bareback' boys, aged between 9 and 15. These boys were racing near the finish. 112

Wrestling was part of the day's entertainment, and winners were given small cash prizes. 114

Several judges ensured that nobody cheated, and the elders distributed the prize money. 114

The food drum, used to feed warriors before a battle, in the Friday Mosque, Herat.   119

The Friday Mosque of Herat (or Masjid-i-Jame Mosque), Afghanistan. It was originally built by the Timurids of mud bricks, with tiles decorating the exterior.   120

The camel train was a common sight on the drive to Kabul.   123

One of the sixth-century giant Buddhas at Bamiyan, on one of the old Silk Routes in the Hindu Kush, north of Kabul.   139

There were five linked lakes near to Bamiyan. The rich blue colour comes from the travertine walls of the lakes.   140

The terrain was harsh near the Band-e-Amir lakes.   141

Barefoot child in Kunduz, northern Afghanistan. There was a wide mix of ethnic groups here including Tajiks, Pashtuns, Hazaras, Uzbeks and even Arabs.   144

Some were better shod.   145

Mehmed, on the left, photographed at the start of his unauthorized trip north to the River Oxus.   146

Impromptu *chai* and a lie-down outside the blue mosque in Mazar.   150

Street barber in Mazar.   150

Local transport – a *ghari*.   151

The mosque in the holy city of Mazar-i-Sharif.   153

Selling watermelons by the roadside, Hindu Kush.   155

The road over the Hindu Kush, northern Afghanistan.   156

Fruit stall and local tribesmen from north of the Hindu Kush.   156

Driving through the Khyber Pass, an essential part of the old Silk Road, into Pakistan.   165

Accommodation was provided at Jahanzeb College, Mingora; since destroyed by an earthquake.   169

The Kombi was well protected by 'pistol wallahs' provided by the governor of Swat.   170

Young girl on bed, Mingora.   171

Driving further north up the Swat valley, pausing 15 miles from Kalam, before driving on to Gabral, some 7,300 feet above sea level, mainly with the Kombi in first gear. 173

Well north of Mingora in the Swat valley, northern Pakistan, was this curious but wary child. 173

Driving in the Swat valley. 174

The custodian at the Golden Temple at Amritsar in India provided suitable clothing before entering the temple. 176

Sikh service in the Golden Temple. 176

One of many university buildings in Chandigarh, a shrine of modern architecture. 178

Dancing monkey at Fatehpur Sikri. 183

Custodian of the temple at Fatehpur Sikri. 184

A typical street in Benares (now Varanasi), the centre of Hinduism in India. 185

Bathing in the Ganges, which is meant to be pure despite the ashes from funeral pyres. 186

Buddhist votive offerings. 189

A Hindu temple photographed late in the day in Kathmandu. 190

Street sellers. 191

Friends playing. 191

Kathmandu 'Orchestra'; they were more photogenic than musical! 193

The enthusiastic young soloist of the orchestra. 195

Busy life on the streets. 196

The British Embassy bungalow at Kakani was said to have some of the best views of the Himalayas. 198

Visits were made to several schools in Colombo. 200

Climbing towards Adam's Peak. 202

Huge elephant about to charge in Yala National Park, Ceylon (now Sri Lanka). 205

Escaping from the elephant, they returned to Colombo in more tranquil surroundings. 206

THE KOMBI TRAIL

Near Arusha, in Tanganyika (now Tanzania), a Masai 'standing guard' over the Kombi.   218

Kombi admirers in Uganda.   219

Enthusiastic students at a school in East Africa.   222

North from Nairobi, Kenya, *en route* to Ethiopia, passing these harvesters …   224

… and one learning to play the drums in northern Kenya.   225

Sunset in East Africa.   227

A warm welcome was given at the Norwegian mission in Alge.   231

There was more than a little trouble *en route* from the Kenyan border to Dilla just across the border in Ethiopia; four-wheel drive was normally considered essential, but the Kombi struggled through.   232

Meeting the camel train …   233

… they eventually arrived on this extremely muddy main road in Dilla …   234

… and there was not another vehicle in sight.   234

At the border town of Kassala, there was a wait for a convoy to assemble, as there was no discernable road to Khartoum!   242

Finally arriving in Khartoum. This was the main shopping street.   242

The government flew Mehmed and Nigel to Gezira – an area between the White and Blue Niles, which was a successful, major cotton-producing project.   243

Traditional Egypt – one man and his camel.   245

The journey onward was by train, with the Kombi on a flat car, to Wadi Halfa in Egypt. Then by boat to Aswan to see the Pharaohs, which had to be moved when the dam was built later.   247

The face of Egypt.   248

Photographs credited to Mehmed Demirer and Roger Sherwin.

PREFACE

Bridging a Half-Century

With the passage of time Tony Thompson had begun to suspect that before long his children and grandchildren would start asking what all those papers yellowing and gathering dust in the loft were all about. Inveterate traveller, former athlete, he still hikes long distances with a 40-pound pack. He graduated from Cambridge in law, only to abandon it for a more rewarding career in teaching the English language to foreigners. Thus the world was, in different ways, his oyster. Hidden amid those yellowing pages of diaries and scribblings from half a century ago was the story of a combination of travels – the Cambridge Afro-Asian Expedition 1961–2, by eight young men from Cambridge (plus one from Oxford) on the eve of different careers. Tony's travelling companions of that time also had lofts, cellars or places under the stairs hiding papers, maps, photographs and other memories of thousands of miles travelled across three continents at a time when officialdom of all kinds did its damnedest to obstruct free movement. After all these years most of them were still in touch. Traicho Belopopski, a swarthy Bulgarian Communist youth activist and former army officer, had died not long before. Anthony Swanwick, the dapper gentleman from Oxford, was lost somewhere in America.

At his seventeenth-century farmhouse on the edge of the Cotswolds Tony hosted the group for a first brainstorming as winter drew nigh in 2008. What should be done with all these papers, photos, files and other mementos? 'How about a book?' And so it was to be.

Work started in real earnest the following summer under the bougainvilleas at the home in Bodrum, on Turkey's Aegean coast, of Mehmed Arif Demirer. Mehmed is a businessman with fingers in several pies, volumes of writing on the state of his native Turkey and elsewhere to his credit, and is now dipping his toes once more in the swirling waters of Turkish politics. He had been the father of the Expedition when he was a restless young Cambridge engineering student. Most available floor-space at Mehmed's house was soon covered with old papers, pictures and newspaper cuttings. Tried and stretched memories were put to work over several days of sorting this stuff out. Tim Parkinson, the expedition's 'chief engineer', with a career behind him in industry ranging from diesels to aircraft, when not dinghy-sailing, applied computers and scanners to all this stuff. Evening sundowners, the delicious Turkish cooking of Mehmed's wife, Gül, or sea-fresh fish at a nearby cove, boosted enthusiasm for distilling life out of these half-century-old mementoes into some form of recognizable shape. Then followed months of writing and related head-scratching. Three of the companions particularly wielded their pens: Roger Sherwin, a former senior executive with major British engineering firms in their heyday, an aggressive rugby wing-forward in his youth, now a sculptor of no mean talent; Tony, as 'supervisor'; and Bob Cox, once a journalist and then a 'Eurocrat', that breed held in high suspicion in today's Britain, working in different guises from diplomatic, to managerial, to peace-keeper. Bob wrote the final edit of this book; Roger, in addition to writing, would mastermind the photographs. Most participants' pens have left their traces. Absent from this Turkish fray were: Nigel Robertson, ebullient historian turned accountant, with a most prodigious memory; and Peter, now Lord, Temple-Morris, barrister and politician with a keen nose for geopolitics.

More will emerge about these characters as the story unfolds.

Oh – and before one forgets – there are two other key characters in this saga, two little ladies: the two vehicles which conveyed the Expedition during its travels and travails – a brace of Volkswagen Kombis whose little engines and rugged bodies, with good nature and occasional protest, suffered the abuse of their young masters over some 28,000 miles and 12 months between them.

What's so special? Well, travel of this sort in those days was not undertaken lightly. It was travel, moreover, in a region fraught today with uncertainty and insecurity and no soft option then. Over the span of half a century the companions of this journey, in the light of their different backgrounds, profiles and professional experience, but of one generation, offer here in this book special glimpses into a fast-changing world.

The Expedition prospectus concluded: '... *with the material obtained, to write a book on return.*'

It took another 50 years to get that book written. Here it is.

Writing it was a great pleasure and educative. Hopefully, it will entertain you, the reader, as well.

PROLOGUE

Thumbing One's Way Through Africa

'I bet I can hitchhike from Cape Town to Cairo.' Mehmed Demirer was never short of ways to shake up a typical, dull winter afternoon in Cambridge. In January 1960, talking travel with friends over tea, Mehmed threw down his challenge. No one seemed impressed. So Mehmed added: '£100. Any takers?' College mate Alistair Pirie across the table held up his hand: '£100 that you can't.'

They set out the conditions: where there were roads and civilian traffic Mehmed would hitchhike; where there were no roads he would use public transportation of his choice. He would make a detailed list of lifts taken and show evidence of public transport where hitchhiking was physically impossible.

The bet was on.

In May 1960, a military junta overthrew the government of Adnan Menderes in Turkey, and arrested all members of parliament, including Mehmed's cabinet minister father. Rather than hang around, and advised to steer clear of Turkey for the moment, Mehmed flew to Johannesburg where he worked for six weeks to earn enough money for his hitchhiking journey home.

In late August, he started out from the Cape. Easy stretches followed via Johannesburg to Salisbury (now Harare). The old green African bus took Mehmed from Salisbury across the great Zambezi River through a bit of Mozambique, where he drank his worst beer ever, to Blantyre where he stayed in the best hotel for £2 and ate his biggest breakfast ever; they served steak with breakfast in 'British' East-Central Africa in those days. In Blantyre he interviewed Dr Hastings Banda in prison and started asking political questions. Banda shouted: 'Get out!' Mehmed did; Banda remained in jail. Six years later Bob, then a working journalist in central Africa, did a survey of Malawi. The now President Banda received him with due dignity in State House. After initial niceties, Bob dug into politics. 'Get out!' shouted Dr Banda. It was the shortest interview Bob ever conducted in his journalistic career. Bob ignored or had forgotten Mehmed's precedent. Banda knew nothing of Bob and Mehmed's shared past.

On from Blantyre, a British lady schoolteacher gave Mehmed a through lift to Dar-es-Salaam, all of seven days on the road. From Dar Herr Leo Rebholz from the Nairobi Volkswagen garage took him to Nairobi. From Nairobi a certain Shafiq Arain took him to Kampala. From Uganda Mehmed took the Nile boat to Juba. And so on to Khartoum, to Wadi Halfa by train, and onwards to journey's end in Cairo.

Mehmed had earned his £100. He did not get his cheque – he settled with Alistair Pirie for a slap-up lunch instead. Alistair at least paid the bill.

But an idea was born in the old green African bus between Salisbury and Blantyre. Mehmed thought: 'Next year and after graduation, a longer journey in my own vehicle to Asia.' In Nyasaland, as Malawi was called then, and in Rhodesia (now Zimbabwe) he had heard from schools and the university about their education systems. Comparative education study could be the key to open many doors.

On return to Cambridge in October 1960, he broached the idea first with his college mate, Tony Thompson: 'Would you like to go to Asia after finals and study comparative education?' Tony jumped at the idea. That is how it all started.

AN IDEA COMES TO LIFE

Various students of Mehmed's and Tony's acquaintance – it was, as so often, all a matter of whom you knew – were invited onto the team. Some common ground was provided by a somewhat nebulous Colonel Penn. This former British Indian Army officer persuaded Shell Petroleum to finance dinners and other gatherings of bright young things from Oxbridge with British and Middle Eastern backgrounds – a sort of culture-bridging nursery for future leaders. Peter and his Persian wife-to-be, Tahere, were members. So were Mehmed, Anthony Swanwick and Tim Parkinson, whose aunt was Controller of Home Division, number two, of the British Council. Shell, in all fairness, attached no obvious strings. But with its incomparable knowledge of the Middle East it did give the Expedition some top-class briefing before departure.

St Catharine's College ('Cats') was the hub of the venture. All who were roped into the venture had specific interests or skills in modern languages, journalism, politics, photography, or had simply travelled. Traicho Belopopski, down the road at Gonville and Caius, was a post-graduate in Serbo-Croat – of all things. For a Bulgarian 'inserted' into Cambridge by 'fraternal exchange', some of us felt, it was a flimsy cover. Traicho had befriended Mehmed through the university darkroom lodged in 'Caius' (pronounced 'keys'). They became drinking and photography friends. Events later suggested that there might be some reason to query Traicho's possible agendas in striking up this acquaintanceship (we will get there in due course ...). Tony Thompson got to know Mehmed through another network, the University Afro-Asian Association and in the corridors of St Catharine's College. A third 'Cats' man, Peter Temple-Morris, the chairman of the Cambridge University Conservatives, another lawyer, was a social friend of both Mehmed and Tony.

Roger Sherwin, also at 'Cats', was a fellow engineer and Mehmed's next-door neighbour; they had coffee together most days. Recruited by Mehmed as photographer, Roger was looking for adventure before starting a graduate apprenticeship. The year before, he had spent three months travelling all over Canada and the USA.

THE KOMBI TRAIL

St Catharine's College
Cambridge in 1960, where it
all began.

Tim Parkinson at Christ's was another engineer rubbing shoulders with Roger and Mehmed in the labs. Tim had thought of visiting Antarctica, but discovered that July–August was winter down there, and gladly accepted Mehmed's invitation to travel in warmer climes. (It took Tim another 48 years to get to Antarctica.) Tim was a VW Beetle addict. Nigel Robertson at Trinity was also bitten early by the Beetle bug. A friend-of-a-friend pricked up his ears in conversation with Nigel over dinner and promptly passed his name down the grapevine to Mehmed. Nigel was a former Royal Navy National Service Russian linguist. So was Bob Cox, across the road (from 'Cats') in Corpus Christi. Bob was inveigled into the project by Mehmed over a soggy plate of Mehmed's favourite *bindi gusht*, with a couple of mutual girlfriends, in a scruffy Indian restaurant on Sidney Street frequented by students with shallow pockets. Bob after the Expedition drove a clapped-out Beetle around Nordrhein-Westfalen on a Reuter traineeship in Bonn. Tony, Nigel and Bob were of the last generation of national servicemen who had done their time in the Navy before going up to Cambridge and were thus a tad older than the others.

Most parents on the whole were supportive. Tony's were enthusiastic. Bob's guardian uncle thought this would 'do him a world of good' even though the aunt thought it was all a bit 'daft'. Mehmed's father was then in jail on the island near Istanbul so Mehmed's mother was more worried about him than about her son. They were less enthusiastic one year previously, when almost immediately after the May 1960 Turkish military coup, Mehmed had announced that he was going to hitchhike from the Cape to Cairo. Both Mehmed's mother and father decided he was MAD (coincidentally also his initials – Mehmed Arif Demirer). Peter's father, a judge, scorned the idea; he wanted his son to press on with Bar exams. It was the only row they ever had. All would be forgotten and forgiven when Peter's parents became riveted as his letters from the Expedition flopped on to their doormat. Tim's Aunt Nancy provided him with a list of contacts in the British Council, and other organizations for some of the cities on the itinerary.

They were all soon busier than they had anticipated – somewhat to the detriment of studies.

Hundreds of letters were written to companies and organizations for help, from film to sunglasses, from food to thermos flasks, from string vests to soap. Companies and organizations responded generously. A major logistics exercise would shortly get into swing. Nigel was impressed by the generosity of local and national companies in the supplies they came up with and how well provided for the Expedition was. Bob remembers hours spent humping cartons up the steps of St Catharine's.

While their goods and chattels were being actively procured, members' excitement grew. Tony three years earlier had travelled for 12 months in the Royal Navy – in the flag-ship of the East Indies, HMS *Gambia* – to over 30 countries, including the Maldives and Seychelles before they had airports. He was particularly excited at the prospect of return visits to some of them, such as Iran, Pakistan, India, Ceylon, Kenya and Egypt, and the prospect of new experiences. In 1959, he had hitch-hiked in a kilt through Scandinavia and via Berlin to Istanbul – 6,000 miles in six weeks. The chance to be involved in an adventure such as the Expedition could not be missed. There was more world to be seen, more people to be met and more to be learned about many different countries. Bob, with his Slavonic languages on board, looked forward to meeting real Slavs in their own environment, and to a first venture into the Middle East, a region hitherto quite beyond his ken.

Tim was 'hooked'. He was also a VW fan having travelled the previous year the length of West Germany down to the Adriatic in an early VW Beetle. The prospect of *new* Kombis was a real attraction. As an engineer, his interest in the education aspect of the Expedition was tangential in that he had been a member of the Cambridge Human Relations in Industry group. And he was 'journey proud', with a mixture of excitement, curiosity and positive anticipation of the difficulties and opportunities ahead.

Nigel was excited by the fact that the first major destination was the USSR, where he had already been with a Cambridge party in 1959. Now he was keen to see more of the country than he had been able to do then. As for Peter, his close college friends Tony and Mehmed both thought it might help to have the current Chairman of the Cambridge University Conservative Association on board. Peter jumped at the opportunity to travel so widely and helped considerably with sponsors and patrons through the Conservative Association and the University Union. Peter recalls that he was not in the least nervous. 'At that age one should not know the word in such circumstances. Excited – yes – and with reason.' Traicho was nervous all the time. In due course, the reasons for this might become more obvious.

Roger recalls soberly that for those Expedition members doing finals in 1961 (the majority) there was the double pressure of finding time to work and revise while sending and replying to hundreds of letters sent to potential sponsors. Thirty-two contributing sponsors and suppliers were involved. 'Frankly I did not have enough time to feel either excited or nervous.' Reflecting, in later years, on the situations encountered, Roger was amazed at the coolness of everyone's nerves. Perhaps hindsight helped.

The members of the Expedition used their own contacts to invite influential people, particularly in politics and the media, to back the Expedition's ideas and to become patrons. A journey of this nature could not be self-financed; financial and material support was urgent. Peter penned a prospectus summarizing the aims of the Expedition, and including the names of the patrons they had meanwhile garnered – a fine palette to be taken on board by undergraduates:

Baron von Adelsheim, Ernst, scion of German nobility
Lord Birdwood, soldier and historian
Muharrem Nuri Birgi, Turkish Ambassador to NATO
Aidan Crawley, journalist and politician

Col Hamilton, Editor-in-Chief, Thomson Newspapers
The Dejazmatch Asserati Kassa, President of the Ethiopian Senate
Professor W. Arnold-Lloyd, Head of the Cambridge Department of Education
Sir Fitzroy Maclean, MP, diplomat, soldier, author of Eastern Approaches

The prospectus in essence said:

One of the greatest universal problems and challenges of to-day is education. The urgent political disputes, and developments of the moment take up most of world attention, and yet it is all too often forgotten that education to a great extent determines the advance of any country, politically, industrially, socially and in almost every other way. The problems of education and youth are to a large extent synonymous and … this is something upon which students are entitled to comment. If there is a duty involved it is for us to study and try to provide some contribution in this field.

Afro-Asia is a continent of change. The future of Afro-Asia is as interesting as it is uncertain. If there is any signpost to this future it lies in the attitudes of youth, and there is perhaps little that is more important in formulating these attitudes than the systems of education in the countries concerned. Education and the attitudes of youth are closely related, if not inseparable, and the potentialities of these need not be further stated. Such a venture – the Expedition – would give not only an insight into problems and trends of the present, but perhaps an answer to those same things in the future. Most important of all it is something the Expedition feels qualified to study in the sense that more might be learnt and discovered on a youth to youth basis than on any other.

So the Expedition aimed: 'To make personal contact with youth and those responsible for their education; and through this contact to make a detailed study of the educational system involved; to study the parallel subjects of the attitudes of youth, their activities, opportunities and ambitions.'

And: 'The Expedition intends to carry out these aims without any national or political bias. The whole success of the project depends on a neutral outlook. Our incentive is to learn to exchange ideas and to better international relations between the youth of countries.'

THE KOMBI TRAIL

Putting It All Together

The Expedition was in fact multiple journeys with core elements in space and time, depending partly on individual commitments. So the first question was – which routes should be taken? Some members had employers waiting for them to start work in autumn 1961. Others still had studies to complete in Cambridge. Mehmed, Nigel and Tony had more time. Two routes emerged: one group would travel for some 12 months; the other, returning in October for jobs or studies, would travel for four months only. Initially both groups were supposed to travel together as far as Pakistan, and then one would head east, the other, west. Visa problems soon scuppered these ideas.

Land Rovers were the vehicle of choice for expeditions at that time in Cambridge. Mehmed, influenced by his African hitch-lift with Volkswagen's Leo Rebholz from Nairobi, argued strongly for the Volkswagen Kombi, a flexible carrier of people and loads, with its simple 1200cc, air-cooled engine and low petrol consumption. And there was a good deal to be had in that two new vehicles could be bought from the factory in West Germany, and sold back at the end of the trip, and this for a total of £1,000. The Kombis would be fitted with *Zollnummer* customs transit number plates. These exempted vehicles from tax if they were destined primarily for export, which the Kombis definitely were. Ideally, they were also supposed to make frontier-crossing easier. Sometimes they did.

Team members' personal contributions were budgeted at £1,200 in total – about £200 each, plus pocket money. Come 1962, some parents had to cough up more.

Peter's father (not surprisingly, given his disapproval) did not stake his son, who thus had to see his bank manager privately and that gentleman put up Peter's contribution with no security offered. Those were the days gone by when you actually had a bank manager who knew who you were and was willing to take a chance on you. Bob had a little inheritance from his grandmother doing nothing much in the bank. He decided that the Expedition was a much better investment.

Roger too was 'well off'. He had been granted an exchange scholarship the previous long vacation to work in Canada for the Winnipeg Hydro Electric Board. Salaries were so much more generous over there that he saved enough to cover his personal costs of the expedition, as well as indulging in the purchase of a spare camera and lenses to support his expedition photographer duties.

Official 'Expedition' status was granted by the university authorities while the hundreds of letters to food suppliers, pharmaceutical companies, equipment suppliers and the media, asking for money, or goods in lieu, were flying back and forth. The Soviet Embassy laid on the services of Intourist; you could not travel then in the Soviet Union without their tender mercies. The Foreign Office obliged with contacts in British embassies, as did the British Council with its extensive overseas contacts. Newspapers supplied other contacts. Student friends would help in several countries *en route*.

Official nitty gritty soon took over. Visas, as one had suspected, became indeed a bit of a nightmare, both then and later. Romanian and Bulgarian visas, for instance, could not be had in the UK.

Personal accident and medical insurance, it was soon realized, was no bad idea either. It cost the grand sum of £22.10s for six of the party for four months. What about accidents, injury, plague, belly upsets with 'Montezuma's Revenge' (and its local equivalents)? The University's Health Service waded in with advice on medical needs and practical tips and generously put together a comprehensive medical kit for each vehicle.

Eclectic goods and chattels started arriving from pestered suppliers. The amount of stuff supplied was vast; it should have been far too much for two 1200cc VW Kombis. Some of this stuff would later be bartered *en route* – particularly cigarettes and coffee – for petrol, food and even for cash. Food was offered in generous quantities: a hundredweight of spaghetti, 75lb of milk powder, 36 tins of Marmite, 60 tins of processed cheese, 4 dozen tins of Ovaltine and 6 dozen packs of biscuits – and more. Pharmaceutical companies provided medical items from aspirins to bandages. Large quantities of soap arrived (from carbolic to Camay), as did toothpaste. There was lots of photographic film too, both colour-slide and black and white. All of this arrived outside the porters' lodge at St Catharine's, addressed to Anthony Thompson Esq., whose college rooms in late May turned into an Ali Baba's cave, and he cadged a storeroom. One afternoon the college porter came to Mehmed's rooms, 'You'd better come to the Porters' Lodge. There's a new delivery.' 'Why,' asked Mehmed, 'can't you just put it in the storeroom beyond the Porters' Lodge?' 'A whole truck full of toilet paper?' Apparently the secretary of the loo-roll company had made a slight error and dispatched 100 times as many packages as foreseen on the despatch note. The truck driver did not appreciate the news that after leaving a small parcel, he had to go all the way back to the suppliers to return the rest. Nothing can surprise the former soldiers and coppers who man porters' lodges in Cambridge.

THE KOMBI TRAIL

At last, British Railways sent a container to shift all this stuff to Ostend Railway station in Belgium, where expedition members, goods and supplies and the brand-new VW Kombis were to congregate. 'How,' recalls Tony, echoing earlier fears, 'we were expected to carry all these supplies in two 1200cc-powered vehicles, together with four members of the team with their personal luggage in each, is beyond me now – but we did!' The long-suffering Kombis' trials and tribulations were still to come – quite quickly, as it happened.

MAPS

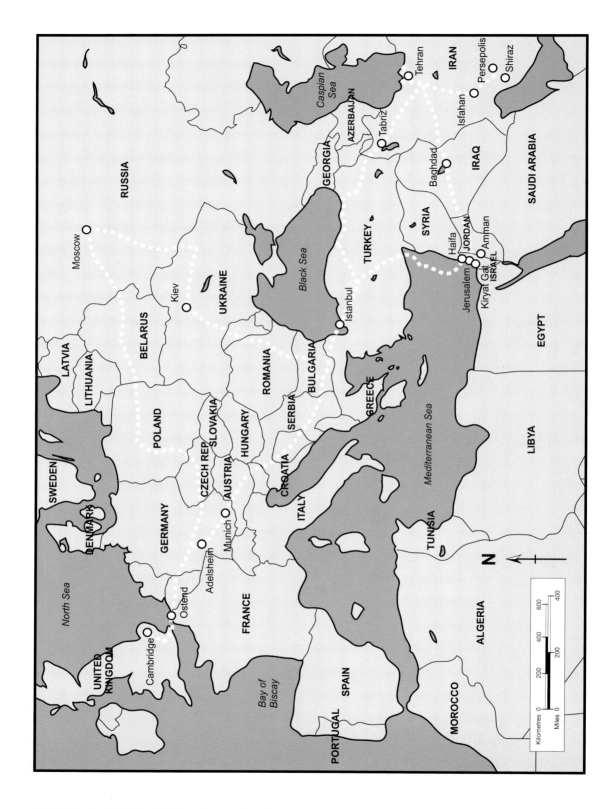

Map 1: The Four-Month Kombi Trail – with current country names.

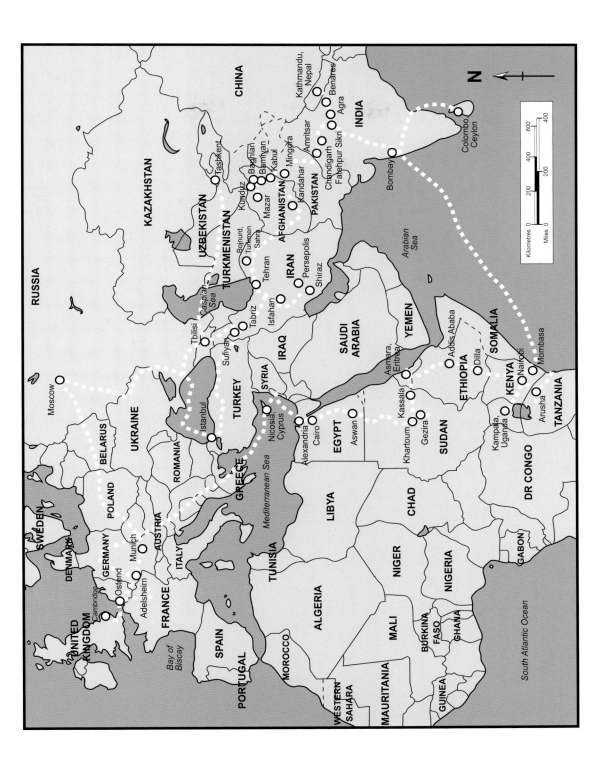

Map 2: The Twelve-Month Kombi Trail – with current country names.

MOSCOW CALLING

1

HICCUPS
AND RUMBLES

Cambridge, June 1961. Finals were over for most Expedition members. The wider world beckoned. Results, posted on the fence of the Cambridge Senate House, could have been better for several of them. Distraction in preparing for the forthcoming adventure had taken its academic toll.

Expedition members left Cambridge in dispersed order. Bob Cox was barred from Russia, and would join the party in Istanbul. Like Nigel Robertson he had trained as a Russian linguist during military service in the Navy. Later, in autumn 1960, a certain George Blake called him for interview at the War Office. Shortly afterwards Blake was denounced, arrested, tried and found guilty of treason. He was subsequently sprung from Wormwood Scrubs jail, and fled to the Soviet Union. Someone in Whitehall, however, feared that the notorious traitor had already communicated the identity of Bob and others to Moscow. 'Steer clear of the Soviet Union,' he was told. So the Expedition started off minus one of its Russian interpreters. Mehmed Demirer and Tim Parkinson, meanwhile, had picked up the two Kombis in Germany.

Earlier, on the train to Cologne, Tim became embroiled in a lengthy discussion with a (West) German about Communism. West Germans were then even more frightened of Communists and their activities than were the Americans – with reason. The conversation became repetitive and boring as the German trotted out the familiar shibboleths. Tim would reflect in due course that the German's moaning was good preparation for much of what lay ahead.

Mehmed, meanwhile, had got himself fined DM33 for failing to stop at a halt sign. Another omen? Tim took what everyone would later call 'his' Kombi – Z 1235 – for a short run along the *Autobahn*. There was a clunk and he was reduced to two gears. This proved definitely a foretaste of things to come. For the moment Tim sorted it out.

Tim supervised the loading of
supplies at the railway station
in Ostend.

Next morning in Ostend there was no sign of Tony, Roger, Nigel or the container. They had left Cambridge a day earlier in a battered 10cwt hired van with the remainder of the provisions, collecting (illegal) roubles and US dollars in London on the way. More such roubles originated, by obscure channels, from Zurich, of all places. They also had to backtrack and recover Nigel's passport which he had conveniently left at home. There was a touch of chaos in the air. At least there was entertainment in the boat to Ostend where the celebrated Alan Whicker and the BBC *Tonight* team were doing a feature on the art of crossing the Channel through scruffy customs and passport sheds, and with ill-kept ferries smelling of stale beer.

Next afternoon nearly everyone met up at Ostend railway station. Nigel and Peter had brought with them more essential supplies – chocolate! Tim arrived with 'his' new Kombi. Mehmed drove in shortly after and promptly succeeded

3

in overturning 'his' Kombi on the Ostend quayside. Stress, it would seem, was setting in. But there was a reason.

The day before had been important in Mehmed's life. He was getting engaged at his cousin's home near Bad Godesberg, the residence of the Turkish ambassador, to Maria Luz, daughter of the Argentinian ambassador in Bonn. He had met Maria a year earlier, on return from his 'Cape to Cairo Hitchhiking' venture. They had shared an 'exciting' last year in Cambridge and during some university vacations.

Now things were coming to a head. Mehmed's cousin, Selma, the Turkish ambassador's wife, was to host a big dinner party for the engagement ceremony with Maria Luz's parents and the expedition members all around the table. The night before, Mehmed had a heated discussion with Maria Luz about how long the Expedition would take. Mehmed would give no definite date; Maria had set a deadline. She was prepared to wait one year and no more. This 'no more' had ruffled Mehmed's nerves. His Turkish-Anatolian cum Mediterranean mind was disturbed that his future wife was setting deadlines. What if he did not return until 15 months later? What had this hard-headed Argentinian girl meant when she said, 'I will wait only one year?'

So it was that a hurried, nervous, tired and stressed Expedition leader, Mehmed, turned the Kombi over the next day at Ostend, like an old elephant. Mehmed now realized that somehow the engagement was off too. He phoned and cancelled the dinner. The next evening he and Maria talked into the early hours of the morning and decided that Maria would wait as long as she chose and no more.

One year later, upon return from the Expedition, Mehmed learned that Maria had married a young American army officer. They had not corresponded while the Expedition was away.

2

INTO RUSSIA'S REALM

Over the centuries, soldiers' boots have tramped back and forth over what many through the years have called the *Heerweg* – the military way across the flat plains of northern Europe from the Channel into the fastnesses of western Russia. Further south, the Fulda Gap, through which NATO planners expected a hypothetical Warsaw Pact armoured invasion, was the other way through. So were other gaps out of the Czech lands. The Expedition Kombis, in their baptismal ride, like a pair of *Valkyries*, took first the southernmost road through the Erzgebirge, before striking east down into the great northern plains and the long, boring and often desolate highway stretching as far as the eye could see. It was nearly 3,000 miles of historical road from Cambridge to Moscow.

Before finally escaping the clutches of Ostend, Tony reluctantly forked out $490 in greenbacks for a customs bond to repossess the container-load of equipment. Some seemingly arbitrary items were rebonded with a lead seal – presumably so that they could not be sold in Belgium. This bureaucracy, together with the need to divide all the stores into roughly equal portions and load the two apprehensive Kombis, delayed things further. At the Belgo-German border, the Germans refused entry because it was then half-past midnight. One forgets now just how closely in 1961 borders between European states were controlled. Cameras, for example, were taxed differently in different countries; one had to carry receipts of purchase. Lorries needed manifests which were checked at each customs post. The Expedition's 'cargo' of camping equipment, food and sundry supplies, exposed it to inspection at all borders – and customs officials did not work a 24-hour shift in those days. Sleeping bags, it turned out, were part of the newly bonded equipment and so everyone spent a very cold night in the Kombis on the Belgian side of the border.

The next day dawned, and the little convoy went straight through German customs thanks to fast talking by Mehmed with his good Teutonic language skills gained from an in-service traineeship with Siemens. Tony, all six foot plus of him, hovered over the little Belgian customs man and got his $490 back – in Belgian francs.

MOSCOW CALLING

More photo equipment was picked up in Bonn where it was much cheaper to buy than in England with its exorbitant taxes. Then on to the Turkish ambassador's residence in Bad Godesberg for an excellent lunch to replace the sabotaged engagement dinner. While Mehmed stayed behind to sort out his 'marital' problems, the rest of the team crowded into 'Tim's' Kombi to drive on a big detour to Adelsheim, east of Heidelberg in the hills of northern Baden-Württemberg, the home of a very distinguished patron of the Expedition, the Baron Ernst von Adelsheim.

Tony had been given a lift by the Baron whilst hitch-hiking in a kilt from London to Istanbul via Denmark a few years earlier. The Baron, intrigued by this phenomenon, had asked Tony to stay with him for a few days and explore the 5,000-acre estate at his sixteenth-century century *Schloss*.

The Kombi and its crew eventually arrived at 11 pm, to be offered chilled white wine served by white-gloved servants, and then given dinner in the hall by a blazing fire. All went off to bed a little the worse for wear. The next day, the Baron lavished grand hospitality on the team, followed by a drive around his estates and a walk to the Roman wall on one of the estate boundaries. It was at the *limes* – boundary – of Roman expansion into Germany. After dinner the Baron's son Cornelius, due soon to go up to Cambridge, and a friend, gave an impromptu recital of flute and cembalo. It was a last touch of civilized living until an evening at the Bolshoi in Moscow.

Peasants going to work in their horse-drawn, wooden trailers gave some colour to an otherwise uneventful journey through Germany the next morning. In Nürnberg Tim, the ever-prudent engineer, had the Kombi given a last check-over by the local Volkswagen garage. Tony, meanwhile, was back in Bonn meeting Mehmed and Traicho, and collecting the other Kombi which had by then been repaired to an almost new condition after its abusive treatment in Mehmed's nervous hands. A little later the duly repaired Kombi and its crew also reached Nürnberg, but this time with a punctured tyre. Mehmed and company called for a mechanic to do the job – after they had tried asking for help from the police who did not quite appreciate the joke. Or was it a joke? With the benefit of hindsight one can only goggle at why a Bulgarian, an Englishman and a Turk, destined for an expedition to faraway places, thought it wise to call for the German police just because their vehicle had a puncture. The learning process was well under way.

Traffic was light through Prague, Czechoslovakia, the first country visited behind the 'Iron Curtain'.

Arriving at about 9.30 pm at the German/Czech border, the first Kombi found another frontier that it was too late to cross. The German frontier officials suggested camping behind their station, with use of their washing facilities, and suggested a place to put up a tent. This was duly done – it was the first time. Nigel, Peter and Roger squeezed into the tent. All was calm until in the small hours it began to blow and rain, and the tent collapsed. Tim, sleeping in the Kombi, stirred briefly and just laughed. The doleful apprentice campers listened to sporadic bursts of gunfire during the night from the Czech side – never explained – and began to wonder what was in store for them.

At the Czech border post the first Kombi to cross had to pay for a Czech *carnet* travel document – funnily enough the second Kombi did not. Now the Expedition was finally behind the Iron Curtain. In the morning, more peasants'

carts crowded the road. The surface was passable; a few six-wheeled lorries made up the industrial traffic. Driving straight through Pilsen – not even time for a glass of the celebrated beer – a brief stop was made in Prague, where the buildings still had many scars from World War II shelling, before pressing on over flat countryside to the Polish border. Another bureaucratic delay ensued, but with the help of a Polish couple returning from holiday who spoke English, a free *carnet* was obtained. Once over the border, the time came to cook a first big meal with ingredients from all those supplies cramming the Kombi space; a first experiment, too, with the state-of-the-art camping stove wheedled out of a supplier. Coming to terms with accelerated freeze-dried meat was another first – it tasted like chewed cardboard. Over the months ahead, experience would refine the basic recipe until a passable *bolognese* sauce of some kind was produced as a suitable accompaniment to the half hundredweight of spaghetti that each vehicle was carrying.

A rough and treacherous road brought the Expedition driving through the night to Wroclaw, the former Breslau. Every town or village passed through was paved with treacherous cobblestones. It rained non-stop – a miserable night's driving. Stopping in the early morning by a café, with no local money, a tin of Nescafe and 40 cigarettes plonked on the counter was rewarded with a good hot Polish meal for four. Mehmed exchanged a sixpenny bar of chocolate for 40 litres of petrol.

On the road further east hundreds of people in the small town of Miedrzyrzec were crowded together in the market – a most extraordinary and colourful spectacle after the long drive through the dreary Polish plains. A weekly rural gathering, like anywhere in Europe, the roads thronged with typical farmers' transport – a horse-drawn, rubber pneumatic-tyred cart, with people sitting on

(Opposite, top) Tony and Traicho talking with a local in Prague.

(Opposite, bottom) Young Pioneers in distinctive uniform in the centre of Prague; they were the Soviet Bloc replacement for our scouting movement.

a pile of straw. Peter and Nigel bought potatoes, and talked in Anglo-Polish-broken-German with the locals. Then, direction Minsk, on to the border itself at Brest-Litovsk, where the Russians staged a thorough customs inspection. Fresh, unpeeled produce was not allowed through so Peter, impeccably groomed as ever, proceeded compulsorily to peel the newly purchased potatoes and carrots in full view of the Soviet officialdom. The underside of the vehicle was carefully examined by the frontier guards – something that happens routinely now, but was most unusual in 1961. It was also made clear that the death penalty for currency smuggling had just been introduced – no one had yet read the story of how that came about in *Hustling on Gorky Street* written by a Russian refugee in New York. Everyone had roubles: Mehmed looked at the sky and put at the back of his mind the fact that Traicho entered the Soviet Union with 2,000 roubles in his pocket.

Between Brest and Smolensk the top gear in Z1235, 'Tim's Kombi', suddenly decided it was fed up, went on strike, and the gear lever jumped out. Nothing could persuade it to stay in other than jamming it in by hand and holding it there. Fiddling with the linkage achieved nothing. Tim finally fixed up an arrangement of his own making with string and a clamping wrench, which allowed third gear to be selected with reasonable ease. All that was missing was sealing wax. The Kombi complied.

After a breakfast of porridge – the first of many – it was time to soldier on along roads which, since Wroclaw, through Minsk, just went straight for mile after mile across the great plains. Their surface became progressively worse towards Moscow. As traffic became heavier, the Kombi again expressed its displeasure as its fourth gear gave more trouble. As the Soviet capital drew nigh, collective farms and wooden-hutted shanty towns of agricultural Russia dotted the landscape. The inevitable policemen took the Kombi's number as it passed.

(Opposite, top) Farmer's transport, east of Warsaw, Poland – market day.

(Opposite, bottom) The friendly face of a local farmer.

MOSCOW CALLING

The two Kombis had been separated in Germany. Tim, Roger, Nigel and Peter were riding in the Kombi with the intransigent gearbox. Far to the west, and a few days behind, Kombi Z1060 with Mehmed, Tony and Traicho aboard, was suffering from neglect.

On the long, straight road between Minsk and Smolensk, on a hot morning, Mehmed noticed a red light blinking on the speedometer of the Kombi. All three of them, Tony the lawyer, Bulgarian philologist Traicho and Turkish Mehmed, himself a freshly graduated Cambridge engineer, assumed long faces and frowns. They stopped, opened the engine cover and watched the engine carefully. Tony watched from a distance. Traicho, more inquisitive, did so from a closer squatting position. Mehmed decided to take a photo and let the other two (non-engineers …) solve this intriguing engineering problem. Having examined all the different parts of the engine from his squatting position, Traicho turned to Mehmed and asked seriously: 'Pasha, how do you say "oil" in German? Is the word perhaps "Oel"?' When Mehmed said 'Yes', Traicho beamed with satisfaction. 'Here, it says "OEL". I suppose we open the cover and pour in some oil.' Luckily there was a spare can of oil somewhere and all this went into the engine, no one being quite sure how much oil was necessary. Obviously – as it emerged later – it was not enough. Several hundred miles later on reaching Moscow on 4 July, the Expedition had effectively burnt out its first engine.

SUMMER IN MOSCOW

A hill dropped behind and there lay the panorama of Moscow, glowing pink and gold in the setting sun. The university, the skyscrapers in the distance, all the landmarks stood out as if flood-lit against the darkening sky, the Moskva River a silver stripe at its feet. It was a breathtaking sight; one could have wished for no better welcome. The summer air was clean. The all-pervasive smell of lignite, so typical of much of Central and Eastern Europe, had taken a holiday together with the power stations that burned it.

Nigel had been to Moscow two years before and was supposed to navigate. Enormous changes had wrenched this great city further still from the grim destruction, dust and rubble of war. Within minutes the Kombi was lost. A lorry driver leaned out of his cab and shouted, 'Follow me!' After a hectic drive through the rush-hour traffic, signs to the camping site emerged on the roadside. Ten minutes later the Kombi thankfully pulled up outside the office.

These camping sites offered the best opportunities for seeing the Soviet Union. Open to all car travellers, Soviet and foreign, they were cheap, mostly clean, and spaced at convenient intervals over European Russia and the Caucasus. The Ostankino camping site was five miles from Red Square with a good bus service. The aims of the Expedition were to see some of the educational establishments for which the Soviet Union was justly famous, to meet professors and, of course, students. And there was sightseeing to do. No time was lost in getting down to business.

Moscow was big and bustling. The city council was building houses as fast as it could. New residential areas were springing up to boost the population of Greater Moscow to more than 9 million. Traditionally centred on 'Red', or more correctly the 'beautiful', Square, bordered on one side by the forbidding wall of the Kremlin and the largest state department store (GUM) on the other, streets radiated for miles, linked by so-called ring-roads.

Nigel realized that during the two years he had been away change had accelerated: the traffic had increased, the girls dressed better, the food in restaurants had improved – though not the service. He recalls the rather curious smell of Russians *en masse*, due to the soap they used – the only type available at the time.

The queue to visit the
mausoleum containing the
embalmed bodies of Lenin
and Stalin. St Basil's is in the
background, at the far end
of Red Square.

(Opposite, top) Ostankino
campsite, Moscow.
Tim was repacking the
extraordinary weight
of food and supplies
that was carried in each
1200cc Kombi.

(Opposite, bottom)
Dominating the Moscow
skyline at the time, the
Ministry of Foreign Affairs.

Part of the
mausoleum queue.
The frocks were
typical of the time.

It was not necessarily unpleasant, just distinct. Across the city many trams and buses now operated without conductors, a prelude to the introduction of free transport. Traffic police were strict and could fine wrongdoers up to $5 on the spot for jumping a red light or taking the wrong lane. The foreigner often got away with it.

But Moscow in 1961 was still dowdy. Row upon row of vast blocks of flats created a great sameness. On first encounter the Expedition's bushy-tailed young travellers looked at but scarcely admired the women. Clothes were drab floral prints lacking real colour in the flowers. Nobody was smartly dressed. The army and the police were among the worst – sloppy, often with a cigarette hanging out of their mouths whilst in uniform. There were virtually no advertisements; this was no Piccadilly Circus. Even St Basil's Cathedral looked as though it needed a lick of paint. But the pavements were hosed down frequently at about 10.30 in the evening, and there was no litter. And it was compulsory to clean cars – such as there were – at least once a week. And the Moscow Metro, fantastically decorated, was fast, efficient at moving thousands of people daily – and all for the paltry price of 5 kopeks, or 5 British pennies of the time.

The British Embassy, in a splendid position overlooking the Moskva River, had superb views of the Kremlin. Christopher Mallaby, private secretary to the Ambassador, was a Cambridge friend of Nigel's brother. Ambassador Sir Frank Roberts had been a Cambridge friend of Nigel's father. All the right connections were nicely in place.

In Red Square, joining the mile-long queue to enter the mausoleum containing Stalin and Lenin, with women dressed in their summer frocks typical of the time, it quickly appeared that foreigners were allowed to push in only 50 yards or so from the entrance. The Cambridge visitors did just that. Both embalmed inmates looked very serene. Photography was strictly forbidden in the mausoleum. As it emerged later, the Russians enforced their restrictions on the use of cameras with grim vigour. Rumours whispered that both Lenin and Stalin's uniforms were regularly renewed. Stalin was to be removed from the mausoleum several months later after the October 1961 22nd Communist Party Congress had rubbished his reputation for good.

This tourism highlighted the extreme contrast in architecture between the relatively colourful St Basil's at one end of the square and the dull, monotonous apartment blocks elsewhere. It was a bit like East Berlin's Alexanderplatz with its furbished facades and ill-kept lodgings tucked away out of sight behind. In Moscow the architect of St Basil's had his eyes put out by the Czar so that nothing so beautiful could be built again.

The Tretyakov Gallery dazzled with its fine collection of Russian Art from the eleventh century to the present. It was most enjoyable up to the Revolution but then fell flat. The contemporary stuff could have been painted any time in the last 100 years. Peter and Roger went on to the Pushkin Fine Arts Museum with its collection of the world's greatest art. Here Roger had a chance encounter with a blonde law student – both of them admiring Rodin's 'The Kiss' at the time.

MOSCOW CALLING

The local petrol station.

There was an abundance of attractive students in Moscow, who were very willing to meet and spend time with the Western adventurers. Peter tactfully withdrew. Somebody, however, had forgotten to tell Roger that there was little petrol in the Kombi. Roger and the young lady got less than a quarter of a mile from the Metropole hotel in the centre of Moscow before they ran out of petrol. Communication was difficult – their common language was German. They walked to the nearest filling station. Petrol pumps were usually hand-operated and the petrol was low grade, which frequently caused 'pinking'. But Roger and Lyudmila had no petrol cans. So the petrol station lent Roger a bucket, which he filled, and duly walked through the main streets with the girl on one arm, the bucket in the other hand, hoping that nobody would think of dousing their cigarette in the bucket. Pouring the petrol into the car was the next problem. Fortunately Roger had various bits of equipment in the Kombi for developing photos – and, rummaging around, found a small funnel. Then the fun really started. They drove towards the outskirts of Moscow to a nightclub Lyudmila apparently knew. They got lost. They asked a policeman on point duty the way. Ten minutes later, appearing to have left the city behind them, they were flagged down by a police vehicle. Roger had been getting a mite concerned after earlier warnings by Intourist not to go outside the city boundaries without permission. It soon turned out that the first policeman had given them bum information; they now had new directions. Roger's impression of Russian police went up a notch.

Eventually they arrived at this nightclub – more like a restaurant with dancing – where there was a queue. As at the tomb of Lenin and Stalin, they were taken straight to the front of the queue, as was the privilege for foreigners, and had an entertaining evening … Hours later, going back to the camp site, after taking the girl home, Roger ran out of petrol yet again. It was three in the morning. A man on a bicycle emerged out of the night; it turned out he was a bus driver on early shift. All this was conducted in sign language. Roger told him the problem. The man on the bike stood in the middle of the road and flagged down the next car to come along – a police car, as it happened. Roger spent the next ten minutes siphoning petrol out of the police car and topping up the Kombi. Roger swears that he has not run out of petrol since.

Back in Moscow, Tim asked the German Embassy what they thought of the condition of 'his' Kombi's gearbox. 'Don't go on to Istanbul,' they said. But no garages in Moscow could deal with the innards of a VW. Flying in spares, said the embassy trade section, would be expensive and a hassle. One idea was to nip up to Helsinki. This, however, meant having all the aggro of negotiating a new itinerary with the dreaded Intourist.

Meanwhile, more rewarding pastimes beckoned. The Komsomol was the Communist Union of Youth (ВЛКСМ), for 14- to 28-year-olds. Its job was to introduce youth to politics. Some two-thirds of the then Soviet population were believed to have been members. Members received privileges and preference for promotion at work. One of the Soviet Union's leading organizations, its control over students was near absolute, covering not only their political but their recreational activities as well. Among Komsomol officers the expedition members met were people with such varied tasks as running the institute choir and acting as representative on a final board of examiners who determined a graduate's future work together with his or her moral fitness for the job.

MOSCOW CALLING

The Chairman of the
students' Komsomol
Committee in his office.

The university was an extremely important institution, both politically and academically. It was the Expedition's good fortune to meet some of the more senior students. A university student was very much regarded as a potential member of the government or of the Academy of Sciences – of the *номенклатура* (nomenklatura) – and as such enjoyed a high status. A meeting was set up with the Moscow Committee of the International Union of Students, actually in the bureau of the Young Communist League at the Lomonosov University, decorated with typical symbols of Communist Russia. This particular day coincided with the visit of President Kwame Nkrumah of Ghana to Moscow. The way out to the airport is the same as that to the university and the streets were thronged with crowds waiting for the signal to cheer. Police blocks were everywhere.

The dinner hosted for the
Komsomol Committee.

MOSCOW CALLING

While in Moscow, Kombi Z1060 usually flew the Turkish flag and the Union Jack from the roof-rack. With flags aloft, therefore, the Kombi sailed through one police barrier after another, listening in vain for the resounding cheers. Evidently someone on the pavement knew his flags.

The 'Cambridge Capitalist Expedition' was warmly greeted at the steps of the university by the members of the Komsomol Committee. Within minutes, all were sitting around a table dug into hard talking. The atmosphere was friendly, the opposition very sharp and the discussion never-ending. The Expedition invited them for dinner in more convivial surroundings the next evening on the sunroof at the Moskva Hotel, then thronged with Gina Lollobrigida, Elizabeth Taylor and other personalities attending the Moscow Film Festival. Somewhat flatteringly for him, Nigel, tall and with his debonair good looks waiting outside the Hotel for the Komsomol, was rushed at for his autograph by several eager Russians thinking him a Western film star. The evening was a success in that a lot of food and vodka was consumed, but the political results did not meet expectations. Many of the students, despite their privileged positions, were unwilling to commit themselves any further; only one of them turned up again. Their generous promises for dialogue of the day before had come to nothing. On the other hand, it would have been hard to find anywhere a group of such highly educated and well-informed young people. Nine out of ten were studying science, and the majority of these were on postgraduate research scholarships. All were extremely polite and friendly, and excellent speakers: a fair index of the cream of Soviet higher education.

For all the warmth, hospitality and even affection shown, official Russia in 1961 was all too ready to bully its way out of any political debate. There was an anti-capitalist argument for everything. Discussion of political subjects soon ran into a sort of dogmatic brick wall. Both sides parted from this meeting believing that the other was sincere about wanting peaceful co-existence. In itself there is nothing remarkable in this until one recalls that at the beginning of the evening Aleki, the very bright secretary of the Komsomol, was asked directly by Tony and Mehmed, 'Do you believe in peaceful co-existence?', and replied, 'We do but you don't!' World War II still cast its long shadow. 'Remember,' said one *Komsomolets*, 'we lost 20 million people in the war. We're still fighting to make that up.' It said volumes.

And yet after hours of vigorous exchanges and some tough accusations, things would return to easy conviviality. Vodka would be drunk, everyone would laugh and smoke, and then stroll together on a lovely summer evening in the university gardens in the Lenin Hills.

The classic symbol of Communism – officially entitled 'Worker and Collective-Farm Woman'; it is now dismantled, and the pieces stored in a lock-up on the outskirts of Moscow.

The university was not the only form of higher educational establishment. The majority of Soviet scientists had at one time or another passed through a single-faculty institute. One such institute was the Moscow Institute of Constructional Engineering, specializing in soil mechanics. In the laboratories the quality of the equipment and the range of the research projects was most impressive by any standards. Some 'pure' research projects were undertaken, but most were initiated at government demand and dealt with specific problems and bottlenecks in development. The tour of inspection was followed by tea and cakes while postgraduates delivered simplified mini-lectures on their own theses, all of which were extremely advanced. The atmosphere of goodwill, the spirit of free academic enquiry and the uproarious jokes of the host, the Chief Assistant, made this an unforgettable visit.

The material results of this high academic level were clearly translated into concrete terms in the so-called Exhibition of National Economic Achievement (вднх), not far from the camping site. A vast area had been set aside for experimental plant nurseries, pavilions of all the Republics, in which national produce was displayed, and pavilions of science, engineering and electronics. A colourful scene was marred only by the incessant blare of canned music from the ubiquitous loudspeakers. The exhibition was massive. Few of the goods on display were always available all over the Union, but one got an idea of the variety and extent of Soviet industry and agriculture.

For a young man life in Moscow was not at all dreary. Soviet young people were highly motivated and dedicated to the success of their country and, rightly or wrongly, their system. They enjoyed food and lots of drink, and they danced and sang as if the problems of the world hardly existed. They swam, played sport with gusto and enjoyed their many parks. A regular sight there, which signified the timelessness of a great country, was the chess area where old men with flowing white hair and beards matched their skills with young schoolboys. All this was way beyond politics and systems of government.

Tim was struck by how well prepared these students were in any political situation – how well drilled they were in familiar arguments. Perhaps, he felt, 'I had the facts to argue in two or three but not six or seven' cases as they did. It turned out that these students were Members of the Committee of Friendship.

At the Ministry of Higher Education Professor Bogomolov, head of the Pedagogical Institute, told us: 'A professor earns 10% more than an engineer.' 'How much does an engineer earn?' 'Ten per cent less than a professor!' It was typical of robust Russian humour.

The People's Friendship University of Russia, founded in 1960 as the Patrice Lumumba Friendship University to provide higher education and professional training for third-world nations, was thought by Western intelligence agencies to be a training ground for KGB activities. Conversation threw up the usual rude remarks about NATO – nearly every Russian student or lecturer harped on about NATO being a threat to the Soviet Union. Nigel was wary of our contact, a somewhat sinister character with a Latvian name – Zhuravels. He felt distinctly uncomfortable in that building. On subsequent visits to the Soviet Union in the

Central Asian republics Nigel would come across 'graduates' – actually drop-outs from the Lumumba University, who had been sent away to these far-flung outposts where perhaps the climate was less severe, but the racial discrimination intense.

Two of the most interesting types of young people in Moscow were the *stilyagi* or *fartsovchiki* (spivs) and the *zolotaya molodyozh* (gilded youth). The spivs were typical of their kind and the more professional of them offered anything from a good dinner to women to encourage a bargain. Their fascination with all things Western was plain to see: one young man introduced himself to Peter because he thought he looked like Marlon Brando and this fellow wanted to get to Hollywood. Western clothes at that time fetched exorbitant prices in an extensive black market. Peter talked to another who liked 'money, clothes and girls' and just would not believe that 'I would refuse to sell my soul for a million roubles'. Talking his language, Peter said that if he wanted a million roubles he was smart enough to get them without having to sell his soul. The spiv and his companions liked that.

At the other end of the scale came the gilded or privileged youth whose parents held good positions making them members of Russia's 'new class'. There were many of them. The girlfriend of one, a minister's son, explained: 'Their antics will surpass even the revels of debutantes on a London tube-train.' All Moscow streets had a VIP traffic lane in their middle. At the time of the famous May Day celebration, when Khrushchev and the government were busy taking their salute, when central Moscow streets were closed, the minister's son, his girlfriend and some companions, were tearing around the VIP lane in the ministerial car, having a thoroughly mobile and alcoholic party.

Mehmed wanted to buy an icon. He had brought a small suitcase containing new cheap nylon shirts, socks and underwear for men, being told that one could exchange these for an icon. Traicho was in on this plan and introduced a new friend, Borya, who would bring an authentic icon (stolen from a church) and take the merchandise. The exchange would take place the next day. Mehmed was already getting nervous and having second thoughts about the whole thing. The next day in the middle of Red Square Borya quietly slipped into the Kombi through the rear door with the icon wrapped in a *Herald Tribune*. Mehmed was at the wheel with Traicho sitting next to him. Immediately after Borya got in, Traicho said 'drive on'. Borya was giving the instructions. To Mehmed's dislike they left central Moscow and drove to some obscure suburbs. It was getting dark. It then became clear that two police cars were following. After about three-quarters of an hour, with each trying to lose or overtake the other, the police cars won. Traicho said, 'Don't move. Stay in the Kombi and don't say a word.' He got out and produced his red Bulgarian passport together with his Communist Party membership card. Borya could not produce an identity card and was taken away. Mehmed and Traicho drove on. The icon stayed in the Kombi. Mehmed cursed himself. Traicho said, 'Don't worry. They won't do anything to you. They are waiting for you to cross the line.' He then explained his story about earlier visa manipulations. He had promised the Soviets that if they would give us the visas, Mehmed, son of a jailed Turkish ex-minister then on trial in Yassıada near Istanbul, would cross the line in Moscow and start working with the famous and dissident Turkish poet, Nazım Hikmet, who fled Turkey in 1952. This was going to be big news in the press both in Moscow but more so in Turkey. In the meantime, Mehmed was more worried about Borya on the one hand and what to do with the icon on the other. Later, before leaving Moscow, Mehmed learned from Traicho: 'They are going to give a life sentence to Borya,' he said, 'and are very angry with you. But don't worry. They will not do any harm to you.' Mehmed would have reason to feel less sure about that on leaving the Soviet Union, some weeks later, at Julfa train station.

During the next two weeks two apparently related incidents happened, one after the other. First, Mehmed met a scholar of Turkish at the Foreign Languages Faculty in the University, an academician called Sergei Alexander Alexandrevich. He was a close friend of Hikmet, who at that time was in Castro's Cuba giving lectures. Hikmet, said Alexandrevich, was inviting Mehmed to join him in the USSR and work with him as a young-blood Turkish Communist. Life would be very pleasant. Mehmed talked several evenings with Sergei in the restaurant of the Hotel National and told him this was not on.

Next came a meeting with Raya Alexandra Alexandrova at the Moscow circus. Mehmed was watching neither the circus nor Khrushchev, who happened to be in the audience, but the very attractive young woman sitting next to him – Raya. Her husband, an army officer, was out of Moscow. Mehmed saw Raya several evenings at her tiny flat. She went out of her way to explain how pleasant life in the Soviet system would be for a young Communist Turkish dissident.

Some members of the Expedition felt that Traicho had another agenda in Moscow. He often disappeared for a few hours, as he did the day before leaving Moscow. Years later – see the Epilogue – Nigel managed to decorticate bits of our colleague's twisted path through life in a talk with Traicho's granddaughter. There probably was an element of truth in Traicho's visa story. Mehmed to this day is unsure of it but remains perplexed about the incoherent behaviour of different bits of the Russian bureaucracy towards him.

It was time to plan getting out of Russia – there had been no time to finalize this before leaving England. In retrospect it was surprising that the Expedition was allowed into the USSR in the first place.

Mehmed now suggested that 'his' Kombi should go by train from Tbilisi or by boat from Baku, while Tim and consorts would head through Romania and Bulgaria to Istanbul and then strike out eastwards. The two groups would thus not meet again until Iran. Traicho's friends then came up with an introduction to the secretary of the Komsomol – and a channel for obtaining permission to drive out of Russia into Iran as well as visa manipulations, about which more would become clearer shortly. After days of bureaucratic fuss, including a premature celebration in vodka until the bottle ran dry, Traicho's Iranian visa was refused, a trip to Leningrad was cancelled, and other hassles intervened. Finally, it was decided that Tim and crew would indeed take the Balkan route, while Mehmed, Nigel and Tony would head due south, the more direct route to Iran – but with what turned out to be interesting 'excursions' on the way. A German embassy engineer told Tim that the gearbox on Kombi Z1235 would get no worse – so carry on blissfully to Iran.

A new complication now erupted. Two weeks after the Borya incident, Mehmed's right gland swelled up as big as an orange. He went into a coma and was taken to Gorky Hospital. The facilities were not impressive – nor the results. Yet this was the No. 2 City Hospital, considered suitable for treating foreigners. Despite misgivings, Mehmed received top-quality care in what the Gorky Hospital called in their medical jargon the 'Nuclear Treatment'. Soon he had almost recovered. He would now fly to Sochi to meet up with Tony and Nigel who, in the meantime, with Intourist on their backs, had by now left Moscow to drive south in the second Kombi. The hospital gave Mehmed a free air ticket to Sochi.

Traicho, Tim, Roger and Peter came to wish Mehmed *bon voyage*. They were leaving for Istanbul via Kiev and Sofia. That was the last time Mehmed saw Traicho, who would leave the Expedition in Istanbul after, in all probability, deciding then that it was time to abscond to the West. And yet, as Bob recalls, during a subsequent last year in Cambridge, Traicho still seemed able to return from day trips to London equipped with bottles of *slivova* and pickled gherkins supplied, apparently, by the Bulgarian Embassy.

Shortly before leaving Moscow, the news percolated that a student friend had lost a holiday job due to being seen around Moscow with the 'foreigners'. He had then found another job as interpreter to a foreign delegation at the dubious 'World Youth Forum' then happening in Moscow, only to leave that with some

MOSCOW CALLING

Traicho and Mehmed
outside a Moscow hospital;
Mehmed was recovering
after 'nuclear' treatment.

excuse as he rejected the odious task of having to make out reports on what the delegates said privately amongst themselves. He thus lost badly needed income to tide him over the academic year. He will pop up again soon in this tale.

The eve of departure from Moscow was a moment to reflect on experiences gained. Roger recalls impressions of Russian women: their old-fashioned clothes; their place in society. On the one hand, plenty of the younger female generation were going to university. On the other, women were employed on building sites, in road mending, painting white lines by hand, etc. Women were also bus and train drivers, before that was generally common in the UK. As Russians recalled again and again,

Women hand-painting
white lines in the middle of
a busy Moscow street.

these were scars inherited from the cull of their males during World War II. Women, as Nigel observed, did everything in the rearguard – and frequently at the front as well. The position of women would continue to improve in terms of careers and opportunities until *perestroika*, when their situation began to come under pressure from endemic Russian male chauvinism. Peter recalls how Western clothes at that time fetched exorbitant prices in an extensive black market. Some Expedition members supplemented meagre funds by selling Marks and Spencer pullovers literally on the streets. And they were snapped up by avid young Russians.

The most bizarre malcontent encountered was a middle-aged housewife who stormed up outside Moscow's National Hotel, a favourite of Western journalists. Almost foaming at the mouth, she stood her ground for ten minutes while one of the Expedition's Russian speakers was hastily extricated from the hotel barber's shop. She was tired of the slum where she and her husband were living. She had been promised a new flat, but the promise had not been kept. She had seen or tried to see everyone from local Party Committees to President Brezhnev to no avail. That morning she had been told to 'go to hell' by a Moscow building organization and wanted to know whether 'the Western Correspondents' would come with her, take pictures of her flat and 'put it in every newspaper in the West so they can see how we live'. It so happened that Expedition members had cards from the *Sunday Times* saying they were 'accredited foreign correspondents'. The reactions of these 'correspondents' were guarded, as police traps were an occasional reality. But curiosity and the temptation got the better of them. The woman's apartment block was very near central Moscow and was indeed a hovel of long, dark corridors, dirty ashbins outside each door and so on. No sooner had she opened the front door than a fast exit was needed. Her husband who 'would kill me if he knew about you' was calmly sleeping inside. If the incident had any value it was to prove that Moscow's housing problem was not quite as solved as everyone would have had one believe, particularly as the woman concerned had done two years service as a tractor-driver on the Virgin lands and her husband was a Party Member.

Departure from Moscow was indeed long overdue; arrangements were finally completed with authorizations dragged out of the obstreperous Intourist. Nigel and Tony left in one Kombi for Kharkov and Tbilisi. Tim, Peter, Roger and Traicho headed for Kiev with the other Kombi. Mehmed was to catch up by plane. Bob was 'lost' somewhere in the Balkans. A first group would meet up in Istanbul. Everybody would reunite in Tabriz or Teheran.

4

HOW TO GET OUT OF RUSSIA

South-west by south from Moscow the road heads straight as a die through the great Russian plains to Orel ('the Eagle') into the Ukraine. Several lorries lay askew, broken down by the roadside, with their sweating drivers attempting major repairs – the engines being removed from their mountings, and being stripped and rebuilt by the roadside. Russian drivers were their own autonomous mechanics. One could not obtain a driving licence in Russia in those days without passing mechanical qualification tests.

Further on to Kiev, the cradle of the *Rus'* or Russian state, the wheat lands stretched to the horizon with the earth painted with patches of gaudy sunflowers. Farm machinery was replacing some horses. Houses were beginning to be quite trim after the drab blocks of Moscow. Kiev's city centre was pleasantly tree-lined and had a mature feel and style, in contrast to Moscow. Intourist had issued vouchers for the Kiev campsite. For some reason – probably Traicho's desire to negotiate everything – yet another debate was to break out with these friends of the tourist on the method and amount of payment. Already when leaving the Moscow campsite, for no good reason an argument about payment had flared up. There was a definite feeling of being told to move on and out.

The following day Traicho disappeared again for three hours. He had fixed an interview with the pro-rector of the Kiev Polytechnic Institute. A bright and friendly student called Viktor turned up to volunteer a quick tour of Kiev with non-stop commentary. Next on the agenda was a trip further up the Dnieper River to one of the youth camps that nearly all students go to for some part of their summer vacation. Viktor, and another student, Lyudmila, rode escort. At the camp everyone was allotted *palotki* (tented accommodation) before a Butlins holiday camp-type dinner, followed by dancing on a rickety wooden floor to tinny music until late, and by the light of a large harvest moon.

Peter judged later that the two days spent at the holiday camp of the Kiev Polytechnic Institute provided the best opportunity throughout the stay in the Soviet Union of getting a feel for the character of Russian students. No

official guides were involved – simply an invitation from an ex-student of the Institute. The camp had a splendid location on the banks of the river. It had been built and run by the students themselves who thus got three weeks' free holiday each summer, a regular practice in the USSR. The greatest hospitality was showered on these unofficial foreign guests – perhaps because they were 'unofficial'. Talk went on throughout the day and long into the evening with the many of them who spoke English and they involved the visitors in their activities, including a trip down the river and an occasion for Tim to show his rowing skills. For an annual holiday these students followed a strict programme each week-day: up at 7 am; breakfast; meeting for the purpose of administration or official discussion; a morning's work on neighbouring collective farms; lunch; two hours' rest; sports training; dinner; free time till lights out at a rigid 12 midnight. During their few free hours there was nearly always something arranged such as a concert or a dance. They seemed to thrive on this organized existence, all the items being compulsory except for sports training which everyone did anyway. Some American schoolboys, who were official guests, had had quite enough after ten days. Tim, Peter, Roger and Traicho were relieved that the full day they spent there was Sunday, the 'day off', although activities still went on non-stop. These students were happy and active, nothing apathetic about them. But the camp provided little challenge to foreign 23-year-olds.

Roger, and an American friend, Dolores, met *en route*, wandered off to take photos in the old district of Kiev known as Podol. All went well for a while, until they noticed that there was one particular Russian citizen who popped up now and again saying, 'you can't take photos'. Roger and Dolores took no notice except to point the cameras up in the direction of the sky and pretend to

(Opposite, top) The centre of Kiev was pleasantly tree-lined, and had a mature feel and style, in contrast to Moscow.

(Opposite, bottom) This small delivery vehicle was on the outskirts of Orel, and normally used for luggage, but apparently occasionally used to take away dissidents!

take pictures of churches merely as a precaution. There was nothing apparently forbidden to take anyway. Just as they were meandering through the market place one miserable, dirty, scruffy, unshaven policeman came up and told them, by various gesticulations, to go along with him to the nearest police station as 'they' did not like 'them' taking photos. They were kept waiting for an hour in a grubby room, then a copper told Roger to open his cameras and expose the film. Roger refused and they were incapable of opening the cameras themselves. All the conversation was in their respective languages, neither party really understanding the other. Repeated demands for representatives from Intourist and respective embassies made the police so fed up with the sight and sound of the determined photographers that they finally let them go, with no more than a vague sort of promise not to come to that area again. Doggedness had paid off.

In a restaurant later that evening, by remarkable chance, up popped Vladimir, a 20-year-old engineering student with whom Peter had briefly talked outside the Moscow Film Festival. He was a typical eager young Russian, and insisted on organizing an animated evening at the Kiev flat of his grandparents. The grandparents were poor, and Vladimir himself spent every kopek he had, not only to entertain his guests, but to give each of them a little present. The flat was poor, but immaculately clean and comfortable. On the wall of his bedroom, converted into a dining room, stood an icon, put there at the express wish of his grandmother, an ardent Christian, 'because English people like the God'. The religious trends of Russia were illustrated perfectly within the family when his aunt joined us, a middle-aged widow who had lost her husband and only love in the war and now lectured for a meagre salary in history, politics and economics. The grandmother was the devout Christian, the aunt somewhere between Christian and agnostic, and he, Vladimir, the complete atheist.

He was no leader of youth, just an ordinary young man, and in his good English rapidly proceeded to sing nearly every known English 'pop' song. He was desperately keen on jazz and asked to be sent English books. So here he was, a Russian, like millions of others. What did he think of the system that governed this country? Each time the conversation swung in that direction he was immediately guarded, if not fearful, and stuck to the party line.

On leaving Kiev the next day, Vladimir came to the outskirts of the city to say farewell. In that final conversation, out came the truth. He expressed dissatisfaction with the leadership, a yearning to be free and a desire for knowledge of the West. Yet, trapped by the system, he said, 'Peter, I have no choice but to be a good Communist because it is by that means that I shall eventually be free!' In other words, it was inevitable that Communism would slowly change as the country advanced and its standards improved, and he had little choice but to go along with it. For poor Vladimir, however, with whom Peter kept in contact over the years, it would not be at all easy. Peter learnt some 30 years later, when able at last to see him again, that he was picked up by the KGB as soon as the Kombi disappeared down the road to Romania. The fact that he was the son of a Red Army Colonel eventually saved him, but not before questioning, putting a book that we had given him down the lavatory and other unpleasantness. Because of his languages, he was later invited to join the KGB, but told that he would have to report all private conversations with, and about, foreigners on delegations. Vladimir refused and was then told that, if he did not join them, they would not support him for any job he went for in later life, i.e. he would go on the black list. He ended up working with his wife on Sakhalin Island, near Japan, to scratch a decent wage. An engineer, he was later sent into the Chernobyl site after the disaster to help clear up, but without sufficient protective clothing. Many of his colleagues have died since, and his own health was seriously affected. He now lives in Kiev on a small pension, his talents wasted. 'How lucky,' thought Peter, 'we have been to be born where we were.'

The Kombi 'got lost' in the early hours of the morning. Shortly, a fine water mill, which was working round the clock, hove into sight. Asked where we were, the miller did not seem to have any clear idea. Such men and places are untouched by change until the time comes when they are either superseded or abolished. Not until five o'clock in the morning did the campsite in Chernovtsy emerge through the early light. Later that morning, a policeman arrived at the tent, enquiring, very pedantically, 'Where were you, last night?' There had been an accident, said he, on a certain stretch of road. It all smelt as if the police really wanted to know what the occupants of the Kombi might have seen. It later turned out that the road had passed close to a military site. Traicho himself was thoroughly interrogated. Finally these people relaxed their clutches, opening the road to the Russian/Romanian border. Getting across was a lengthy business, on a hot and sultry day. The only real difficulty was when Tim fished out of his pocket a £1 note that he had not declared on entering Russia. He lost it. At least the Romanian border functionaries had had something to do that day – they packed up shop once formalities were complete.

Once in Romania, the Kombi, flying the Union Jack and the Bulgarian flag, attracted a lot of curiosity from the locals. The traditional white costume worn by the northern Romanian peasant-farmers was quite distinctive and set them apart

from the Russian peasants with their rather drab clothes. In Bucharest, after much hassle, one of the best hotels came up with a couple of rooms. Nowhere else was available to stay with official vouchers. Over dinner a dissatisfied Romanian doctor struck up conversation. He introduced some alarming if unlikely figures. He claimed there were 2 million political prisoners; that 30 out of his year in medical school were in jail for demonstrating against the invasion of Hungary (for which Romania had sent troops); he would have to work for a year as a doctor without eating in order to be able to buy a car. Perhaps with the benefit of hindsight his lamentation deserved more notice. And Ceausescu was not even in power yet.

Dusk fell on the rough road to the Romanian/Bulgarian border. Peter nearly mowed down one of the numerous and unlit carts drawn by oxen or bullocks. In the last town before the border it was too late to change any remaining cash. There was nothing for it but to blow the lot on local *konyak* and wine generously offered in a border boutique for purchase at inflated prices. It then emerged that everyone had differing points of entry marked in their visas for Bulgaria. Traicho again performed and soon fixed that little problem with the officials. Camp was set up by the roadside shortly beyond the frontier.

Over rolling hills some atrocious and some good roads led ultimately to Sofia, where Traicho squeezed everyone into the Hotel Grand. It lived up to its name. Traicho was host for the brief stay in Bulgaria. Too much *slivova* in too large glasses was washed down with dinner. The party just about managed to stagger to bed. A short tour the next day revealed a city that was not as beautiful as expected. Traicho, funnily enough, did not seem to know the more historical

(Opposite, top) In Romania, the Kombi, flying the Union Jack and the Bulgarian flag, attracted a lot of curiosity from the locals.

(Opposite, bottom) The traditional white costume worn by the northern Romanian peasant farmers was distinctive and set them apart from the Russian peasants with their rather drab clothes.

places of interest at all. The centre of Sofia was curiously soulless in the manner of Bucharest. Worse still, an important member of the government had just died and all day long small and large processions trouped past for all the world like so many sheep.

At last it was time to head down the road on the last stretch to Istanbul. Dinner *en route* was eaten expensively and in style in Plovdiv in a restaurant recommended by Traicho – the biggest and best in the area. 'Some Communist state!' muttered Tim. It also seemed, with the benefit of hindsight, that Traicho was happily offloading some spare cash before making a definitive exit from his native land. The Kombi swept through the Bulgarian side of the border in about five minutes, helped by some sweet-talking of the official by Dolores, our American passenger, who had been with us since her photo episode with Roger in Kiev. Peter, meanwhile, was following behind separately with her companion, Howard, in a Volvo. They came within inches of their lives when the Volvo's back axle collapsed sending them spinning all over the road.

The Turkish side of the border was reached at 2 am. Four hours later customs were cleared – not bad given that this particular Kombi had no *carnet* and its papers were in Mehmed's name. Everyone huddled by the roadside until the sun became too hot.

The Thracian countryside here was completely different from back across the border. It was arid, dotted with the poplars that Turks lovingly plant for baby sons so as to provide timber to build their houses when they mature and marry. Such grass as grew was yellowing and sparse. A first taste of genuine Turkish coffee was served in a kerb-side café in Edirne. Turkish military were very noticeable and abundant about this sensitive big city on the marches of Greece and Bulgaria. The shadow of the recent Turkish army coup lay long.

Arriving in Istanbul in late afternoon, the first call was at the house of Ridvan Mentes – an old family friend of Mehmed. Mehmed's co-expeditionaries had been expected two days earlier so no one was at home. A policeman offered to show the way to Mr Mentes' office. The *poste restante* arrangement, previously set up in Istanbul, revealed that Tony and Bob had both arrived, but they were nowhere to be found. An army cadet helped find a room for three in a small hotel.

It was a first taste of Istanbul. Part of the city, particularly on the Pera side, was markedly Western, with streets winding down to the Golden Horn waterfront, dating from Genoese and then Ottoman days. All around was an abundance of private enterprise, a refreshing change from the Soviet bloc. *Hamal* porters bore huge sacks of merchandise on their powerful backs; reputedly the strongest of them could carry a piano. From the Galata Bridge men coaxed fishing lines for supper. And everywhere was the bustle and liveliness of a thriving port at the foot of two continents.

5
YUGOSLAVIA'S ZENITH

Bob Cox, meanwhile, had made his own way to Istanbul. The Royal Navy had told reservist Bob to steer clear of the Soviet Union. By chance he had picked up a working knowledge of Serbo-Croat in Cambridge. Tito's Yugoslavia was no problem for the Navy. So Bob had set off in July on his own one-man segment of the Expedition.

'Why you come to Yugoslavia?' the immigration man asked in broken German when the Tauern Express drew up in the border town of Jesenice. Bob replied in Serbo-Croat, 'To see your beautiful country'. The man looked at him a bit puzzled, paused, muttered with an equally unshaven colleague (reluctance to shave seems to grow as one progresses further east) before grudgingly stamping his passport. Yugoslav gruffness, it soon turned out, was largely superficial. Balkan hospitality was legion.

Zagreb, capital of Croatia, had bustle and smelled of some noisy tolerance. The market was gorged with produce, much of it from little old ladies selling their fruit and vegetables from improvised stalls. The loosening-up during the previous five years of the hard grip of the state on Yugoslav economic life was starting to tell. Café conversation was loud and – up to a point – uninhibited. Balkan addiction to tobacco and coffee was manifest. Bob knew that political dialogue in Yugoslavia was less fettered than further east. But Belgrade was still nervous about Croatian hankerings after greater autonomy, if not more. Serbs dominated the Croatian police, as other sectors of government. An introduction to the Croatian Writers' Union, a major cradle of Croatian self-determination, gave Bob opportunity for franker conversation with little apparent inhibition.

Bob lodged with the family of Frano Abramović, a secondary schoolteacher with a broad culture, inherited from generations of Austro-Hungarian civil servants. Frano needed 24 hours to offload inhibitions and engage in unstinted conversation with his Western guest. He wanted greater Croatian autonomy. As he was a teacher, this suggested that Party control of educational staffing was either lukewarm or sloppy. In any case, Frano stopped short of the dreaded 'independence' word. But, as his family name suggested, Croatian self-assertion was overcast by the wartime *Ustaša* fascist past of willing collaboration with Nazi persecution of Jews. Frano's family had covered their traces during this unhappy time, holed up in a remote village towards the multi-ethnic Vojvodina, too miserably poor for the authorities to bother about. Frano was clearly bothered that a new-found freedom would come at the price of resurgence of the old fascist demons never far below Croatia's surface. Behaviour by some in the ruling HDZ party in the early days of Croatia's fight for independence in the 1990s would prove him right.

Belgrade, Yugoslavia's capital, was more homespun than Habsburg Zagreb. But both cities shared that particular pre-Great War architectural *kitsch* typical of *Mitteleuropa* and the Balkans. Where was the distinction? Serbia and Belgrade saw themselves as Balkan – not so the denizens of Zagreb. An introduction to the Serbian Writers' Union, and to some university circles, provided insight into current feelings. The similarity between these Zagreb and Belgrade temples of intellect and academia was striking. Both were at the heart of nineteenth-century emancipation and rediscovery of their Slavic roots in the teeth of Austrian and Ottoman imperial domination, but even more so in Belgrade, where barely a conversation went by without evocation of Serbian history, suffering and sacrifice for the South Slav cause – ultimately rewarded by leadership of Yugoslavia. The League of Communists had pretty well taken over the prerogatives of the royal Karageorgević dynasty.

At Belgrade University, Bob's contacts with a new generation of graduates revealed how they had profited from recent relaxation to complete their studies abroad, in Western Europe and the USA. They acknowledged the excellence of Soviet technological education, but there were few takers for a stay in Moscow. Nor, not surprisingly, was there any encouragement in that direction from the Yugoslav authorities, themselves then engaged in offering university places to youngsters from their Bandung Non-Aligned partner states (right then gathered at a summit in Cairo) in competition with Moscow's Lumumba University.

Bob was to experience, some 30 years later, the sequel of what he experienced in 1961.

✻

The Yugoslavian drama in the making exploded in 1991, creating an unfinished test for today's Europe. Bob became professionally involved on the ground, when detached to the European Community Monitoring Mission (ECMM) sent in to try and create some dialogue amidst the warring parties. In vain. By the spring of 1992, Bosnia-Herzegovina plunged into the viciousness that culminated in the torture of Sarajevo, the massacre of Srebrenica, and other horrors Europeans visited on each other. Europe's political immaturity was there for all to see in the face of a major conflagration on its own doorstep, less than two hours' flying time from Brussels. NATO stuttered in the face of a dying cold war. The US-sponsored 1995 Dayton Agreement brought peace – but with the seeds sown for future outbreaks of violence in the western Balkans, where efforts to heal wounds and create confidence and prosperity progress painfully. Ideological and racist rubbish smoulders on; grievances, self-pity and paranoia gnaw away. The republics of the former Yugoslavia excel in non-cooperation. Croatia may become the 28th member state of an EU already farcically overstretched.

*

The overnight train from Belgrade climbed into Skopje in the early morning. Here was a real eye-opener of a cultural shift. Shortly before Skopje the elderly ticket collector was in lively conversation with an equally elderly and distinguished matron, complete with fur collar in mid-July. Their conversation veered back and forth from Serbo-Croat to Turkish. 'Alas,' said the ticket-collector, 'we are both of the last generation that still speaks Turkish down south here.' That last generation was still abundant in Skopje, where one side of the railway track was modern and the other side was the old Turkish administrative and merchant city of Yugoslav Macedonia. So much of it was tragically destroyed a bare two years later in 1963 by an earthquake.

Leaving behind the pleasant atmosphere of Skopje, Bob bussed across Macedonia towards Priština. This, to many Serbs, is their historical and emotional cradle of Kosovo where, in 1389, the Ottomans crushed them. One is mentally at odds with the idea that a major defeat is celebrated as a central piece of national mythology. But that is what Serbs do. In 1991, Bob, with the European Community Monitoring Mission, was to get earfuls of that paranoia (what else do you call it?) when trying to engage in dialogue with Serbian officers.

More even than enjoying the superb medieval Serbian Orthodox monuments of the region, Bob wanted to test the theory that Albania was a hermetically closed country – as a week earlier the British Embassy in Belgrade had bluntly told him. So early one morning he took an old bus and set out from Ohrid to Struga, followed by a lift down the road on a bullock-cart and a final walk past curious bystanders to the barrier on the Yugoslav side of the border. 'And what is your business?' asked the duty lieutenant, poking Bob's rucksack – but quite amiably when he heard that he could do business in Serbo-Croat. Bob explained his ambition, pointing ahead down the rutted road to the Albanian side. 'Forget it!' said the lieutenant. 'The barrier is rusted into place through disuse.' He made it clear that he would arrest this intrepid traveller before he did anything stupid, but first a cup of coffee together was in order. He seemed quite happy to accept that this was just a bizarre English student trying his capricious luck and not something more sinister. The lieutenant's job was boring; this was unhoped-for entertainment during his shift. After coffee, conversation and the obligatory slug of plum brandy, Bob was courteously bundled into a truck to return to Ohrid town with the compliments of the Yugoslav People's Army.

*

Albania in due course blundered out of its cul-de-sac in the general rupture of Communism. In the spring of 1997, Bob was co-opted into the OSCE (Organization for Security and Cooperation in Europe) team under Austrian former President Vranitsky, despatched to Tirana, with French and Italian military back-up, to restore some semblance of order. The place had collapsed in a vortex of general sleaze and a *Ponzi* pyramid scam (à la Bernie Madoff). Albania continues to struggle with its inheritances of clan-violence, corruption and poor governance. Its next-door neighbour, Kosovo, is another unlanced boil in the European Union's neighbourhood emergency ward.

*

After a stopover in Salonika, including a chance to drop in, uninvited, to a typical sumptuous Greek Orthodox wedding with bride, groom, priest and cheerleaders cavorting around icons and ornaments, Bob was on a battered train clattering through Thrace towards Turkey. Just as hunger started to bite, a smell of grilled meat wafted down from the head of the train in competition with the smoke from the wheezing locomotive. Treading gingerly over a couple of planks covering the couplings, Bob lurched into a freight van with doors wide open on both sides to the passing countryside. In the middle was a blackened charcoal grill tended by the huge, profusely sweating figure of what looked like a blacksmith or a denizen of Hades. It was an introduction to several months of successive kebab – hot off the grill and wrapped in unleavened bread with a handful of salad thrown in for good measure.

A few hours later Bob was on the dockside in Istanbul, welcoming Tony to Turkey.

MOSCOW CALLING

Meanwhile Further East …

Tony and Nigel had finally got out of Moscow on 18 July. Mehmed was recovering in hospital before flying to the rendezvous in Sochi. From Moscow down the long road south the rolling plains fed into the heart of the Ukraine with its vast wheat lands. Maize and sunflowers, too, sprung from the rich soil for miles on every side. It was harvest time. The women laboured in the fields; the men drove the horses and trailers. Villages on the main road had the slogan 'Comrades, let us use our skill to increase production'. 'This farm,' posters said, would produce 'so many *tsentner* (hundredweight) per hectare' to honour the *Plan*. New industrial combines emerged here and there. This was already the Steppes, the lonely plains of Southern Russia, being tamed by mechanized equipment and large-scale techniques. But horses and carts were still aplenty. Women outnumbered men in the fields, another legacy of the war when every man was at the front. An all-night drive ended in Kharkov, centre of the Ukraine's industry. It still bore the marks of heavy fighting. It was the second city in the Ukraine, but the cobbled streets and dilapidated appearance gave it a provincial air.

Further south, Rostov, also heavily battered in the war, had made a fine recovery and enjoyed a certain atmosphere of southern gaiety. Vacationing crowds thronged the pavements. Across the thriving port, the Flying Ferries passenger craft on hydrofoils skimmed over the smooth surface of the quietly flowing Don. The city had long been a melting-pot of nationalities: Greeks, Armenians, Georgians, even some of Caucasian extraction, who came here in the past to settle. Even then, although the Armenian town no longer existed as such, the few old buildings that still stood witnessed the prosperity of those times.

(Opposite, top) Harvest time in the Ukraine, with mainly women in the fields, little mechanization, and men driving the horse and trailer!

(Opposite, bottom) The vast wheat lands of the Ukraine.

MOSCOW CALLING

A football coach and a lawyer's assistant, bumped into at dinner in the Hotel Rostov, offered to be guides to the city and revealed its interesting detail. The sun went higher towards the middle of the day, and pavements were strewn with drunk men. The football coach laconically commented, 'I wonder why people find it necessary to drink so much!'

The call of the south is very strong in Rostov. Thousands of people pass through the city on their way to the summer resort of Sochi on the Black Sea. It was a relief to arrive there. This famous Black Sea resort was stacked with sanatoria and holiday-makers. It was a place for promenading and admiring the scenery. Dress styles were less than inspiring. But here a foreigner could feel more or less anonymous and inconspicuous; the whole atmosphere was at arm's length from officialdom. But no one would talk politics, such was the risk at the back of people's minds.

Mehmed, discharged from his hospital bed in Moscow, had now flown to join Nigel and Tony in Sochi. A three-day rest followed in this ideal location – a sort of short summer holiday, before driving on to Tbilisi (the 'warm springs'), and the southernmost stopping-place, in late July. This was a far cry from Moscow. Capital of Georgia, Tbilisi was a fast-growing town and the pride of the effervescent Georgians. It oozed zip, colour and culture. It boasted broad streets, and well-stocked shops with Western-style window displays. The men appeared especially well dressed. Unlike the Russians, they exuded panache and gaiety. Georgia was a rich province. Georgians had the highest per capita income and the highest number of university graduates or their equivalent in the whole of the Soviet Union. Tbilisi got to one. It was the ideal place for meeting the students on informal ground – a swimming pool reserved for higher educational establishments. But here too the followers and shadowers were conspicuous every day. The students had warned of this.

The campsite in Tbilisi was a collection of comfortable tents near the hippodrome, amid tall pine trees. Intourist was still the unavoidable 'big brother'. Nearly every day someone turned up from the local office, mostly saying 'why are you still here?' On one such visit, they recommended taking a trip up the Georgian Military Highway to the *Daryalskoye Ushchelye* on the Terek River. This was the gorge described by Russia's great poet Lermontov in his *Lullaby*, as the place where the 'wicked Chechen crept along the ditch and honed his dagger'. Some things, it would appear, do not change. This was spectacular scenery. Pigs and sheep were herded together in one body on the road up into the mountains near Kazbegi, the tallest mountain in the Caucasus.

At the gorge, the bridge was down due to a storm and flash floods. This dramatic scene naturally lent itself to being photographed. Whereupon the eager-beaver cameramen were duly arrested by a certain, pint-sized Commandant Chitiri – because 'you took a photo of the Devil's Bridge!' Chitiri added an opaque comment about it being a crime to speak with non-Communist Uzbeks – 'when did we do that?' the 'prisoners' wondered. In the command post, there was a long argument about why the travellers had such 'sophisticated photo equipment' and what were they doing there anyway. The issue was that, on the way up, they had passed a police car that had ordered an about-turn as the road was closed. Ignoring that brought the foreseeable result. Films were confiscated and exposed – thus destroying the record of most of Mehmed's photos of the journey thus far. Nor did they have any luck in getting the unexposed films back – at least the cameras were not seized. Nigel had to sign a 'confession' admitting 'insubordination' before a long drive back to town. Did Intourist, in suggesting this trip, knowing the security sensitivity about the Military (*sic*) Highway, deliberately seek to screw things up, or was it just old-fashioned incompetence?

Next day, the Intourist minder jumped up and down and put (another?) spanner in the works. After that, most attempts to walk around town were followed by a young student, Tengiz, who was nice enough, but a nuisance. Now, the agency minder said, it was impracticable to put the Kombi on a platform wagon of the train to Julfa (now called Nahchivan) and thus follow the planned route onwards through Julfa Iranskaya, one of the few frontier crossings on the Soviet-Iranian border, crossed only by train.

Thus Tony had to take the Kombi out of the Soviet Union by way of the Black Sea, while Nigel and Mehmed would ultimately take the train to Iran as simple passengers. On 1 August, Tony duly drove the Kombi by himself back to Sochi – some 375 miles and a 15-hour drive. There he caught a boat – the *Feliks Dzerzhinski*, named after the Bosheviks' notorious secret police chief – for Istanbul, via Yalta, Odessa, Konstansa and Varna. Tony remembers that the Russian crew was not allowed to land in Istanbul, so paranoid were the Russians about defectors.

Tony met up with Tim's group on 9 August in Istanbul. The Expedition's two hard-worked Kombis, like a pair of separated donkeys, were reunited too. Donkeys, as any French or Spanish peasant will tell you, do not like solitude. Mehmed and Nigel, left to their own devices back in Tbilisi, were to embark on further escapades before meeting up with the rest of the expedition in Iran. More of that in due course.

FROM ASIA'S EDGE

6

ANATOLIA

Eurasia's Crucible

The history of the great upland mass of Anatolia, like its sister, the *Heerweg* in northern Europe, has seen peoples, civilizations, cultures and armies go back and forth, fight, create and settle, for as long as human history has known. For many historians Anatolia *was* Greece. Herodotus, the great Greek historian, was born in Halicarnassos – today's Bodrum – where Mehmed in 2010 would host a gathering of the Expedition members that laid the groundwork of this book. The great city of Ephesus was just a few hours' drive 'down the road', so to speak. The Expedition's route would take them through Trabzon (*Trapezon*) and Samsun (*Amisos*), and then through Erzurum known to the Greeks as *Theodossiopolis* and to the Armenians, who once populated much of eastern Anatolia, as *Garin*. The Silk Road passed through, and so did Alexander. The Selcuks and the Ottomans came back the other way to lay the grounds for Turkey.

It was now 9 August. With help from host Ridvan Mentes, Tim and Roger met up with Tony and Bob to coax Tony's vehicle out of its bond at the notoriously tetchy Turkish customs. Tim by now knew that the number plates had been wrong since Germany. They did not match the vehicle documents. An attempt to get a *carnet de passage* from the Turkish Auto Club, and so ease passage through various future customs posts, got nowhere. Both vehicles were registered in Germany with these special 'export' number plates. Somehow, the Kombis were released. Then there was no common-sense alternative but, once out of sight of the customs officers, simply to swap the number plates on the vehicles. Duly re-baptized, both vehicles were then taken to VW Service – Tony's to have a proper engine overhaul and Tim's to fix the jumping gears. Two days later, nothing had been done to Tim's, but Tony's had been fitted with the last two pistons available in Istanbul.

Ridvan Mentes, it later emerged, had to bribe officials in order to 'correct' the records, and get Tony's Kombi released. Ridvan not only eased the way through officialdom, but also entertained and fed everyone royally throughout the stay

An abundance of fresh
food outside the Iron
Curtain – fish sellers by
the side of the Bosphorus,
Istanbul.

in Istanbul. When asked what he did for a living, Ridvan shrugged his shoulders ever so slightly, touched his moustache and said – 'import-export'. You could draw your own conclusions. This was, after all, Istanbul.

A certain Mr Bayazid, known to Mehmed, was the first Turk to go to Cambridge, where he had a very happy time. He helped sell some of the Expedition's surplus goods for some useful cash. He, too, dealt in import-export, was politically respectable, and very successful.

Tim went fishing one evening with the lawyer who defended Mr Menderes, the ex-Prime Minister of Turkey. Menderes was to be executed just over one month later. At this time, Mehmed's father, Arif Demirer, was still in jail.

Istanbul continued to enchant. The light across the Bosphorus caught the minarets of both the Blue Mosque and Hagia Sophia to give a surreal effect of shape and colour. The usual tourist visits to these mosques, as well as the Grand and Spice Bazaars, lived fully up to expectations. The Istanbul market stalls groaned under a great abundance of fresh food. Unlike behind the Iron Curtain, Istanbul then was not the target of mass tourism that it is today. Even less of a magnet for travellers was the great land mass of Anatolia into which the remarkable Kemal Atatürk had consolidated his country, abandoning Istanbul for the new landlocked capital of Ankara, after the debacle of 1918 and the collapse of the Ottoman Empire.

Bob felt keenly that Turkey was caught in an impossible situation – and one liable to last for a long time yet. This was – and is – a complex society. No practical solution to its difficulties looked to be on the cards. The intelligentsia was a small group of men and women whose education had been almost entirely European. Probably European governesses had nurtured them while young. They had then been educated in one of Istanbul's 'European' schools or *lycées* before going abroad to study and become even more firmly fixed in European ways. But the vast majority of the nation (some 80 per cent of it), had never seen the inside of a school; they tilled the land, bred army conscripts, and lived in Anatolia. The rift between these people and the small elite of European-trained intellectuals, or merchants, was enormous. In Turkey (as indeed elsewhere) this upbringing, alien to much of the country's history, became an obstacle to reform and improvement, even with the strongest will and deepest patriotism. There was indeed the bond of the nation, cemented with a modernized language – both inherited from Atatürk. Many educated Turks had little taste for the plaintive Turkish melodies pouring out of Istanbul taxi radios or tenements, and more for crisp American 'hot' tunes. The psychological difference between the two layers of Turkish society erected a high wall. The top layer, one felt, was like a bad piece of skin-grafting that had not taken. One could easily be persuaded that the Istanbul elite was more European than most Europeans further west. The fraught saga of Turkey's bid to join the European Union is a product – also – of this mismatch of identity.

A short story, in Turkish storyteller's idiom, about a little girl from Anatolia, gleaned from a conversation in Istanbul, told much:

> The little girl from Anatolia cannot read or write. And her eyes are distorted. She approaches the table hesitantly, hardly daring to look at the faces she is to serve. The vague chaos of her world intimidates her – all those people with clever faces and fine tongue. Yet their words differ little from those spoken

to her before she left for the great city where the houses touch the clouds, where machines clatter through crowded streets. In the big, cool house slim, benevolent ladies would correct her with a fleeting frown when she performed her small tasks properly. As she approaches the table she hesitates as if the 20 faltering paces from the kitchen to the table carried her into a different world mysteriously evoked by the elders of her lowly village.

Her mistress had sent her to another, more lowly gentleman who tried to teach her the strange symbols these people put on paper which were painted over the walls of the great city. The gentleman rarely smiled as his pen moved from sign to another and the little girl tried to follow.

She recalled how the brown-skinned mullah in her village had made signs on paper for the boys of the village. How could she, with her misformed eyes, which the lady had promised to have cured by a great doctor, dare to share the secrets of the mullah, the clever boys and the clever gentleman?

The meal over she approached the lady and waited a small distance away until she should be noticed. The lady turned and beckoned her to speak. The little girl whispered: 'Please, Madame, what shall I do now?' 'Go and play with little Aysha,' said the lady. The little girl from Anatolia walked timidly down the garden between the clipped flower beds to be a playmate – or a toy?

One day back in the village she had fallen and struck her head upon a stone. A spear of pain jabbed across the back of her eyes and she sobbed while her body lay across the stone. Two men grumbled and picked her up. The flame flashed suddenly to white heat and darkness fell more quickly than it had ever fallen before. She woke as if thrust out of a deep well into daylight, revolving as she rose. Two strong hands held her head and two eyes penetrated hers but she could not fix her gaze upon them, try as she would. The head of the man shook slowly and deliberately, then turned to utter a few words to half visible figures in the dim background: 'her eyes will not serve her well.'

Now in the great city the same chaos bubbled behind her eyes. The great doctor had come, as the lady had promised, to look at the little girl's eyes. After a while he rose. 'I cannot mend those eyes. And even less can I look beyond those eyes and mend the gap between the two worlds in which she lives.'

The thread of the storyteller's tale would come to mind during the weeks ahead while travelling through the fastnesses of Anatolia and Persia.

✻

Turkey is one of the few countries visited by the Expedition that has much to boast of in the last century. But it has been a hard ride. Its current spreading of wings is fraught with risk. Two of the Expedition members have close ties with Turkey: Mehmed, of course, because it is his native country, where he is active politically and economically; Bob was the European Commission's man in Ankara for four years at a crucial point in Turkey's modern history. In 1961–2, Mehmed's father was languishing in prison, following the military coup which threw him and colleagues out of government. In September 1980, Bob and Mehmed were in Ankara when the Turkish military struck again amidst growing anarchy. Only in September 2010, following a referendum, was much of the generals' real and constitutional power contained. Turkey enters the new century a much-changed and more self-confident country than was evident in 1961. Why, many ask, is Turkey asserting itself? Bloody-mindedness towards a Europe that drags its feet over Turkey's potential membership of the club? A 'neo-Ottoman' vocation in its key geopolitical situation? Or just a refusal to be kicked around in great power war-games where NATO took for granted a plentiful supply of Turkish conscript bayonets? None of these theories suffice for a country with a proud history and proven capacity to reject defeat. Mehmed wrote in the Cambridge University student weekly *Varsity* in 1960 under the title 'Where Is Turkey Anyway?': 'Turkey is neither European nor Asian. She will remain what she has always been, a bridge between the two. And she will continue to be proud of this.' One of Bob's Turkish local staff, an educated Istanbulite, said of his native city: 'It's being overrun by Anatolia.' The same guy, after a traineeship in Brussels, said about young Greeks he had met there, 'They're the same as us!' Two truths and realities which, paradoxically, could contain the seeds of a greater regional sobering-up – if the politicians let it be so.

✻

It was time for the Expedition to move on. With the help of American fellow-travellers from the Balkans, Dolores and Howard, depleted provisions were restocked at the Istanbul American PX – then a goldmine for fancy and other US goods accessible to Europeans by invitation only. Both Kombis left Istanbul in the early evening after a splendid lunch at the home of the Mentes family, who escorted the little convoy to the Ankara road. Before dawn, camp was set up outside Ankara, the capital city. Mrs Demirer – Mehmed's mother – could not be found.

It was a hot day in mid-August. The endless Anatolian plains baked in brown remoteness ahead. A cool beer fortified the sense of endeavour before tackling the long haul over mountains behind the Black Sea to Samsun. Roads of uncertain surface quality spiralled ahead. Soon there was a nasty noise from the front of Kombi Z1060, now 're-baptized' with the registration number of 'Tim's' Kombi. A shock absorber had come loose. Three men on a rope took two hours to pull it on again.

The road took a turn for the better. The countryside was the wildest yet seen, with great plains giving way to bare mountains and ultimately hills of many different hues of green before dropping to the coast. Mountain villages with flat-roofed, stone-built houses provided solid refuge for the inhabitants against the notorious storms rushing out of the Black Sea and the harsh Anatolian winter.

The road grew worse, the shock absorber now decided to slip off the other way. Tim tied it up out of the way with string. For the Kombis, like real pack animals, there was a lot of laborious climbing on a twisty, gravel-surfaced road. Finally, a halt was called in the early hours of the morning on top of a mountain and a tent rigged up between the two Kombis. The sun allowed little sleep. Tim bought some washers for the Kombi in Samsun, a town with shops full of useful commodities, and with them fixed up the shock absorber. This repair, as luck would have it, would work perfectly all the way to Teheran. The empty road went in a straight line along the flat littoral, with fertile land and with ample water all around to feed the abundant produce it yielded.

By this time Kombi Z1235 had forged well ahead of Tim and Roger. At one point Tim and Roger noticed some rather bad skid marks round a corner. They found out later that this was another of novice driver Bob's efforts– the first being a gentle collision with the behind of a grumpy donkey in Ankara. Both Kombis were now playing a sort of involuntary cat-and-mouse game.

The littoral receded and the road began to wind along the shore. Supper was in the only restaurant in Ordu. Camp was set up for the night by the shore.

Roger and Tim were up and away by dawn. A lovely excursion inland followed, then back to the twisty coast road. There were heartstopping moments when lorries came at full pelt round corners, where there was just room for them alone, and forced the Kombi into the ditch. Turkish lorries frequently carried the painted sign 'Masallah' above their windscreens as a charm of trust in the protection of the Almighty against disaster when driving against all odds of survival, particularly around blind corners or over hilltops. Asked what the sign meant, one driver answered, 'This is a bloody good lorry!'

The end of the day –
sunset on the two Kombis
by the Black Sea coast,
northern Turkey.

(Opposite, top) There
were many spiralling roads,
of uncertain surface quality,
in the mountainous areas
of central Turkey.

(Opposite, bottom) A
typical mountain village
with flat-roofed, stone-built
houses, in eastern Turkey.

Arriving in Trabzon mid-morning, a search for the Atatürk Museum proved fruitless; no one seemed to know where it was. Instead, a big US Air Force base emerged around a bend. From Trabzon the route continued to Erzurum; the coastal mountains were almost alpine, the road splendidly engineered through the challenging terrain. Along the way were small, compact towns with bright paintwork and the occasional Roman bridge against the backdrop of a fine vista. They reached Bayburt in the early evening. This was supposed to be the meeting point with the other Kombi. It was nowhere to be seen. Camp was set up for the night on a haulage site with the sidelights left on, in case the others came along.

Most crops had already been harvested, but farmers were still busy. Threshing the grain crop was still done in the old style using an ox roped to a beam and trudging round in circles. Nut and fruit crops were spread on the ground by the side of the road to dry in the sun. Mechanical implements were few and far between.

Enquiries the next day in Bayburt revealed that the other Kombi had left for Erzurum the previous night. That would be it until Tabriz. To Erzurum the road followed the flat plain between smooth hills with few trees in sight. The underside of an oil tanker provided welcome shade for a quick lunch. Erzurum was obviously a big centre for the military. Now it was broiling hot in mid-summer glare. In winter the temperature could drop to minus 30 degrees and lower; sentries at barrack gates were changed every 15 minutes to prevent them from freezing to death. After Erzurum a chance meeting with some of Tim's friends from Christ's College, Cambridge driving from Karachi to London in a Land Rover, elicited dire warnings about how terrible the road was in Iran. A puncture shortly after leaving Agri meant putting back a spare tyre which already had a slow puncture. It was time to pull off the road and camp at the foot of Mount Ararat, just before the frontier town of Doğubayazit, to wait for daylight.

Meanwhile, near Bayburt, for the other Kombi carrying Tony, Peter and Bob the evening meal nearly ended in 'alcoholic disaster'. In the smallest of chow houses on the main road and only street a mad cook rustled up steak in two minutes flat to a half-drunk waiter wearing a wide, floppy Turkish cap like his other clients. They were all very excited by the odd arrival of these creatures from afar and the hand and the neat black moustache of the waiter gave frequent twitches of pleasure. In the ordinary downtown Turkish restaurant the menu was limited so no one bothered to write it down. You merely walked in, reserved yourself a seat and then strolled into the kitchen to see what was cooking. A brief consultation, grimaces and gesticulations ensued and then you returned to your seat for a beer. The cordial waiter friend retired into a small cubbyhole behind a low table, frowned and then disappeared for two minutes. He returned, smiled, and left his new guests to quietly separate the fiery peppers from the salad. They hoped that no one was watching too closely as they did so. One pepper needed at least four bottles of beer to accompany it, for the Westerner at least, as the tongue temperature experienced a rapid rise after these pernicious little white things had done their worst.

The door flew open and in came the fellow from the place down the road with fresh beer in the usual unlabelled bottles. Meanwhile, our friendly waiter had helped himself to another slug of the cause of his cheerfulness – *Yeni Raki 45* – the Turks' favourite anis-based drink, whitened sparingly with water. He then splashed *raki* into the glasses of the foreign guests but added beer instead of the customary water. Bob and Tony exchanged a brief, doubtful glance without changing the polite smiles on their faces and clinked glasses with the happy waiter. Cigarettes were exchanged and more *raki* appeared. The situation began to grow serious. Peter made steering wheel gesticulations with his hands and excused himself on the grounds that he was driving. At the same time, a grandly moustachioed gentleman, who appeared to be something like the local constable, walked in, eased his not inconsiderable weight into a chair besides some of the locals and occupied the waiter's attention as he took his evening few to fortify himself for the night's beat. Tony, Bob and Peter prepared to take off, but one more glass of Anatolian firewater had first to be consumed and with handshakes all round they swiftly but tactfully managed to get out onto the street, amused but relieved. As they drove out of town, a fairground shrieked and grunted noisily. Only men were actually on the swings – the women sat packed like sardines on benches, with just their eyes showing through their *chador*.

The border was now close. Convoys of military lorries and jeeps passed; camps were frequent. Turkey then had 1.5 million men under arms. Persians and Turks, from the Seljuks down to the Byzantines before them, had more often than not been at each other's throats. The border had ping-ponged back and forth a few times. And the Red Army, too, was just up the road.

Roger set the alarm for dawn to take photos of Mount Ararat. It was cloudy for once – a good excuse to go gratefully back to sleep again. There was better luck later. With its upper mantle of snow and attendant cloud the mountain looked timeless.

Driving – or leading – a
herd of goats, in eastern
Turkey.

But it must have looked different when Noah was around, what with all that
swirling water. Then, after driving over a slight ridge, there was Iran. At the Turkish/
Iranian border it emerged that the others had spent the night in the 'Border Hotel'
and had just passed through. 'Not very intelligent,' grumbled Tim, who still had
the wrong vehicle number in his passport. One person could not take two cars into
Iran. This threw up a documentation hitch at customs on the Turkish side – this
Kombi had the 'wrong' engine and chassis number. On the Iranian side, Tim had to
declare that he was 'driving the vehicle out of Iran' before they would let anybody
in. Various imprecise written undertakings finally did the trick and the barrier into
Iran was duly raised.

The first 12 miles ran alongside a dried-up river valley and then across a wide,
arid plain. The road surface was reasonable and as long as one kept moving
the heat was bearable. Every so often there was a small township built round

a spring. The buildings were one storey of mud and straw and formed into one mass by tall walls of the same material. A few trees to provide shade for all and sundry made the whole scene into a blurred hotchpotch of colour from a distance. The plain looked like shifting sand, having the same wave-like formation, but actually was quite permanent. The rivers that flowed in winter and spring cut deep gullies in the otherwise uniform terrain.

On leaving the last town before Tabriz a soldier blocked the way for what looked at first like a security check. 'Could you take my sergeant into Tabriz?' 'Well yes.' Then in jumped two soldiers. 'Oh no you don't!' There was nothing for it but to adjourn to the nearby cafe for *chai*. Suddenly, two goats and half a dozen chickens materialized. These were also travelling to Tabriz. 'Oh well, tie them on the roofrack.' A soldier climbed up on top and lashed the goats down. The chickens were quiescent, having been carried around head downwards. The Kombi groaned with this additional load and set off with all aboard. Soon a stomping noise was heard from the roof; on leaning out, Tim saw that the billy-goat had cast off his lashings and was standing facing forward with an expression of disgust on his face. This, it appeared, was how he liked to travel, so the journey was completed with him walking about on the roof. The poor chickens were almost flattened by the wind across the roof of the travelling Kombi and had to be brought inside, where they lay in a motionless heap.

Soon the lights of Tabriz beckoned. A tour of the streets looking for the others ended up in the garden of a hotel where they were found drinking cokes with four Australians. After food and a shower, an hour was passed talking with an Armenian engineer who built barracks for the Iranian army. According to him, the Americans and the English were equally disliked. As for the Iranians, said he contemptuously, and short-sightedly – they were 'donkeys'.

It was Roger's 21st birthday – celebrated in Tabriz with a coke.

7
A BIT TOO FAR EAST

Meanwhile, 1,250 miles away as the crow flies, still in the Soviet Union, Mehmed and Nigel were seeing life their way.

Tbilisi was the southernmost and cheapest jumping off-place for Tashkent in Central Asia. The expense was prohibitive, but having got there the cost, for once, could be considered last. A TU-104 aircraft rocketed Mehmed and Nigel through the night to Tashkent where they arrived before dawn. Here was at once a different world, but one becoming half-familiar. Russian architecture still disfigured what might once have been one of the most fascinating cities in the world. But Tashkent – the 'stone city' in Turkic – remained a place full of surprises.

In a restaurant for breakfast that morning, in a long, thin room with a narrow carpet down the middle, Mehmed and Nigel shared a table with a one-eyed writer called Ignatyev (an exile?) and his ethnic Korean companion (minder?). On discovering that these were foreigners, Ignatyev ordered what he called *portveyn* (a lethal concoction of red wine and probably methyl alcohol). As this concoction went down, his companion became more and more agitated as Ignatyev grew more and more vociferous and before long they were chucked out of the restaurant. Nor could Mehmed and Nigel stay – they had to meet their mandatory Intourist guide later – but how after such a breakfast does one walk straight down a restaurant on a very narrow carpet?

The Intourist guide was not your regular sort – he spoke fluent Turkish and knew more about English football teams than Nigel did. He was actually a Ukrainian. Being driven around Tashkent gave our travellers an opportunity gradually to sober up. In those days, Tashkent was typical of the old Russian colonial era with a 'European' and a 'native' quarter. Once the tour was officially over, the guide was persuaded to leave Mehmed and Nigel on their own. Thankfully there was a *chaikhane* in the ethnic quarter close by and severe dehydration was corrected with copious cups of tea.

A young Uzbek at the next table noticed the medallion hanging from a chain around Mehmed's neck, and could actually read it. After some time in conversation, in Turkish, Russian, Uzbek and English, Kazym, for that was his name, invited Mehmed and Nigel to his house. This was a first introduction to a proper Central Asian family with all the formalities which apply and also very interesting company. The next day came a new invitation from the family to an 'Uzbek Pilau', a dish specially prepared in honour of guests. On returning to the hotel that evening, however, the guide was waiting. Kazym was grilled about why he was with these strangers, etc. On a subsequent visit to Tashkent, Nigel found the family again and discovered that this event had had consequences. Kazym's elder brother lost his job, and the whole family were in difficult circumstances.

One cannot live indefinitely in a place at the rate of one pound sterling an hour, so the next night Mehmed and Nigel flew to Baku. Baku was a closed city. How they were able to go there in the first place is a bit of mystery. They were followed most of the time, sometimes more obviously than others. Capital of the Azerbaijan Soviet Socialist Republic (SSR) – another Turkic province – Baku was big and bourgeois, floating on oil. Economically the town was far ahead of the rest of the Republic. It claimed to have the best petro-chemical institute in the world and also had many other top-level higher educational establishments. Unlike the Georgians, the Azerbaijanis were more willing to travel to other parts of the Soviet Union, and many surplus graduates were sent to Kazakhstan and Kirghizia. An atmosphere of boom pervaded the oil-laden air. The town was also situated in a strategic zone. A special permit was required for photography. During lunch Mehmed and Nigel were closely observed by a rather unpleasant-looking couple and found, on return to the hotel, that Mehmed's camera had been opened, and all the film which the intruders could find had been exposed.

The old quarter of Baku had its charms and was apparently a popular filming location. At the entrance of some old buildings there were still the sculpted medallions proclaiming the identity of early British insurance companies which had exploited the presence of oil and the wealth it created. At a jazz concert in Baku the most popular piece was *The American Patrol*. Chatting with a young man playing backgammon outside his house, Mehmed found that Azeri and Turkish are extremely similar. This led to an invitation to go to the beach, a few miles out of town, the following day. On arriving at the rendezvous, Aga Selim, the young man, showed up with a book under his arm and the excuse that he had to study for an urgent assignment so could not take them to the beach. It was worth trying to go out of town anyway and eventually a taxi drove Mehmed and Nigel north across a sandy plain covered with oil rigs. 'Where do you come from?' asked the taxi driver. 'East Germany,' said Mehmed, on the

Market stall in Tashkent.

basis of his excellent German; 'Czechoslovakia,' said Nigel (apparently referring to his alleged accent in Russian). 'Oh yes, I was in hospital in Prague for some months,' said the driver. Abrupt end of conversation. The silence was broken when a policeman jumped out from behind a bush, yanked the door open and said (in Russian), 'Who have you got in there, idiot?' 'One East German and one Czechoslovak,' came the reply. 'That's what you think – turn around and go back to the hotel.' With the policeman in the car, there began a seemingly interminable argument about who was going to pay for the return trip. Unaware that Mehmed and Nigel could understand him, the policeman told the taxi driver all the details as they rode back. 'The signal went out from Headquarters,' he said, 'to stop this car wherever it might be.' He was so excited. Mehmed hoped he got promoted.

Soon it became impossible to do anything. A row with the Komsomol resulted in such pressure being exerted that it was a pleasure to leave, as it was indeed, one suspected, what they hoped. With mixed relief Mehmed and Nigel caught the night train to Tbilisi on 6 August.

Tony had already gone to Istanbul with the Kombi. Mehmed and Nigel were left in Tbilisi on their own for a few days, before catching the train to Julfa and the border. They visited the mosque (under surveillance), while Mehmed got into conversation with other Turkish speakers in the bazaars, who were less than polite about their treatment at the hands of the Georgians.

Nigel found buying train tickets to Julfa quite eventful. The only currency he had left was in black market roubles – and, moreover, in large denominations of 100 roubles, an infrequent sight. On trying to pay with one of these notes, the woman in charge went downstairs and walked up and down chanting, 'Who's got change for a hundred rouble note ...?' The local Intourist manager, called Edermann, caught Nigel's eye; it was clear he knew or guessed where that banknote came from, but said nothing. (A year or two later, Nigel was in Tbilisi with a small tour group and it was also clear that Edermann had not forgotten.)

The charm of Tbilisi restored spirits and a few more days were spent dodging the escorts – to the intense amusement of the spectators – watching football matches, and thoroughly enjoying life. Attempts to study the educational establishments of Georgia failed after relations with the Komsomol broke down. There was no way of hanging on any longer in Tbilisi – visas had already been extended twice. A farewell supper, with Intourist minder Tengiz and his stunning girlfriend from Leningrad, gave Nigel food poisoning, which made the impending train journey a little difficult.

So began the two-day-long train journey, in a very comfortable compartment. Down the line to Yerevan, Nakhchivan, along the Turkish border, past Mount Ararat and then into Julfa, the border town with Iran. Nigel slept most of the time. Mehmed talked to curious renegades, quasi-dissidents, who were holed up in the restaurant car.

As a parting shot, the Soviet customs were particularly attentive. After seven weeks in the Soviet Union, they must have felt that it was no less than their duty. Personal papers, diaries, postcards, any scrap of paper were carefully scrutinized. Addresses were confiscated. Nigel had to translate handwritten notes, diary entries and scurrilous poetry dictated to Mehmed in the restaurant car. Worst of all, they discovered the last of the dollars (fortunately no roubles) for which, of course, there was no currency receipt. Forty dollars confiscated – 'You can have it back if you come within the next three years,' they said. 'Thanks,' murmured Mehmed and sighed with relief as the train rolled slowly over the bridge into Iran.

*

Thinking back to that time, as Julfa receded down the railway line, provokes thoughts as to how Russia is evidence that governance may change while underneath the people remain the same. The massive rape of state assets under Yeltsin yielded to the new state thuggery under Putin. The Cold War has given way to a more subtle regime of East–West mistrust. Russian pride and Slav emotions smart at being perceived, so they think, as some sort of Third World country. Mindful of its former power and glory, Russia wants to be respected in its own backyard or traditional spheres of influence. In the last analysis, in place of fear, 'Europe should realise how much it has to gain from a sound relationship with what is a very remarkable country', as Peter Temple-Morris learned over his years as a parliamentarian with active links to Russia. He hosted the celebrated visit to the United Kingdom of Mikhail Gorbachev in December 1984. Soviet Russia in 1961 was a ruthless dictatorship, with dreary Communism and all the rest of it. But the warmth of the Russian people shone through.

*

It was an abrupt shift to the amazing atmosphere of Julfa on the Iranian side. Music, a sense of freedom, and normality. It was then that the news broke that the Berlin wall had just been built. Once together again, Expedition members in their conversation instinctively turned to the subject; a new barrier, physical and psychological, and above all brutal, had sprung up across the Europe that in both their travel and imagination they had sought to cross.

8

IRANIAN DYNASTIES

While Nigel and Mehmed were ensconced on the train from the border, the others walked in the crowded streets of Tabriz. After six weeks of Russia, it was a relief. People moved about with noise and animation, the streets were full of traffic – and accidents. Shops were full of imported goods costing not much more than in the country of manufacture. But this was far from a prosperous capital for Iran's 5 million Azerbaijanis. It somehow did not look the second biggest city in Iran that it was supposed to be. There were only one or two real restaurants, apart from kerbside eateries. 'Tabriz is on the decline,' said one merchant; people had moved to Teheran and other booming centres. It was fast losing significance. There were no German or British Consulates in Tabriz, and the existing French, Turkish and American ones had little to do. Tabriz's only significance was as a transit centre through which went all traffic to Turkey and further west. Sometimes people stopped to buy the odd carpet or inexpensive, fine silver work. A grumpy local Azerbaijani with anti-Western feelings said that people were listening to Baku and Baghdad radio rather than Radio Teheran, and from time to time listened to Radio Istanbul for the music. Russian stations were easy to pick up, and their propaganda was impressive. The Azerbaijanis' discontent was palpable.

With no trace of Nigel and Mehmed, both Kombis left Tabriz for Teheran. The asphalt road soon degenerated to loose macadam with its characteristic corrugations. It was like driving over a monster washboard. There were trucks everywhere and even more abysmal drivers. Over the bad surface in the two Kombis, it was a case of the faster the better. You could not do more than 40 miles per hour and the more fragile Kombi rode better with the engine spinning in third. Camp was set up for the night off the road half-way to Teheran. When the occupants awoke, it turned out that the impromptu campsite was on top of a small hill and well off the road, so they were bothered by nobody for a change. The day promised to be hot again, the arid desert scenery stretching out monotonously ahead.

After an hour's driving, calamity struck. In a game of silly buggers Kombi Z1060, attempting to re-pass Kombi Z1235, after they had already overtaken, threw up a stone from a rear wheel, smashing an offside windscreen. They did

not stop. While Tim was fixing up a temporary screen of polythene, Eric, one of the Australians encountered over coke in Tabriz, came back in his battered Austin to announce that Kombi Z1235 was stationary a mile or so down the road, with what was probably a broken half-shaft. The polythene proved useless. Dry drinking flasks were filled up with dubious water, vouched for by a friendly Iranian Army officer, in preparation for a lengthy session under the midday sun. It was time to catch up with the other Kombi.

Tim tried to find out what was wrong with Z1235 by starting the engine. It was funny – she seemed to be effectively in gear. But the gear lever seemed curiously detached. The whole gearbox had gone wonky. Tim finally found a way to select any one gear at a time – which could only be done from under the stationary vehicle. Third at least allowed a moderate cruising speed.

Off again and with Roger feeling the heat after exerting himself on the tyre pump. After about 95 miles, the road started to boast a fine asphalt surface – thoroughly welcome as the poor Kombis were not going to take much more of the rough stuff. Off the road in a village 20 miles from Teheran a touring strong man was doing his act, swinging weights around using his teeth, and then trying to break a chain tightly fixed round his torso. He was interrupted by two cyclists who collided, threw their bikes at each other, and then started fighting in the middle of the street.

The outskirts of Teheran hove into sight at dusk and Tim selected a lower gear to spare the clutch in the chaotic traffic. It was carnival night in town; the sidewalks were crammed with sideshows, banners were everywhere and huge lorries carrying a mass of shouting, gesticulating humanity raced along the streets. It was the anniversary of the Shah's return to power from his voluntary exile eight years previously. It was also the anniversary of the accession of his father, Reza Shah. Through this din of hilarity a strange convoy of two Kombis, one mini-minor and the battered Australian Austin crawled to the British Embassy.

(Opposite, top) Tea break, northern Iran. Left to right – Peter, Tony, Bob, Tim, Roger.

(Opposite, bottom) Typical village spring in northern Iran, forming the centre of village activity.

Outside the Embassy by chance were Mr and Mrs Treeves, a British couple living and working in Teheran, he as a UNESCO engineer. They offered their garden as sleeping quarters. Meanwhile, someone stole the clothes that were hanging behind the front seat in one wounded Kombi by leaning through the broken front windscreen, despite the four Australians keeping watch on the vehicles. Tim's birthday ended with a very welcome drink in the Treeves' house.

Kombi Z1235 was emptied and towed to a VW service garage. Tim was delighted to deal with a firm having Germanic standards of efficiency again in the shape of a young mechanic from Dortmund. Roger retired to a horizontal position with a mild attack of heat exhaustion. Everybody else went to lunch at the house of Mr Amir Hosein Khozeime Alam. One of his daughters was Tahere, a student at Cambridge, who subsequently married Peter. Their house was in Shemiran, set in the foothills of the 18,600-foot Mount Demavend ('Bride of the Gods'). Mr Alam was a very senior member of the Shah's entourage and one of the biggest landowners in Iran. He provided many contacts, and planned the Expedition's outline for travelling in Iran.

Traffic in Teheran was arguably the world's worst. The guiding principle was to neglect anything that happened, or was likely to happen thanks to your own actions, behind a line drawn at right angles to the car through your own driving position. Once this principle was mastered you then had to realize that anyone who overtook you was actually insulting you, in a like manner to spitting in your face. Then driving became fun. This chaos produced any number of collisions which in local parlance were known as 'coincidences'.

A 'Cooks tour' of Iran was arranged by the Pahlavi Foundation. This organization was controlled by the Shah; the nearest Western equivalent would probably have been the Rockefeller Foundation. Mr Yussefi, the Tourist Chief of the Foundation, would personally be the Expedition's guide virtually throughout the stay in Iran. A short, well-built man, his mastery of English was impeccable and his knowledge of the history and civilization of his country was thorough and enthusiastic. Of natural discretion, almost demure, he showed great skill in navigating between the rocks and quicksands of Iranian politics in discussion with the Expedition members. And – such a contrast from the Soviet Union – he was neither inclined nor instructed to shadow their every step.

Educational contacts were set up. Tim and Peter went to the Red Lion and Sun Society – the Iranian equivalent of the Red Cross – where a dozen very cultured men sat round a table talking and dealing in measured tones with any business that turned up. They obviously performed this stress-free duty on a regular basis.

Mr Yussefi set up a visit to the Shah's Golestan Palace, entry to which was granted only by special permit. The throne room had a very long backwards walk for anyone who had to take counsel with the Shah. It was crammed with the riches of centuries; a bit of a bazaar, really. Then to the inner apartments, the intimate holy of holiest, where few outsiders ever penetrate. Tony recalls how 'one left such an apartment knowing you are leaving an enclosed world of a few square feet where few breaths from outside can penetrate. The drug wears off and you step from the delicately patterned carpets past the blue fountains to cars running on poor-grade petrol'.

At the university campus law students said quite bluntly: 'there is no free speech'. Students, they said, were not allowed to talk politics – that was the government's prerogative.

The Iraqi Consulate was being decidedly unhelpful about visas for the onward journey, so time became available and the opportunity arose to leave the Kombis in Teheran and set off to the Caspian in two chauffeur-driven Mercedes – by courtesy of the Pahlavi Foundation, of course. A fine drive over the Elburz Mountains led up to the massive Kharaj Dam, supplying Teheran with hydro-electric power and water. In Ramsar everyone was put up in a magnificent hotel, owned by the Pahlavi Foundation and not far from the beach that was sparse and somewhat bleak but provided a first swim in the Caspian Sea beneath the shrouded sky and amidst heavily forested hills.

Next night in Babolsar Persian caviar and vodka were served up plentifully for dinner. Much Iranian caviar was sold to the USSR, where it was then sold as Russian caviar. Russian *émigrés* in Teheran told how the Bolsheviks had commandeered the Russian fishing fleet, and how the Soviet fleet later persisted in invading Iranian waters in high-speed launches with which local fisherman could not compete. These were indeed rough waters.

At the beach Tony spotted a very attractive young lady in a one-piece white swimming costume lying face down on the sand. 'Do you speak English?' 'Yes, so what?' she replied. Tony sat down next to her on the sand and later ended up having a drink with her and her mother in the hotel. Days later in Teheran, Mehmed, Nigel and Tony were invited out to dinner by Goli Farman-Farmaian, as was her name. Her father was an ambassador in Europe somewhere. Her mother – one of 32 children – was a Qajar, the people who ruled Iran for over 100 years until the 1920s when the Pahlavis took over.

From Shahi on the Caspian a nine-hour train journey back to Teheran rose to well over 9,000 feet *en route* and crossed the Victory Bridge, so called since this was the supply route for the Russians from the south in World War II. Different levels of track flashed into view as the train wound up the mountain, and even seemed to double back on itself at one point, among fascinating rock formations.

In Teheran there was a note from Mehmed and Nigel who meanwhile had been travelling south in another train on the very new Tabriz–Teheran line. But, elusive as ever, they were nowhere to be found. The next day, however, the pair, looking thin and slightly haunted, turned up just in time to see off Tim, Tony, Peter, Roger, Anthony and Bob who were booked on an early morning flight to Shiraz. This cat-and-mouse game was getting long.

The famous gardens of Shiraz, lush and in full bloom in contrast to the bleak landscape surrounding the city, lived up to expectations, as did the tombs of Sa'di and Hafiz – the famous Persian poets, masters of enchantment. Lunch was in a hotel, which turned out to be the residence of the former British Consul in Shiraz, when such creatures still existed.

With the sun dipping, now was the time to set out for Persepolis over a small pass and across a wide, flat plain between the mountains. At first there was nothing. Then the first outline of Persepolis looked like nothing much more than a few slender columns as one approached. Soon the true enormity of the place was revealed. It was breathtaking. The Achaemenian kings (600–300 BC) had levelled out a huge platform measuring, in places, some 60 feet above the present level of the plain, accessible by the Grand Staircase. Here were the palaces of Cyrus the Great, Darius and Xerxes; arguably the cradle of Western civilization. No photographs do Persepolis justice.

Staring at this huge monument to a past civilization one of us was prompted to recall the awesome words of the poet, Shelley, about immortality:

> My name is Ozymandias, king of kings:
> Look on my works, ye Mighty, and despair!
> Nothing beside remains. Round the decay
> Of that colossal wreck, boundless and bare
> The lone and level sands stretch far away.

Darius' palace at
Persepolis, which had been
excavated only 30 years
previously.

We were, albeit, somewhere about a thousand leagues westwards, but the idea
was right.

As the sun dropped over Persepolis, a magical time of the day, with shadows
skimming over the desert in conflicting patterns, dinner was preceded by several
glasses of *arak*, a drink made from grapes in Iran (and/or dates in Iraq) and
flavoured with aniseed. This proved too much for Tony and Anthony who missed

a splendid dinner. This was the time when booze was freely made and drunk in Iran – as it had for centuries since the great Persian poets quaffed it and praised its virtues. Iranian wine was labelled by numbers – none of this *château* nonsense. Some wine is apparently still made there.

The morning was spent 'on location' at the palaces. Until excavation about 30 years earlier the masonry had been buried under soil washed down from the hills in the previous 1,500 years. Thus much of the fine relief work had been protected from the ravages of the weather and also from the attentions of the Arabs who dislike the human face being portrayed and accordingly disfigure any sculpture they find. The reliefs were in such fine stone, smooth and black, that they could have been sculpted yesterday. As the midday sun rose to its zenith, the swimming pool of the hotel provided welcome relief. The cool of the late afternoon was ideal for a drive to the tombs of the other kings carved out of a perpendicular cliff – known as 'the city of the dead', which is where Darius, Xerxes and Cyrus are entombed. The tombs were in remarkable condition and readily evocative of their incumbents' past.

Meanwhile, after nearly one month of each other's company in Georgia, Central Asia, Azerbaijan, and Iranian Azerbaijan, Nigel and Mehmed were still going strong – and talking to each other. Such was their enthusiasm that they drove to Shiraz and back to Teheran in a Kombi without even as much as a pair of pliers. Nigel worried about getting stuck if there was a puncture. But they were not going to give up. This was an Expedition of endurance. Their main aim seemed to be to measure the strength of their nerves. The Kombi, after 25 days of separation, made them feel like being back at home. They now pick up the story of the journey south.

Qom was the first stop, the holy city where the sister of the eighth Imam lies resting in her tomb in the majestic shrine – a breathtaking sight. It could also have been life-taking, as Mehmed and Nigel nearly crashed on the dusty road, their eyes fixed on the two illuminated domes of the shrine that stuck out with all their golden splendour amidst the sleeping town. 'Where is the eighth Iman?' He is at Meshed, they were told; that was on their route. They camped for the night outside Qom. Five hours of fresh air and sleep made men of them again. Unbreakfasted, unshaven, they packed and drove into the town. Mehmed was told

(Opposite) The size was breathtaking. This shows one of the four flights of stairs forming the Grand Staircase.

he must have police permission to use his camera. He thought that only happened in Russia. But this was a holy city.

The man at the gate of the shrine sent them packing. With a few words of Turkish Mehmed understood that they had to go and get written permission from someone or other. Up a flight of stairs and through a door they found two desks and a typist. The one with the spectacles behind the desk in the far corner looked as if he might do the trick. He got up, smiling, shook hands, offered seats. He was very obliging and kept smiling at Mehmed whenever their eyes met. He asked Mehmed his name. Mehmed was careful to spell Mehmed as Mohammed. Tea came. Nigel suggested a proper meal, but a second lot of tea arrived. The man with the spectacles still smiled when he lifted up his head from his work. Mehmed smiled back, but was ready to explode, his teeth clenched. So was Nigel – and then they would probably be deported from Persia. Everyone in the room was busy with work; they went on drinking their tea. They could not take a third one. If he had ordered it, they would have protested and left; they could keep their blessed shrines to themselves. Never in his life had Mehmed, who could not stand the stuff, started the day with two glasses of tea. At last, still smiling, the man looked up, rang a bell and within seconds the courtyard of the shrine opened up. It was rich in colour and in beauty. The golden domes were so high that, across the great courtyard, people looked like beetles against the fantastic walls. Mehmed could enter the shrine; not Nigel. People round the tomb were crying. All ages, both sexes. A very old man, a scarf round his neck, which was tied to the tomb as well, wept vigorously; next to him a boy of probably 12, also kneeling before the holy lady, wept too. They were all crying loudly, so there was quite a noise going on. Mehmed and Nigel could stand it no more.

Leaving for Isfahan on a very bad road, Nigel looked grim and in trepidation about the ailing Kombi. But it was nice to be in the open air again. That shrine had been suffocating; why did that young boy cry that way? The mouth-watering sight of watermelon provided a good excuse for a wayside stop. It could have been redder, but the day was hot and dull. Soon Isfahan was on the horizon. The Omar Khayyam celebration brigade was there, in their hundreds. At the 'Red Lion and Sun' (RLS) a letter of introduction to the boss produced bed and board in the best hotel. Whisky was drunk solemnly at the expense of the RLS

(Opposite) Seventeenth-century Lutfullah Mosque, originally a ladies' mosque, on Maidan Square.

and Mehmed and Nigel ate their first European meal since Moscow. It felt good, especially as they were not paying for it. They slept like babies for nine hours.

Meanwhile, the rest of the party had a rougher flight back to Isfahan; a sandstorm was howling below and the plane bucked and swung. Between the airport and the hotel they saw a familiar Kombi, gave chase and found Mehmed and Nigel at the RLS building. Together they all visited the Jum'a and Shah Mosques with their wonderful tiled and mosaic work and then went to a reception given by the RLS at their newly built youth club centre. In Isfahan, the modern premises of the RLS seemed a bit too extravagant. With half the money spent on the premises they could have opened another orphanage of the sort they ran for boys, or nursing schools, and maternity hospitals. An orphanage visited in Isfahan seemed to be working very well, but as was usual all over Iran, it was still partly under construction. A German related how the Iranians were great at starting new projects before completing the old ones.

Dinner that night reunited around one table all eight members of the Expedition; a truly historic occasion in its annals.

The next day, a rapid tour of the rest of Isfahan took in the Shaking Minarets and careful peeks into sundry other mosques. The bazaar was crowded with pedestrians, porters, pack-donkeys, sellers, the deafening rattle of the coppersmith's mallet, small caravans of camels loading and unloading their goods, mile upon mile of labyrinth-like, roofed alleys with shafts of sunray piercing through from the sky-holes, and the great bustle of trade and craft. Mehmed, oddly enough, felt that Isfahan was not a beautiful city as such: 'Take away the works of the Savafid dynasty, it was even ugly. But you could not ignore one of the most beautiful sights my eyes ever saw' – the wonderful ensemble of the *Maidan-e-Shah* (the Imperial Square), Shah Abbass's old polo ground surrounded by the majestic *Masjid-i-Shah* (the Shah Mosque), *Ali-Qapu* (the Royal Booth),

(Opposite, top) Uniquely decorated cream tilework and lattice windows on the dome of Lutfullah Mosque.

(Opposite, below) Islamic decoration.

Food vendor, Kombi and
mix of clothing on a typical
Teheran street.

Sheikh Lutfullah (the Lutfullah Mosque) and the entrance to the bazaar. The Shah
Mosque, with its two main portals, a smooth and simple transformation from the
north–south to the Mecca axis, the beautiful blue dome, the imposing portals – for
Mehmed one of the few pieces of architecture he could not stop looking at.

Roger, too, felt that 'Isfahan had some of the most beautiful sights I have ever
seen'. But it contrasted strongly with the living environment of the ordinary
citizen. 'Persepolis was an education for me to realize how advanced civilization
and architecture were in this part of the world in 500 BC and that civilization
there probably helped to start the golden years of Greek civilization.'

Back in Teheran, a spruced-up Kombi Z1060 was recovered from the VW dealers.
A loose nut in the gearbox had been the guilty party. How they had been so lucky as
to get all the way from Minsk in Russia to Teheran with that fault beggared belief.

Teheran – with nearly 2 million people – was a flourishing, boisterous, modern city, resonant with appalling traffic and accidents. Characterless architecture tried to be half-modern and half-economical; the end result was unpleasant. It was extremely hot between 11 am and 4 pm so people slept on the sidewalks in front of their shops or stalls; then the city began to wake again as food vendors plied their wares. New accidents, new traffic jams and a new atmosphere. Coming from Russia, the thing that struck one most was that Teheran was a city full of rich people – and even more poor ones. The rich lived on the hills of Shemiran, north of Teheran, but in none of the numerous restaurants in the area could one find Persian dishes; Cappuccino or Pepsi Cola ruled. People here spoke at least two foreign languages; they had been to Europe or America or both; they had flashy sports cars and colourful shirts. 'Speak with them, you will find no depth,' said a fine young lady who had studied in Paris and London and who was frustrated with the superficial Teheran society of the day. There were big parties almost every week. It was always the same people, the same set-up, the same topics of conversation, gossip or the latest designs. Barely a few miles away to the south, in the slums of Teheran, people lived in mud houses, or huts made from corrugated iron sheets. There was a rehousing scheme for these slums; but could it ever catch up with the ever-growing numbers of the needy?

Standing in central Teheran, you saw all sorts of things and types of people. At Tophane Square Tony and others watched three criminals being hanged for various crimes.

At this time, more Iranians were getting university education abroad than at home; co-education did not exist. The students of Teheran University had aligned themselves with the then famous National Front, the secular opposition movement founded by former Premier Mohammed Mossadegh, bent on nationalizing Iranian oil and combating British influence. In 1953, after two years in power, Mossadegh was overthrown by a combination of the British and the CIA. In conversation a prominent leader of the National Front and a shrewd politician, Mr Saleh, conceded that the Front was not the ultimate solution. They had no real alternatives, but they did press for elections, and he maintained that a government representing the middle classes and their needs would then solve the problems of the country. High school graduates were unemployed, as were graduates of non-technical disciplines; even at times in Teheran engineers and doctors could not find jobs. And in the meantime, these same people were sought after in the far away provinces like the Turkmen Sahra, where many towns had no doctors at all and the death rate was unbelievably high. A graduate felt that, as obviously a more educated person than the villagers or small townspeople, he would not be able to stand back and shut his mouth in the face of semi-feudal landowners. That could be dangerous.

The Expedition met many prominent Iranians, saw many lovely places, witnessed various welfare projects and, importantly, talked with students. As ever, Teheran University was discontented. But then, as our hosts explained, it was always discontented about something or other. But there was a definite feeling that all was not well. The students were careful in what they said but, compared with the Soviet Union, were very free indeed. They obviously had no depth of affection for the Shah – a general problem with students and others throughout his reign. A shy man who, to the Western eye, posed as more powerful than he was, the Shah attracted criticism on everything because he insisted on ruling and claiming responsibility for everything. The advantage of gradually becoming more constitutional as a monarch, and letting the politicians carry the blame, was a democratic card to play quite beyond his thinking.

✳

In Iran one could identify, even in 1961, some of the fault lines that cracked open into revolution and subsequent shockwaves in that country's already turbulent history. Not that the consequences were obvious. Peter, former Chairman of the British Iranian Parliamentary Group and married to an Iranian, has watched the drama unfold over many years. On the eve of the Iranian Revolution in 1977 to 1979, British and American intelligence boffins and others completely missed the underlying seriousness of what was happening. Iran's struggle to westernize disguised the fact that two countries and systems actively opposed each other. The Shah and the elite espoused the West. The latent powers of traditional Iran and its clerics gnawed away at the woodwork. Frustration fumed among a rising generation that, for some at least, now bitterly regrets youthful enthusiasms.

✳

Meanwhile, on 16 September, Mehmed heard that his father had been acquitted and released from jail in Turkey. Sadly two of his father's colleagues (Polatkan and Zorlu) were hanged. And on 17 September 1961, Turkey became the first country to hang an elected Prime Minister, Adnan Menderes. Mehmed's father's friend, foreign minister Zorlu, defiantly donned the noose himself and kicked away the stool.

Mehmed, Nigel and Tony eventually left Teheran in Kombi Z1235 on 17 September. This narrative will catch up with them later. Now begins the homeward journey, back through the Middle East, of the shorter part of the Expedition.

9
CHILDREN OF ABRAHAM

Tim, Peter, Roger, Anthony and Bob left Teheran on 2 September, spending the first night in the desert near Hamadan towards the Iran/Iraq border. Kombi Z1060 had now clocked up some 16,000 kilometres (10,000 miles) and was feeling somewhat prematurely aged. With renewed courage she now attacked the long drive westwards from Hamadan to the Iran/Iraq border through great open spaces dotted with the odd shepherd's hut.

Embassies had warned that in all Middle Eastern countries customs formalities were severe. In Iraq, so they said, no exposed film could be taken out of the country – and Roger had the entire stock from the beginning of the Expedition's travels. The British Council kindly offered to get it back to England in a diplomatic bag, which was gratefully accepted. Roger recovered it for processing shortly after returning to the UK.

In fact the Iranian customs waved the Kombi through with a tired gesture. The officials did not even look at the vehicle, let alone search it. Procedures had been stiff on entry, as they logged all valuable articles such as cameras and radios into passports. On departure they could not be bothered. Crossing now into Iraq too passed off with a minimum of formality and camp was set up for the night near the customs post.

A hot drive across the desert along the route of the oil pipeline brought the group to Baghdad on 4 September. The local YMCA offered the use of their roof overlooking the River Tigris for free accommodation. Lamia Gailani, an Iraqi student friend from Cambridge, arranged lunches and dinners, and a meeting with her brother, who in turn introduced several useful people in education. He set up a guided a tour of the only mosque that Westerners were allowed to visit – it was their family mosque, the Gailani Mosque. The contact in the Embassy turned out to be an enterprising secretary called Ross Thomas who really turned up trumps. He arranged a cocktail party one evening, set up a long list of people to see, and briefed with insight on the political situation.

A relatively minor hazard
for the fully laden Kombi
en route.

(Opposite, top) The long
drive westwards from
Hamadan to the Iran/Iraq
border.

(Opposite, bottom)
Shepherd's accommodation,
western Iran.

85

Peter recalls how 1961 was but the early days of Iraq's independence and nationhood. With the British mandate not long ended, and its influence steadily declining, the country was run until 1958 by Nuri es-Sayid, the Prime Minister, and others from the established families of the country. The young King Feisal II sat uneasily on his throne, to which he ascended aged 17 in 1953. In 1958 came the brutal revolution, which killed him and ended British influence. In place of a traditional government, with British advisers on hand, the Iraqi Army imposed its power in a coup led by General Abdul Karim Kassem. The Army was key to the deadly political game that then followed, a complicated business including the competing influence of the Ba'athists, or Arab nationalists Iraqi-style, and the Communists. By 1961, the 'Sole Ruler', as General Kassem liked to describe himself, held power until he duly and literally lost his head in another military coup. All the usual ingredients with which we are now all too familiar were there: dictatorship; army power; political manoeuvres from the Ba'ath who eventually took over, with Saddam Hussein increasingly prominent, and the Communists who eventually lost out; the ethnic tribes and deep divisions between the Sunni and Shi'a; Kuwait, then as now, an opportunity for the Iraqi leadership to show its macho propensities. Kassem in 1961 threatened Kuwait several times, leading to the deployment of British troops.

Remnants of quasi-colonial rule abounded. In the Finance Ministry an alert member of the Expedition looked at the information shelves in detail. Underneath booklets of the current regime were great bundles of the same booklets, but bearing the murdered king's photograph and saying lots of nice things about him. This caused due embarrassment with the officials in charge.

Many English families still lived and worked in Iraq. As the Ba'ath and Saddam Hussein steadily took over, many would go into exile for their own safety. At that time one could still go out to dinner at the old 'Jockey Club', a place symbolic of faded years gone by. The servants, still in attendance, greatly outnumbered the few guests.

The British Embassy in 1961 was led by Sir Humphrey Trevelyan, one of Britain's best diplomats of the past half-century. The Embassy arranged meetings at the Ministry of Education, Baghdad University and the British Council, still managing to be active in the country. But clearly this was a deeply troubled country in a state of transition, but with little control over the direction of that transition. Its only quality was to be comparatively subdued under firm dictatorship – so disparate was the country the British had created with arbitrary lines on a map.

Apart from bestowing kingdoms on the Hashemites and oil on the West, British efforts did little to foster a potentially cohesive state.

The visit to Iraq was the only time during the Expedition's long journey when everyone felt really ill at ease. In the Soviet bloc there was at least organization and direction. One knew where one was and, within the necessary parameters of the system, one could both learn and enjoy. Iraq was something else – hot, sticky and unpleasant, with a certain feeling of menace in the air. Kassem, the sole leader, was in constant danger of assassination. Indeed, shortly before, his convoy had been attacked and a car within it blown up. Kuwait caused tension and the resulting roadblocks and inspections on the road to Baghdad all added to it. People the Expedition met were delightful, and largely Western-educated. But they were not happy or relaxed. Thus it was that on 8 September five rather jaded figures set off across the 400-odd miles of desert to Amman in Jordan. Jordan customs were cleared with a cheery minimum of formality and they were allowed to set up camp next to the local police station.

*

A brief four days only was spent in Iraq but it was enough to feel ill at ease about the present and what was in store. Endemic violence wreaks continued havoc with the fabric of that unhappy country. None of the Expedition companions have ever rushed back to Iraq in spite of, in the cases of Peter and Bob, several opportunities to do so. Half a century after the visit, the US army has gone home while Iraq's factions fight over the country's future governance. Few are ready to put any bets on the future – nor on the sharpened, wider Sunni-Shi'a schism. Security and development throughout the region risk paying the price.

*

The contrast between Iraq and Jordan could hardly have been greater. The border-crossing was in the evening and the reception there said much about the two countries. On the Iraqi side, there was at first just one rather idle official with a large stomach, for whom it was a considerable effort to get to his feet. A fan in the ceiling slowly turned and flies, no doubt reluctantly, inhabited most parts of the room. That said, the officials were far too lazy even to examine the Kombi, loaded as it was with a formidable amount of gear. Crossing over to Jordan, the Expedition was met by several lively young men, dressed in sports jackets and ties, speaking fluent English and cracking a number of jokes along the way.

FROM ASIA'S EDGE

Bedouin encampment near
the Roman city of Jerash
in Jordan.

In Baghdad sleeping accommodation was on the YMCA roof overlooking the wide expanse of the Tigris with beautiful long shadows cast in the moonlight. In Amman it was on another roof, this time of a private house, by courtesy of Mr Goodison, the British Embassy press attaché. A visit to Jericho was heavy with history. More visually interesting was the Roman town of Jerash with its remarkably preserved amphitheatre. Anthony managed to get himself arrested on the main street of Amman by two military policemen for taking pictures of something apparently sensitive; it was never quite sure what. But somehow he talked his way out of their clutches.

The close relationship of Jordan and Iraq was – and is – perhaps surprising, until one recalls the practical grounds. In Jordan's case, dependence on Iraq for trade and finance was considerable, then as now. Jordan, a rare example of an

Arab country without oil, depends on its larger neighbour, and has no wish to upset it. In 1961, Jordan was a smaller, but more homogeneous entity than Iraq. It was lucky to have a wise and respected branch of the Hashemites in charge, beginning with King Abdullah bin Hussain, veteran of the war against the Turks and brother of King Feisal I of Iraq. Under British influence, he headed the Government or Amirate of Transjordan from 1921, becoming King of Jordan in 1946. In 1948, the mandate ended and, in July 1951, he was assassinated by extremists in Jerusalem. He was succeeded by his young and able grandson, King Hussain. Further Middle East crises were still to come and, thanks to the tradition of General Glubb 'Pasha' and his Arab Legion, Jordan had the best fighting army in the Arab world.

The Amman of 1961 was small, but already appeared as a beacon of security to the Western visitor. It seemed remarkably normal after Iraq. Most interesting of all were the days spent in Jerusalem and in the West Bank. The war of 1967 was still six years away as was the Israeli occupation of the West Bank. In 1961, it was under Jordanian control with no visible Israeli settlements dominating every horizon and much work being done, with international participation, to develop the area. In 1961, the Palestinians were still largely in Arab Palestine. They had not yet spilled over in large numbers into Lebanon and Jordan, creating massive instability in both countries.

The Dead Sea provided the inevitable, unusual swimming experience. They say you can sit in the water and read a newspaper; they don't say you must not get even the smallest drop of water in your eyes – it stings like mad.

Everybody bought a *keffiyeh* – the 'tea-towel' headgear that Arabs wisely wear against sun and sand. Roger, with his ready suntan, dark hair and chiselled features, could by now, after exposure to the elements, have been mistaken for a local. His temper occasionally became a bit frayed when the others got into the habit of calling him 'Abdul'.

One night was spent in an Arab Development Scheme farm and school, founded and run by one Musa al Alami, a man of remarkable energy. A major problem in the Arab world at the time was to obtain and train skilled men and craftsmen. Alami's project was aimed primarily at orphans and boys from the poorer frontier villages, who lived at this place for up to ten years, receiving a full education and then practical training in either a machine shop, carpentry shop or various aspects of farming. The next morning at the farm was celebrated with a slap-up breakfast with eggs and the first glass of fresh milk since leaving Germany in June. This was the only place in the whole of the Middle East – excluding Israel – that produced pasteurized milk.

A guided tour of Old, or East, Jerusalem meandered down the narrow streets past tiny shops which almost seemed to fade into the walls. East Jerusalem under Jordanian control was much as one experiences it under Israeli occupation nowadays, but without the large settlements that dominate the Arab part of the city from the heights around and the steady nibbling away of Arab homes through frequently opaque financial dealings in which the Greek Orthodox Church has dipped sticky fingers. In 1961, there were two cities in two countries; the East, unchanged for centuries and containing the holy sites, Jewish, Muslim and Christian; and the West, a bustling, modern, westernized Israeli city. Incongruous splashes of modernity cropped up, like the sight of Jordanian children off to school in their smart uniforms, just like kids in Britain.

The two parts of the city were still joined by the Mandelbaum Gate, which was part of the old truce line after the 1948–9 war of Israeli Independence. In 1961, it was the only place to cross from Jordan into Israel. Israeli visas and stamps were issued on a form separate to passports, so that nobody would be denied entry subsequently to any Arab states. On 13 September, the Expedition party crossed to the 'other side', as it was known in Jordan, escorted by no less a person than the HM Consul-General, Mr Burgess, whose secure presence compensated for the shrapnel scars and bullet holes all over what was left of the buildings alongside. What a contrast stared one in the face on reaching the modern city of West Jerusalem.

One left Jordan with the thought that it was doing a good job to the best of its ability in the West Bank, and that it was helpful to have Jordan in place next to

(Opposite, top) Jordanian children off to school, smartly dressed, on the eastern outskirts of Jerusalem.

(Opposite, bottom) Going through the Mandelbaum Gate, accompanied by the British Consul – the only way to go from Jordan to Israel in 1961.

a strong and increasingly strident Israel. Jordan gave the impression of being a voice of sanity and, when necessary, an intermediary between the Arabs and Israel over the years.

*

King Hussain was still finding his feet in 1961. His successor still sits uncomfortably on his throne, despite the strength and sense that has preserved Jordan as an entity. Unwise Arab heads would prefer war to development and the whole balance shifted dramatically in Israel's favour with Palestinians spilling over into Lebanon and Jordan, creating massive instability in both countries. The Syrian upheaval further undermines the prospects of all concerned. Today, Palestinians form a majority in Jordan where they have been contained and absorbed as far as possible. Those left behind on the West Bank and in Gaza never had the chance to get away.

*

Once in Israel, the Expedition was immediately taken in hand by the Jewish Agency with a rapidly organized itinerary, but carefully leaving a day free – the Day of Atonement – spent by the Sea of Galilee near Tiberias. An invitation was provided to a concert given by Pablo Casals, probably then the world's leading cellist, who was making his first return visit to Israel for a long time. Introductions from the Agency included two of major intellectual importance: the Hebrew University, where discussions with senior people could not fail to impress with their sheer intellectual, cultural and humane qualities; and the world-famous Weizmann Institute for scientific research at Rehovoth – doubtless pivotal in producing Israel's alleged nuclear strike capacity (but that was not on the agenda). Other valuable introductions included Israel's ever-present Army, the all-powerful *Histadruth* trades union congress, and the Technion City at Haifa.

A student called Sam provided agreeable and unobtrusive company on many of these visits and proved knowledgeable about general conditions in Israel, particularly for students. At the time, the majority of students at university had to work during the day to pay for their studies. This was despite the fact that the USA was pouring money into Israel. Why could not some of those dollars be diverted to help finance struggling students? The answer given was that the buildings erected with American money were to be part of a new heritage, a new culture that the Jews had to build for themselves, to establish themselves; the buildings would remain, the students were merely in transit.

First sight of modern,
westernized Israel.

No wonder Israel stood out like a sore thumb compared with the then Arab world. Arriving in West Jerusalem from the East, one leaped from developing to developed, from the Middle East to Europe in one fell swoop. Medieval East or Old Jerusalem suddenly gave way to familiarity; this was the modern European world.

Would Israel's reinsertion into the Promised Land foster development and progress for the whole or would the sheer level of difference be too much to bridge? That question is still open. In 1961, these were valid thoughts about a newly established Israel, rapidly developing and asserting its independence and nationhood. The sheer efficiency with which the Expedition was received was a case in point. British Jews were much involved, making one feel at home. Hosts were high-level and competent. Two meetings at the Israeli Foreign Ministry were run by experts under the eye of the heads of the relevant departments. A talk on refugees, always a difficult subject for Israel, was given by the resident specialist, as was a session on Africa. There was nothing that any mandarin back at the Foreign Office in London could teach these people, such was the professionalism of their presentations. In a way, it was if Europe were grafted onto the Middle East. At that time, one was a Friend of Israel and its creation, but suddenly exposed to the realities of the creation and its effect on the region. One could not help but be impressed. Now one wonders. Then one admired it all, if with questions gnawing at the back of one's mind.

Israel was governed then by the founding Israeli Labour Party. The people in charge were overwhelmingly of Western and Central European origin. The big shifts and changes in the geographical and cultural make-up of Israel's population were still to come. Many Jews of distinction offered their services to Israel in their later life; many young people came out to be part of the great new adventure. It was almost eerie to hear a talk about journalism from a former assistant editor of *The Times*; or a meeting with the *Histadruth* conducted by a former British trade unionist.

Pride in the State of Israel and the absolute determination to establish the State, were tangible. The 1948–9 war was a recent memory and the old battle lines from before the ceasefire were still on show. These were strong people. Even the often strikingly attractive Israeli women soldiers confessed privately how their training took over their lives. One told how in her dormitory in the early days they had to sleep with their Uzi sub-machine guns under the covers with them; this rapidly overcame any reluctance to handle weapons.

At Kiryat Gat *Kibbutz* near Beersheba Jews were establishing farming settlements on the less fertile parts of the country – the Lakish project. *Kibbutzim* had played a big part in the establishment of the state of Israel. Here educated immigrants from Europe and the USA led an almost spartan existence. New mothers returned to work quickly after the birth of a new child; a crèche was provided – something unheard of in the UK at the time. After eating, drinking and discussing with Jews from all over the world, one departed somewhat relieved not to be Jewish and dedicated to early mornings and hard, agricultural work. The experience included joining a night-time patrol checking security, squeezed in trucks against *Kibbutzniks* clutching *Uzis* with safety catches off. At the Gaza Strip the forlorn UN control post had one foot in Israel, the other in Egypt.

The UN post at the Gaza Strip. Visitors could stand with one foot in Israel and one in Egypt.

Tel Aviv yielded more agreeable contacts in that largely westernized Mediterranean city. The locals promenaded up and down the main thoroughfare in the early evening, just as they do in the Arab countries, and as people do in the *corso* throughout the Mediterranean world.

The Day of Atonement, Yom Kippur, was spent safely out of the way by the Sea of Galilee, with time to relax, to swim, water ski and briefly visit the ruins at Capernaum. Behind loomed the Golan Heights, then full of Syrian gun positions totally dominating the area below. Driving during those 24 hours of a major religious holiday was a bad idea – unless you wanted to get stoned by the Orthodox. Departing for Haifa the next evening there were no stones, and the traffic came pouring back onto the roads as soon as there were two stars in the sky.

FROM ASIA'S EDGE

The Kombi being loaded
onto a boat at Haifa, destined
for Turkey.

At the Haifa Technion – the original technical university in Israel offering
engineering degrees – conversation was mainly in French, and the drinks were
mainly brandy. Comfortable beds for a last night in Israel helped to get over the
effects.

The next evening, Kombi Z1060 was loaded onto a boat in Haifa, bound for
Iskenderun in Turkey. Everyone ate and slept on deck. There was no other way
out of Israel given the Arab blockade of the frontiers.

*

The contrast of Israel with Jordan, or indeed the then Arab world, was enormous
in 1961. Israel was also then a cosier place for Westerners. Mass immigration
and settlement of Oriental and Russian Jewry was still to spur the rise of Likud,

Crossing the Bosphorus at Istanbul, this boat looked in imminent danger of sinking.

today's more right-wing Israel and a progressive coarsening of Israeli politics. One hopes for an enduring peace settlement with Palestine and common sense elsewhere. What will prevail in Israeli politics? The deep-rooted instincts of culture and civilization that the Expedition felt in 1961? Or the thug instincts too often manifest in 'what remains of our once-vibrant society', as former Israeli ambassador, Alon Liel, put it in December 2011? May Israel – and others – choose well for the sake of the region and the world, as a whole.

*

After Iskenderun came the long journey back across Anatolia. In Ankara Mehmed's mother and brother, Ahmed (who subsequently went to Cambridge), were warm hosts. But with room short at their flat, everyone dossed down in a students' dormitory block – a bit like British Army accommodation at the time.

On to Istanbul where, to cross the Bosphorus, the Kombi perched on the deck of a rickety ferry, generating flutters of nerves all round. Once the Expedition was on dry land, the British Consulate offered the use of its summer cottage at Tarabya – which turned out to be very basic, even by Expedition standards. But the spot was idyllic and the view of the Bosphorus impeccable. It was now time for a prosaic, trouble-free ride through the Balkans and Austria. And finally to Munich during *Oktoberfest*, where Roger was impressed by two things: the number of large *Steins* of beer that a waitress could hold and serve and the discipline of the German youth who, even at the end of a good night's drinking, would wait for traffic lights to cross the road, unlike jaywalkers in the UK. On to Bonn to part with the faithful Kombi and sell it back to the original suppliers. They were clearly surprised to see this bit of the Expedition back in one piece. Peter collected the cash, which he found rather burdensome. To avoid a hotel bill, he opted to spend the night in a nightclub and ended up pursuing European relations with, of all people, a Dutch belly dancer. Roger thinks that Peter nearly got waylaid by a charming young lady later on the way through Brussels. But memories do get clouded. Somehow everybody met up again in Ostend before crossing the channel to Dover. Roger found £1 left in his pocket, not enough to buy a train fare home. There were no credit cards in those days. Tim kindly invited Roger to stay with his aunt in London, and to borrow the train fare home from her.

The first part of the Expedition had made it safely home – 11 October 1961 – just under four months after setting out. But the story continues.

(Opposite, top)
Accommodation at the British Embassy's summer cottage, on the outskirts of Istanbul, overlooking the Bosphorus. Bob was never photographed without a cigarette drooping from his mouth!

(Opposite, bottom) Last tea break on the way home after four months. The Colman two-burner petrol stove performed dutifully throughout the trip.

TO ASIA'S HEARTLAND

Now is the moment to switch back across space and time and pick up with Mehmed, Nigel and Tony in Teheran as they depart on the next and longer leg of the Expedition.

10
TURKISH CONNECTIONS

Eastwards from the Caspian lies the Turkmen Sahra spilling over into Soviet Turkmenistan. Half a million Turkmen lived in the Iranian part of the old Turkistan when it was divided between Iran, Russia, China and Afghanistan. With their *telfeke* Turkmen hats made from *karakul*, the Turkmen had always fascinated Mehmed: they are racially most akin to the Turks of Turkey and speak more or less the same language. They were thought hostile towards foreigners. A while before, some tourists wandering in Turkmen lands were mysteriously lost for good. Well-wishers back home advised Mehmed against going there.

Armed with letters of introduction – Iranians prized them – Kombi Z1235, with Mehmed, Nigel and Tony aboard, left Teheran for the Turkmen Sahra, and ultimately to Meshed and Afghanistan. After the Elburz Mountains the road dropped dizzily to sea level before heading to Gorgan, the door to the Turkmen Sahra and its main town. The land was green and fertile, studded with palm trees, smiling peasants, among the richest in the country. There was enough to eat, and work for all. Not all of Iran could boast such wealth.

A beautiful, clear morning shone on Bandar Shah where the Turkmen tribes start. It was a military zone, calling for redoubled prudence – not always the Expedition's greatest strength. At midday, in scorching heat, the place was almost deserted. It was siesta time.

The first letter of introduction was to Murad Shomali, a young, energetic businessman who owned much of Bandar Shah's industry which he had built almost single-handedly after the war using British, German and American equipment. His friend, a Mr Iranpour, had at one time been a member of the Iranian Communist *Tudeh* party and suffered five years in jail for his sympathies. He was still the political big shot for the area as the elected member to the *Majlis* – the Iranian parliament.

The Expedition members' 'circulation cards', were now a month out of date. Where should they be renewed – in Teheran? 'What the hell can I do?' Iranpour asked, frowning, when Murad Shomali suggested he take these 'illegals' to Gorgan to get new cards. Then discreetly in Persian, Shomali told Iranpour that Mehmed was Turkish. … Before long everyone was bowling down the road to Gorgan, Mehmed at the wheel, Iranpour beside him, already old friends. During an obligatory stop at a police station the chief said everyone should have checked out of the police station in Bandar Shah. This was a frontier zone with the Soviet Union and checks were pernickety. A fugitive who had just crossed the border that night was huddled under the stairs. Nigel started negotiations in French and got nowhere. Iranpour just sat still. Then Nigel had a brainwave and in 'his best' Turkish asked – 'Do you speak Turkish?' 'Evet, efendim,' said the chief enthusiastically and Nigel promptly passed the buck to Mehmed. Now with Mehmed in the driving seat (metaphorically and physically) everything got straightened out. A Turkish colleague up in the frontier area had once given the chief a very good dinner. New cards were issued at once.

Gorgan was the centre of this fertile farming area. Modern agricultural methods were boosting its importance and wealth. Iranpour, a movie fanatic, suggested seeing *Perfect Furlough* at a new cinema. This was followed by kebab washed down with beer and vodka. Talk over the table ranged eclectically from such things as the Turkmen marriage system, their 95 per cent illiteracy rate, how there were 300,000 of them but their numbers were static due to tuberculosis, how they kept to themselves, how the elders were the 'police force', and how they had no doctors or hospitals for the whole area – 'people just die!' They were a proud, tough, strong race of fine-looking people – but you could get killed just for looking at their womenfolk.

Iranpour had a new idea. The next day was the bazaar in Akkale. Why not go there this evening and stay with Mehmed Dürdü (yet another letter of introduction)? They arrived in the darkness in front of Mehmed Dürdü's house at about 10.30. The small town of Akkale slept soundly. Iranpour rang the bell. To someone upstairs who asked what the hell he wanted at this time of night, he said importantly, 'Tell Dürdü Iranpour has come.' Iranpour had indeed come, bringing with him three foreigners, one of them a Turk from Istanbul. Mehmed Dürdü, a short man of about 40, opened the door, wiping the sleep from his eyes.

Dürdü looked well off, judging from the collection of beautiful, dark red Turkmen carpets that adorned his house. Respectfully leaving shoes at the door, everyone sat down to tea in the true Central Asian manner, despite the hour. The cups were made in Japan, with no handles. There was no sugar. You sucked sweets while downing pots of tea, black or green. Morad Shomali had seen almost every capital of Europe and its nightclubs. Iranpour had seen Teheran many times. Mehmed Dürdü was a local Turkmen grown rich with his small cotton trade. These unexpected guests clearly amused him. He could understand Mehmed's Turkish, or newly acquired *Türkmence*, but insisted on talking via Iranpour, and referred to Mehmed, Nigel and Tony as *bunlar* (these).

Dürdü originated from Uzbekistan. He had trudged over the high Pamirs away from Soviet oppression. He had walked for over a year. He proudly showed a full-length fur and sheepskin coat which the Kyrgyz wear as protection from the bitter cold. The samovar bubbled as everyone sat round talking. The women floated around in the background. The girls were really beautiful – as the sly and furtive glances of the young Cambridge-men betrayed. These women had clear Mongol features. Turks, Turkmen, Mongols, etc. all originate from the same Central Asian stock. The host had a wonderfully expressive face, a slight beard, a bald head and an amazing wit. The local schoolteacher came in and joined the cross-legged throng talking till well after midnight. Could 'these men', asked Dürdü, sleep on the floor? He then made the most comfortable beds the guests had slept in for a long time. They slept like sultans, covered by thick quilts to keep out the early morning chill.

The next morning there was the richest breakfast to be had anywhere in the world. There was butter (a rarity since leaving Cambridge), jam, eggs, fresh bread, pots of tea and, finally, about one pound of the best caviar in the world.

The dusty, uneven streets around the bazaar were already crowded. Turkmen men wore a *papak* or cap. They had come, each from his nearby *oba*, or summer village, bringing carpets to sell and to buy food for the week ahead. They rode in on horseback, tall, stately men, some with straggling beards, proud, in rich clothes, with their black or grey *telfek* or *papak* headgear. Their even prouder women, in rich red, also rode in on horseback. The odd horse misbehaved and jumped; the young Turkmen controlled them with masterly, nonchalant efficiency.

Tractors, lorries and carts jostled for position along the street. Herds of bleating sheep and goats waited to be sold. Clusters of chickens lay tied up on the sidewalk awaiting bidders. The women and children wore fantastically colourful robes with reds, yellows, mauves and blacks predominating. A large pushing and shoving crowd of people offered their various wares: carpets, rugs, hats, chickens, fruit, etc.

From Akkale the road ran north through the desert. The Elburz mountains rose through the bluish haze to the south. Alexander had marched along this road

'Doctor' Thompson administering to the local tribal chief who had wrenched his hand driving the first tractor to come to his village.

with his armies. The emptiness was broken by the occasional small *oba* with its typical Turkmen tents, noted by a former traveller as the 'most ingenious ever designed, cool in the summer and warm in winter'. Refreshment at a *Tomach* tribal village, squatting on the floor of the headman's hut, was pure yoghurt made from camel's milk. Water is scarce in an *oba*. 'Doctor' Thompson administered to the headman's swollen hand – he had wrenched a joint overturning on his new tractor. This was much appreciated. These were real nomads. They had no problem about their women being photographed at work making carpets. Two women took a month to make one 3 feet x 5 feet carpet.

Education had brought big social change to the lives of the Iranian Turkmen. Reza Shah had brought it to these lands 30 years before, although with brutality.

Once completely tribal, many people now lived in towns with their primary and even secondary schools. Fewer now came out to the plains with their animals in the summer. Even girls were educated to prove that the Turkmen, like his brother, the Turk, could become quite secular and even reformative about religious matters. Mehmed had been to several Muslim countries, but only with the Turkic people did he sense the existence of a pondered balance between religion and a more secular appreciation of society's priorities. Here he could feel relaxed about the atheism that was at the core of his philosophy of life.

In Gomishan *chai* was drunk in the local headman's cloth shop, followed by an invitation to lunch at his house. The house was built vaguely in the Swiss chalet style, with wooden verandas going two-thirds of the way round its girth. The tin roofs drained the scarce rain off into storage tanks. That was the only water supply; ever deeper wells only brought up salt water owing to the closeness of the Caspian Sea. Many people owned no water supply of their own and bought it. No wonder they rarely washed! Their sanitary conditions were primitive in the extreme; they just defecated on the ground, so collecting hundreds of flies, which in their turn carried the dirt and germs and deposited them on the food and the people themselves.

While everyone reclined barefoot after lunch on cushions spread out on a superb Turkmen carpet, the local frontier-guard officer turned up with his notebook. Foreigners being here at all, it seemed, was a privilege. This was a military zone, normally forbidden to anyone but local inhabitants. These were the first Europeans seen here for a long time and they were a natural object of curiosity. The proximity to the Soviet border was intriguing. One small boy, in one of the groups of boys who sprung as if from nowhere to surround the Kombi wherever it went, proudly announced in Russian – 'Yuri Gagarin is a Soviet sailor!'

After rice and sturgeon, fried eggs and camel's milk, Iranpour talked about the problems of the area – especially insufficient educational facilities. Decades earlier, Reza Shah had killed many recalcitrant Turkmen while introducing education. Now the Turkmen thought they deserved more. They wanted to send more students to Turkey, to Germany, but passports were hard to get. Doctors were very scarce and this, together with lack of hygiene and water, accounted for the high death rate. Tony, as Expedition 'medic', noted that Gomishan, with a population of 8,000, had only two semi-doctors who were about his standard.

In Bandar Shah the security police gave permission to cross the military zone to an island for a swim. It was nearing sunset, with the sun's dying rays a burning red, flashing across the still waters. The deliciously warm water washed away the dust of the day's driving. A visit to the caviar factory followed. The next morning the best caviar in the world would make for a sublime breakfast. One pound cost £4. Mehmed, Nigel, Tony and Iranpour got through at least one pound between them.

After dinner Iranpour coaxed everyone to go to his beloved cinema again. This time it was *The Fall of Rome* with Sophia Loren. The cinema had a sheet, patched in many places, for a screen. The audience became part of the film itself, clapping, shouting, and screaming gently when excited. The night was spent at the house of Mr Sheri, the first Turkmen representative in the Iranian parliament – when it sat.

Next morning a motley, gloriously colourful crowd milled round a Kazakh house for a tribal wedding. The women were in their finery – the bride's family womenfolk wore a white turban hanging down at the back of the head, and other regalia. There was positive encouragement to take the women's photos, followed by an invitation to the bride's house for *chai* with all the men. The men sat in one room, ranged around the four walls, the women in another – drinking their *chai* and eating bonbons. Suddenly the bride was approaching, so everyone hurriedly put their shoes on and dashed outside. Small 'bridesmaids' held banners. Close behind them came the older women, with the bride firmly settled in their midst, her head and whole body covered by a long, white shawl. Only the bride wore the '*chador*'. The other women left their fine faces uncovered. The bride disappeared into her house and large cauldrons of rice and meat were given a few more stirs ready for the big feast.

Now came a customary throwing away of money. The bride's family threw away about 1,000 *tomans* (some £50) into the assembled crowd of friends, neighbours, beggars and children. They threw not only actual money, but also shoes, bits of tin, etc. The agile retriever got a *toman*. As part of the wedding celebrations, there were horse races for 'bareback' boy riders, aged between 9 and 15. The celebrations went on all day and in the evening music blared out.

About 2,000 Kazakhs lived in Bandar Shah. They had fled from the Central Asian steppes of Soviet Kazakhstan in 1934 because, as comparatively rich people, their belongings were forcibly taken from them by the Russians in their anti-*kulak* drive. Kazakh men were taller and thinner than the Turkmen, usually with impressive moustaches. Their language, Kazakh, belongs to a different Turkic group. They had come far from Uzbekistan to settle on the last piece of Turkic land to the west.

TO ASIA'S HEARTLAND

It was time to move on. After a superb lunch of rice with tender meat and salad, which the Turkmen call Istanbul Pilavi, Iranpour bade farewell. The Expedition had yet another letter of introduction to a Mr Nejjari. This was to be the start of a hilarious wild-goose-chase around the Turkmen Sahra.

Behind Mr Nejjari's front door his young servant was obstinate, and his wife was having none of these strange men crossing the threshold without her husband's permission. A student who was cycling by came to the rescue and an 'acquaintance' of his kindly let the party sleep in his new house. Erhan, 23 years old, still in the local high school, was already married; he had paid the princely sum of 10,000 tomans (£500) to the bride's father for the privilege.

Erhan tagged along next morning as guide and interpreter in the search for Mr Nejjari and everyone headed further into the desert, along rough, bumpy cart tracks. The Kombi was on test to prove its versatility. It was extremely hot. Only later did it become evident that the engine had been driven too hot, thereby melting the piston rings and consequently the cylinders. That was going to cost a lot of hard cash later on in Meshed. No tourist ever ventured along these routes and the few tribesmen on their horses had difficulty in controlling their steeds which got bouts of nerves at the unusual sound of a mechanized vehicle.

At every village the question was: 'Has Mr Nejjari been by?' – to little avail. Just then a Jeep drove up. At the wheel was a certain Ahmedi who had learned that foreigners had been looking for Nejjari. His Jeep was old, its steering wheel was loose and the tyres were in an awful condition. He looked much older than his 30 years; an impetuous person who acted on the spur of the moment and took life easily. He piled everyone into his Jeep. Ahmedi was a good driver but you sat bolt upright and said your last prayers. His Jeep took corners at greater degrees of inclination than you would think possible. Then he would barge off the road into the desert, drive after terrified Turkmen riders whose horses were trying to throw them off their backs, and laugh loudly while the poor Turkmen would swear and get into contortions.

There was going to be a big wedding, said Ahmedi, and horse-racing too. A rear tyre got a great big hole in it, and the spare did not look very healthy. Outside a village a slim Turkmen woman in red stood in the middle of a field. Ahmedi in a joking voice asked her if she had seen a Jeep, obviously more interested in her than in the answer that was not forthcoming anyway. He shouted back to her that she was very nice and he wished he could … The word he used was the same in Turkish. When Mehmed showed signs of understanding, he looked up and said, 'Be careful otherwise the men will cut your throat'. Mehmed believed him.

Another Jeep now arrived – it was Nejjari. He was a quiet man, with short grey hair, and, with his rifle, he looked like a typical traditional landlord. He spoke little but knew when to laugh and joke. He was a good shot, a good driver, much saner than Ahmedi, but even more courageous when it came to shouting at women in the fields that 'he would die for them'.

At Pishkemer he told people to kill chickens and grill them, and sent Ahmedi to fetch vodka. Everyone sat down to eat and drink, and afterwards, with almost childish pride, Nejjari wanted Mehmed to watch him shooting perfectly, and laughed for minutes when a small girl started crying when Mehmed wanted to take her picture. Afterwards he jumped into the Kombi and showed his guests a school that was being built for a village at his expense.

Next day the poor Kombi was moaning and groaning. A trip to what passed for the local Volkswagen dealers to try and locate the 'strange' noise in the engine came up with the same old story – the piston rings and the cylinders were *kaputt*! There was nothing anyone could do but pour in litres of oil as had happened in Russia and press on in hope.

In the small Turkmen village of Sulfiyan the new arrivals and their long-suffering vehicle were greeted by the sound of the pipe and drums of wandering musicians. An acrobat did cartwheels, and then went around the onlookers with his cap, telling them how good he was. People sat ranged round the room with a solitary oil lamp in the middle. Two musicians perched on cushions played traditional Turkmen folk songs. Shadows flickered on the walls. Smoke fumes gradually filled the room. Villagers peered through the closed windows. This entertainment had been laid on especially – no other Europeans could have been so privileged. Nigel taped the whole proceedings, and the villagers were thrilled to hear it played back and asked again and again for a replay. Crowds of boys pushed each other through the door in their eagerness to listen to this weird machine. Nigel tried to change the tune and played them the 'American Patrol' from the Glenn Miller Story. 'Did you like that?' '*Yok, Baba,*' was the dismissive reply.

Suddenly a man's raucous cry called everyone to come and watch the wrestling. Everyone joined the throng in an open space. It was now pitch black and only the rays from the moon gave light to the scene. The contestants looked ghoulish as they waltzed round, kicking up dust and sand onto the spectators. They grimaced

Male-dominated group
posing for the wedding
party. Westerners were
seldom seen in the
Turkmen Sahra.

as they strained for supremacy. Three or four of the elders wielded sticks and
whips to keep the crowds from closing in too much. Shouts and cries greeted the
sweating wrestlers as they pirouetted in the dust. Often the apparent loser jerked
his feet to bring his opponent down with a thud.

At six in the morning a wake-up call of drums throbbed throughout the village.
The sun pierced the early morning mist. The horses were being loosened up and

Preparing *pilau* for the all-
day wedding feast.

already men were dancing to the pipes and drums. 'The Big Day' had come, with
horse-riding, wrestling, dancing and – a wedding. Small groups of men stood
around the beautifully groomed horses with cloaks over them to keep out both
cold and heat. A large circle formed and the wrestlers started the morning's
entertainment. Then came the horse-riding around a one-kilometre circuit. The
winner of each race got 50 *toman* for each circuit completed; the last race of the

111

morning was eight times round the course and the winner got 400 *toman* (then £18). The whole day's entertainment, including the wedding itself, cost the bride's family about £800. The setting was perfect – an endless plain with a few low sand hills seen through the horizon's haze. At the finishing posts a crowd of about 2,500 people had gathered, most of them standing, some sitting astride superb horses. A group of elders sat with the prize money in envelopes in front of them on the carpet making sure no one cheated.

Excitement mounted at the first race. Several riders were disqualified for cutting the staked-out corners. Once or twice a rider-less horse would come thundering in, having thrown his young rider at a corner. The inevitable happened when a rider, unable to turn his steed in time, galloped straight into a cluster of men sitting on the ground, badly cutting one man's head, wetting the sand blood-red. No women were to be seen. No human description could adequately portray this superb panorama of men and horses sharply outlined against the desert and the clear Persian sky. When the races ended, Mehmed, Nigel and Tony climbed onto sweaty horses to have their photos taken.

Back at the village more innumerable cups of tea were drunk before a rice and kebab lunch, followed by bowls full of grapes. This oppressed Turkmen minority could not have been more hospitable. The foreign guests ate first, and the remains were for the other guests, who sat round the bowls swooping up the rice and meat with their fingers. After lunch an animated general request brought the tape-recorder out for a new concert of the previous night's music. Then everything subsided into a quiet hour. Later came the opportunity to give the locals another surprise as three young men got out their stove and started boiling up some washing. The women looked up from their wooden fires on the ground, amazed. Given the Kombi's sickly state it made sense to leave later when it was cooler for the engine. As it drove eastwards into the gathering gloom, mountains closed

(Opposite, top) The men did prepare some food.

(Opposite, bottom) As part of the wedding celebrations, there were horse races for 'bareback' boys, aged between 9 and 15. These boys were racing near the finish.

in all around with fertile land covering their slopes. At a babbling brook in the shade of the trees water containers were filled. The full moon rose above the mountains. Minor oil troubles punctuated the journey as the Kombi was nursed along. The sleeping town of Bojnurd emerged out of the gloom just before midnight and the darkness made finding the address for a promised night's stay at Reza's house a hit-and-miss affair. By then midnight was past but the door was opened. Such was the sense of hospitality.

Next morning Reza, the 18-year-old host, was mustard keen to show his guests around the town and countryside. Everybody embarked in his Jeep, with three of his young friends, to drive to his country house, outside the town in an orchard of apple trees, grape vines and tall poplars. Grapes, apples and fresh walnuts garnished the table and at a local flour mill, where a stream drove the wheel, an old Kurd and his wife poured in the wheat grain and collected the flour in dirty sacks. Flour covered them from top to toe as they worked in almost complete darkness.

'Would you like to swim?' Further south appeared a veritable haven of an oasis in the desert. There was a tomb of an old 'lord' of Bojnurd, in the form of a mosque, surrounded by large, shady trees. At the foot of its steps was a pool of deep, clear water, full of enormous trout. A wonderful opportunity to strip off, dive in and swim across to the rocks and the source, a spring. It was paradise. In the shade, under the leafy trees, the local Kurdish women in long, black pantaloon-trousers under their dresses, hid behind *chadors* and did their weekly washing. Then back to the orchards to lie under the trees on an enormous carpet, drinking tea from a samovar and listening to recordings of Moscow jazz and Turkmen wedding music. Another recording was added of one of the boys singing and talking. They loved hearing their own voices.

(Opposite, top) Wrestling was part of the day's entertainment, and winners were given small cash prizes.

(Opposite, bottom) Several judges ensured that nobody cheated, and the elders distributed the prize money.

TO ASIA'S HEARTLAND

It was a black night on a bad road and eventually a makeshift campsite was set up in the middle of a cold, windswept plain. Nigel and Tony shivered all night despite layers and layers of clothing. By the morning Tony felt feverish, glad when dawn broke and he could sleep fitfully for an hour or two. Mehmed, typically, had slept perfectly.

Arriving in Meshed at noon, they cruised around in search of the power station, where the department boss, Mr Harari, would, hopefully, be their host for a few days. Sure enough, he invited them to stay and dump their kit while the Kombi was being mended. He was head of the electrical department. He and his Armenian wife, who spoke the worst Russian Nigel had ever heard, and three children had a bungalow on an estate nearby. After a good lunch, Tony, a little 'off', lay down while his temperature climbed to 103. Mehmed sat with him while he sweated it out.

Meshed, Iran's holiest city, once its second biggest, had sunk to fourth place in 1961. Mehmed and Nigel got the Kombi mended – £28-worth of damage – with a new shock absorber, piston, piston rings, etc. Tony, meanwhile, meandered across to the estate's dispensary where he almost fainted, and they laid him down and gave him three penicillin jabs and various tablets and pills. He went back to bed for another sweat. Tony rose from his sick bed the following afternoon and helped, or possibly hindered, the packing up of the Kombi. The whole family had been very kind, especially the wife of Johnny, our host's best friend. There was a terrific mixture of nationalities – Scottish, Armenian, Iranian and others. She was part-Armenian, part-Syrian. She wanted Tony to stay in Meshed where she would find him a nice girl for a wife. Tony asked her just to find him a nice girl, and not get carried away by such complicated things as marriage. The next day they wanted to make an early start from Meshed, anxious not to miss the *bushkazi* in Kabul – the national game of Afghanistan due to be played in honour of the king's birthday.

But Tony still wanted to see Meshed, so off the three went to the centre of town, to the famous mosque and shrine of Gauhur Shad. On trying to walk straight into the mosque they were stopped by the faithful. After much talking and Mehmed swearing madly that he was an extremely devout Muslim, he was allowed in, in the afternoon, when there were no prayers being said. Nigel and Tony were jealous, but had to make do with Mehmed's description of the holy place.

They left Meshed soon after noon, Tony lying in the back all the time, feeling acutely aware of every bump encountered on the terrible road. They missed their turn-off and were racing down the road to Teheran until some lorry drivers put them straight. Midnight came, and time to camp. It was cold in the night and someone had a revolutionary idea of how to use the tent to its best advantage. Instead of sleeping in it, they put it on their camp beds, and then folded the other half back on top of them. Not the brightest idea as it turned out.

On 1 October in Yussofabad, on the Iranian-Aghan border, they met a German student who had just driven from Kabul. He brought good news – the Khyber Pass was closed to all normal traffic but was still open for tourists. What a relief, both as regards money and time – Delhi could now be reached by 12 November as originally planned. The Iranian police and the customs took their passports, and all looked straightforward. The police chief, however, was in the middle of his afternoon siesta, so they had to wait a few hours till he shook off his sleep and was ready to sign their papers.

Off into the 10 miles of no man's land with, for company, the occasional long camel-train. A solitary white stone with 'Afghanistan' written on it in English proclaimed that at last it was there. A few more miles later over the *dasht* (desert) was the Afghan customs post. It was already 5 pm. Private vehicles had to stay the night at the border 'hotel' as this was a military zone open only from dawn to dusk. The customs officer seemed to have no problem with the story of the stolen *carnet* but extracted a solemnly worded letter promising that the Kombi would not be sold in Afghanistan. The camp-beds were spread out on the floor of the hotel, and it was time to cook up one of the Expedition's famous 'gruels' – a packet soup, two handfuls of dehydrated meat, an Oxo cube, salt, pepper, some spaghetti and water. Tony was now succumbing to the dreaded fever again.

11

TESTING AFGHAN PATIENCE

Up to the border, the road had been little more than a cart track; inside Afghanistan it disintegrated into wandering sand ruts, bordered by patches of desert scrub. Nights in Afghanistan were bitingly cold and Tony's fever persisted. These factors and the cheapness of Afghan hotels led to abandoning camping for most of the stay in the country.

Along the sandy roads only an occasional bus or lorry came the other way. Herat produced a doctor – trained in Paris. He prescribed more penicillin jabs, more tablets and pills, and plenty of water for the suffering patient. Tony was to spend most of the next few days in bed.

The only hotel in town was very pleasant, set at the end of a tree-lined avenue amid flowerbeds and tall pines. It was a fine reflection of Afghan contradictions; the beautiful gardens were obviously intended for a high-class hotel; but the building and rooms were dilapidated, and services were non-existent. But it was cheap and so it was an opportunity to be rash and book a room with beds at 3 shillings and 8 pence a night (a fiver in today's money) each. Some New Zealanders, who had just driven over the southern route, had bashed up their car and were trying to sell it. An interesting Dutch-Australian had sold his motorbike in Kabul and flown across to Herat to escape the clutches of the police. They confirmed that one could get out via the Khyber Pass.

Russians were everywhere. About 320 families of them lived in Herat where they were mainly involved with building roads and bridges, but had not got very far. Some of the shops now had signs in Russian, as well as Farsi and Pushtu, and many in English also. It later emerged that many of these Russians were there for a very specific purpose – to buy up dried fruits, especially grapes, which were being flown out at the rate of 12–15 plane-loads a day. The only other Afghan exports were wool and skins. There would be more encounters with Afghanistan's Russians in due course.

Herat was once the capital of the Timurid Empire and was a centre of learning, art and religion, but it had declined greatly during the past two centuries. The

The food drum, used
to feed warriors before
a battle, in the Friday
Mosque, Herat.

Friday Mosque of Herat (or Masjid-i-Jame) was originally built by the Timurids
of mud bricks, with tiles decorating the exterior. A huge food drum, used to feed
warriors before a battle, was among its prized possessions.

Sitting cross-legged next day in a *chaikhane* and drinking tea provided a good
vantage point for watching the activities in the local market, with everyone
shouting their wares. Occasionally someone lost their temper which was the sign
for a few 'fisticuffs'. Fruit was cheap. One kilo of grapes, two of tomatoes and
some pomegranates (and plenty of bread) came to a total of seven Afghanis – just
1 shilling.

Afghan ponies pulled along the numerous, colourful and highly polished *gharies*,
or carriages, at a tremendous pace. A curiosity trip to the Russian compound in

The Friday Mosque of
Herat (or Masjid-i-Jame
Mosque), Afghanistan. It
was originally built by the
Timurids of mud bricks,
with tiles decorating the
exterior.

the back seat of one of these *gharies* proved precarious in the extreme and one
had to hold on for grim death. The Russians were not at all unfriendly, but no
one paid any attention to their casual visitors, not even to ask them what they
wanted.

Back at the hotel the manager was more than happy to buy 25 tins of coffee,
from the Expedition's original English supplies, at 30 Afghanis a tin, so providing
enough petrol money for a while.

An Afghan aged about 22, Nasser Hanefi, who sat in the hotel foyer playing his
portable radio – usually tuned to Radio Ceylon – seemed very hurt at not being
spoken to more often. He seemed to think he would be taken in the Kombi to
Kabul, his home town. The Kombi's crew was equally certain he wouldn't, owing
to its overload and the rough roads ahead. He would soon make a pest of himself.

The Prime Minister had two years previously issued an edict to the effect that all women were to discard the *chador*, or rather at least the part that completely covers the face. But women still to a large extent wore this kind of visor, through which one could just glimpse the outline of their eyes. Iranian women were less inclined to wear this visor-piece. Few in Kabul itself did, but outside the capital it was common.

In Herat Mehmed and Nigel tried to persuade the police and the Governor to allow the Kombi to travel the northern route to Kabul, across 300 miles of desert. Apparently an American boy and a Swedish girl had been killed there a few years earlier so the answer was 'no' – even though some Oxford blokes had come through that way in a Land Rover a few weeks before.

On a drive out to the *Mosalla* (mosque) of Gandar Shah, Mehmed and Nigel climbed up the only surviving minaret of this once imposing building, claimed by many to be the finest edifice of the Muslim world. Eighty years earlier all the minarets partly stood, though in decay. In the face of a threatened Russian advance from the north, all buildings likely to afford cover to the enemy were demolished, under the advice, if not the direct order, of the British. So perished, but for its minarets, the *Mosalla*. Two of its four minarets were destroyed by an earthquake in 1932; a third had fallen down about five years earlier. Only one remained to illustrate the glory of the whole building. The dome of the shrine, still preserved, retained its beautiful form and some of its magical colour – a cross between deep blue and green. The young trainee mullahs from the *Madreseh* were terribly eager to help the visitors, and about ten people followed each other up the minaret like flies climbing a wall, some 250 feet high.

To Kandahar

Along the Russian-built tarmac road, by-passing a new bridge the Russians were putting up, the Kombi suffered a puncture, and became almost stranded in the deep, soft sand on a 'detour' off the main road. Even in two years of roadworks the Russians hadn't got very far, and soon the Kombi was twisting and turning and bumping along the narrow 'road', past occasional little villages of flat-roofed, mud houses clustering amid groves of green poplars on the bare hillside. There were no railways in Afghanistan, so it was just as well the roads were gradually being improved; road and air travel were the only two reasonably fast methods of transport, compared with donkeys and camel trains.

Two more arrivals after midnight stretched the patience of local hoteliers, first in Farah and then in Girishk, where the annoyed hotel proprietor needed much persuasion to open the door. The next morning was a good occasion to wash some clothes by boiling them up in a 'Dixie'. Just then the needle in the stove broke, leaving everybody, so to speak, stoveless. Nigel gathered a collection of tools and set to fiddling around with the nozzle, all of which provided him with yet another worry for his already careworn brow.

Mehmed and Tony drove into town along the main street, which was lined on either side with small, often colourful open shops selling almost every imaginable commodity from grain and tea to Japanese teapots and Russian hats. There was a definite lack of fruit, especially grapes and tomatoes, which were becoming part of the companions' basic diet now; they filled themselves up with *naan* bread instead. Most of the men were Afghans in their long, loose shirts coming down below the knees and sandals, plus individual variations like pullovers and old army jackets; all this crowned by a turban, frequently embroidered on top with brilliant silver and gold thread. Mehmed and Nigel intensely annoyed a camel-driver by driving up and down the main street four times while looking for some tomatoes, disturbing his beast so that each time they passed it 'got up' and the driver had to continually coax it back down onto its haunches, a procedure which became increasingly arduous as time went on.

Arriving at Kandahar in the cool of the evening of 8 October, the companions found a guard standing outside the hotel. There was room to be had and herded together in the lounge were eight Russians. They were buying dried fruits. Asked where one might eat, they had no idea. Finally, down a dark street emerged quite a clean place, a former barber's shop, run by an Uzbek who had come out from Bokhara many years ago, travelling rough by mule and horse across the mountains out of the USSR. He had come via Kashgar and Sinkiang in Chinese Turkestan, taking 15 years to cover a distance of 1,000 miles. He, his son and a friend were very welcoming and everyone sat for hours talking, eating kebab off spits, with bread and *chai*. The proprietor provided addresses of his friends up in the north of the country for the trip that Mehmed, Nigel and Tony proposed from Kabul. After supper they bought a melon from an Afghan sitting cross-legged in the middle of his fruit, his face lit up by a swinging lamp and his birds twittering in their covered cages.

The Americans were in the middle of resurfacing the main road; the police were having great fun keeping the locals off the new tarmac. Tony wanted to cash a traveller's cheque but the bank, it seemed, didn't open until the afternoon. He

The camel train was a common sight on the drive to Kabul.

and Mehmed went for a walk instead via some ruined buildings, which appeared to be one of the city's public conveniences, up a narrow, foul-smelling road to the bazaar. In a sort of antiques shop Tony fell in love with an old Russian knife, reputedly from Bokhara, and 200 years old – but US$20. It looked genuine enough, so back they went to the bank to await the usual slow method of changing money. A fellow with a shabby uniform and a sleepy face showed them into the manager's room. Portraits of Premier Daud and the king, a desk, two easy chairs, a map of Afghanistan and a short, fat manager were the total contents of the room. The ceiling was so low that Tony, all six foot plus of him, had to bend forward in order not to break his neck. Changing a $10 bill was a horrendous process. All sorts of papers had to be signed, passports shown several times and one's name spoken loudly so that it could be written down in Farsi – as *Anti Jan Tomson, Ingilizi.*

The town had no set plan – buildings and streets ran haphazardly in all directions. Half-naked, barefoot children followed everywhere; noisy coppersmiths beat out their masterpieces; kebab sellers blew the smoke away from their grills, while fruit sellers nibbled their own grapes. Before getting to the hotel Mehmed was seized by a vital desire to relieve himself. The locals did not understand his agitated enquiries for a toilet, until one youngster led him through a narrow alley to a path by a stream where, quite undaunted by the local women passing by in their *chadors* and a running commentary kept up by some children, he did what was necessary.

Once back at the hotel, the dreaded Nasser – who had turned up from Herat – elected himself guide and everyone drove out to some rather pleasant gardens and small waterfalls outside the town. After an evening meal at the Uzbeki 'barbershop', on returning to the hotel, there was Nasser again, who proceeded to get well and truly drunk, insisting all the time that he was coming to Kabul with everyone in the Kombi. Again he was assured that he was utterly mistaken! Then he changed his mind and promised Mehmed any amount of money if he would go to his room. Mehmed went, for the hell of it, but soon returned without even one Afghani. Nasser admitted that many Afghans, himself included, much preferred boys to girls, mainly because you could ask a boy to your home but not a girl. At midnight, Nasser woke everyone up and threatened to kill Tony if he went to his room.

They paid the bill and sped away from the hotel and their drunken friend early in the morning. The road was good asphalt, and when they arrived at the airport, there was a road junction with a rather worn signpost. It did not look worth bothering about so they sped off down the asphalt road which the Americans were busy making, past the houses of the ICA (military Intelligence Corps Association) people. Living with their deep freezers, with their bourbon, especially compared with the more adaptable Russians, the Americans left unfavourable impressions on the Afghans. They isolated themselves socially and in Afghan eyes they lived pretentiously. Quite apart from the standards to which they were used, perhaps these were also sorts of defence mechanisms.

On out past the new International Airport and still the surface was excellent. That was odd – the New Zealanders met in Herat had said that only 15 miles or so was asphalted; surely even Americans could not do 15 miles of road in a week. Just over 60 miles later, a barrier suddenly appeared across the middle of the road. It emerged that instead of heading north-eastwards along the road to Kabul the Kombi had gaily sailed down to Spinbaldak at the Pakistan border. In addition, just to make it a really good day, they ran out of petrol, incurred two punctures, and had to toil through the midday heat to mend them. While Nigel struggled with the 'help' of some of the locals, Mehmed and Tony sat down in the *chaikhane* to fine tea flavoured with dry lemon leaves. At last both wheels were back on and appeared to have more air in their tyres, a little petrol was cadged, and so they drove all the way back to Kandahar.

On to Kabul

After a hearty meal and fill-up, they set off for Kabul, this time deliberately turning left at the signpost. It soon got dark. Every now and then the road would abruptly diverge to right or left and go down a short, steep incline, thus avoiding a bridge which had long since caved in. One needed to concentrate very hard in order not to carry on over the non-existent bridge. At Kalat two American boys and a Spanish girl in a Citroen 2 cv caught up with the Kombi – its inmates were maliciously pleased to hear that the *deuche* crew and two Germans and two Dutch boys had also gone down to Spinbaldak by mistake.

After getting into Mukur at 2 am, Mehmed and company were stretched out contentedly, if not exactly comfortably, in the four-storey national hotel, with still a bed spare in the room, when the local bus rolled into the yard below, and two English journalists from Teheran burst in, as well as an Afghan army officer. They were all looking for somewhere to sleep. The officer grabbed the spare bed.

They awoke next morning to a superb sunrise flooding the scene over Mukur with its backdrop of the Ghazni mountains. It is almost impossible to describe the morning beauty of the high Afghan plateau. The crisp blue air outlined every shade and detail, as if on an artist's canvas, against the background of the cloudless sky, the brown hills, the yellow villages and the green trees. The bus left again at 6.30 am so the 'friends' didn't get much sleep. Once awake, the Kombi seemed to be sulking and didn't want to work. Nigel almost crawled into the engine in an attempt to diagnose the trouble. The solution was relatively simple; Mehmed suddenly decided it was lack of petrol, and, lo and behold, once the reserve was turned on, she worked. After they had filled up with petrol, the inside of a *chaikhane* revealed the American and Spanish friends of the previous evening who were eating. One of these 'characters' was Mathias Opersdorff II from Rhode Island, the smallest state in the USA. He strode along the road, all 6 feet 5 inches of him, a karakul hat perched on his head and two cameras hanging round his neck. He subsequently became a professional photographer. At one time later he left his London black cab at Tony's house having spent three months on the road with the travelling people or 'tinkers' in Ireland, and subsequently wrote an article about the experience for the *National Geographic*.

He was the son of an Austrian count, who could trace his family back to at least the thirteenth century, and a mother whose ancestors went to the USA on the Mayflower. His parents met in Paris and fled to America in the 1930s in revulsion over Hitler's policies.

Trying to reach Kabul that night, Mehmed, Nigel and Tony were soon bumping their way on to Ghazni, too late to look round this particularly old, historical town. It got nippy at night, not surprising at 7,400 feet above sea level – 1,400 feet higher than Kabul. Dinner that evening was in what at first sight appeared to be a very ordinary restaurant, but which turned out to be the meeting place of just about all the possible racial mixtures in Afghanistan – Pashtuns, Uzbeks, Tadjiks and Hazaras being among the main ones. Good kebab and bread were brought, washed down with tea, and enormous platefuls of grapes. The locals here, as everywhere else in Afghanistan, repeatedly got out their little round tobacco tins and took a pinch of *naswar* – an extremely powerful stimulant. It was of a greenish colour, and was administered either as snuff up the nostrils or in a pad under the tongue. It smelt vile, but it was very cheap, and was the most popular and widely used drug in the country. On the way out of the town Afghan Radio was blaring out anti-Pakistan propaganda in English.

12
KABUL BEFORE THE WINTER

Only 6 miles to go to Kabul. At last the few flickering lights of Afghanistan's capital appeared across the dark plains. As midnight struck, Mehmed, Nigel and Tony drove slowly down the main street of Kabul. The engine's roar echoed eerily as they hunted through the deserted streets for a place to stay. A solitary figure stood on a street corner swathed in blankets against the sharp night air. 'Hotel koja?' Nigel shouted in faltering Farsi. Half an hour later they were thankfully installed in the Maiwan Guest House for 15 Afghanis, the best doss-house in town.

Austere Kabul was a small town with an animated history at the centre of one of the world's major platforms of contest – Afghanistan. Yet Afghanistan was never really a state, rather a collection of mutually suspicious fiefdoms. A first taste of this suspicion was evident the next morning when Mehmed, Nigel and Tony hotfooted it to the Afghan Tour office, the first tour operator in Afghanistan, licensed by the government. It operated a bit like Intourist in Moscow, in that all tourists had to have agreed itineraries.

The Turkish Embassy now turned up trumps with an offer of space in their compound. Once a royal palace, the embassy was quite old. It had an Ankara cat which, like all its breed, had eyes of different colours; a proper specimen, it seemed, had to be deaf as well. Mehmed and the Ambassador, Mr Talat Benler, hit it off very well. A little room round the back of the embassy provided a long overdue opportunity to unload and sort out crumpled and scruffy gear. Within an hour the empty room on the veranda was graced with a carpet, four chairs and a table, with a toilet and wash-basin next door. The ambassador and his wife, a charming couple, speaking faultless English, despite a five-year sojourn in the States, set extra places for lunch. In the middle of lunch in walked a long-lost first cousin of Mehmed's – Lütfi Coşkun. A little later in came a member of the Turkish military junta that instigated the coup in Turkey in May 1960, but who fell out with the rest and was exiled – a certain Colonel Akkoyunlu. The junta had put all the Democratic Party members of parliament – including Mehmed's father – on the prison island of Yassıada near Istanbul. Soon after the coup Akkoyunlu and 13 other renegades were sent away from Turkey to various embassies as 'consultants'.

At the Ministry of Education the Head of the Secondary Schools Department, in a mixture of French and English, said he would be only too delighted to help the Expedition's studies – 'just write out a questionnaire' – like a good bureaucrat anywhere.

Back to Afghan Tour for visa photos. A large collection of fellow travellers were hanging around, including two Dutch boys already met in Moscow, trying out the new Dutch car, the Daffodil, and the two English boys who had appeared out of the woodwork at Mukor. Outside was Colonel McLean, the cousin of one of the Expedition's patrons, Sir Fitzroy Maclean, author of *Eastern Approaches*, to this day still the greatest travel book of the 1930s. He was to be very helpful.

The embassy of the British, who more than any other outside power had burnt their fingers in Afghanistan's turbulent modern history, was in a very large compound some way out of town – that was probably a useful extra margin of security. It was a large, grand, white building, beautifully situated and furnished. Lord Curzon, Viceroy of India, had been responsible for all this splendour. Now that finally, he had said, the British were to have a permanent mission in Kabul, they should ensure that it be the most magnificently housed. This was in the 1920s, just prior to the Third Anglo-Afghan War, or the War of Independence as the Afghans call it. The Ambassador, Mr Gillette, had dwelt beyond the mountains, so to speak, as Representative in Sinkiang for many years, and several valuable maps and antiques of that area adorned his residence. David Hannay, the 3rd Secretary, was an old school friend of Nigel. Suave and sharp, he would in due course become one of Britain's outstanding diplomats, including stints as ambassador to the EU and the UN and tasked with trying to sort out the intractable problem of Cyprus.

Tony and Mehmed were standing quite innocently outside the Kabul Hotel waiting for Nigel, when a rather attractive girl walked by with her escort. They paid her the due amount of admiring attention that she deserved. She quite rightly ignored them and just carried on walking. Her escort obviously hadn't liked this unwanted attention as he came back and, swearing something in Farsi, pointed his fingers in a V-sign just short of Mehmed's eye. Mehmed and Tony were too surprised to do anything for a moment. The lady dragged her escort away just before everyone became aggressive.

Colonel Akkoyunlu and his daughter set up a tour of Kabul's highlights. The late Nadir Shah's mausoleum, set on a hill, dominated the city. A soldier on guard kept beckoning rather slyly. He wanted money in return for letting anyone take photographs. At Babur Shah's Gardens and in front of his tomb a national scout jamboree was just about to take place. Various hectic scout-type activities rampaged, from putting up tents and roping off fences, to making every manner of wooden structure, such as tables, chairs and cupboards. Scouting in Afghanistan was new, with about 600 boy scouts and 400 girl guides, and growing in popularity. Somehow it felt culturally out of context up here on the high Afghan plateau. The campsite was meticulous and tidy; whether it would stay the same way once the jamboree got going was another matter.

Western facilities abounded. An International Club, with a cosy little clubhouse, in Shehr-i-Nau, the new city of Kabul, swarmed with Germans plus a few spare French and Americans. Western-style houses were large and expensive; shops sold Western groceries and canned foods at prices that had become even more exorbitant since Pakistan had closed the border; coffee, washing powder, cornflakes; anything you wanted, at a price. By stark and gaudy contrast, in the bazaars the old city impinged on the new. Narrow, labyrinthine streets; tiny stalls, one tended by a cross-legged little boy who bargained like a fully fledged tycoon; noise, colour and squalor. Curious eyes followed the strangers here. Veils were lifted to allow a quick glance, and then hurriedly dropped again.

Mehmed, Nigel and Tony had deliberately forced the pace of their journey to Kabul in time for the celebration of the king's birthday, at which the national game of *bushkazi* was normally played. Alas, it hadn't taken place for at least two years, owing firstly to the large number of people killed, and also because of some alleged disease of the horses in 1961. *Bushkazi* is a game between two teams, which do battle on horseback to get the carcass of a goat over their opponent's line. They each have a whip, partly to 'stimulate' their horses, and partly to attack their opponents – not a game for tender souls. It is in fact not an Afghan game as such, but came down from the Central Asian tribes, including, in Afghanistan, the Turkmen and Uzbeks. 'How about a basketball match instead?' asked some joker. There was an alternative – try and get permission to go up north and see a game at Mazar-i-Sharif, where the season was just beginning. This was to be the source of major headaches.

The generosity of the Turkish Ambassador and his wife in offering frequent lunches or dinners provided a welcome alternative to the repetitive Expedition diet of gruel, alternating with spaghetti and dehydrated meat. A good briefing was had over pre-lunch whisky and sodas on the lawn of the American Embassy with its 1st Secretary, a tough, pleasant ex-Marine, who walked with a permanent limp; he had been badly wounded in the leg in the Korean War. Mehmed earned his lunch one day through interpreting services rendered in a discussion about Turkish politics between Colonels McLean and Akkoyunlu. Mehmed's cousin, Lütfi, not only offered dinner every evening at his house, but acted as chief salesman of the Expedition's surplus coffee, chocolate, shoe-polish, spaghetti and porridge, as well as obtaining letters of introduction for the still evasive trip north.

A certain Dr Kardesh, the Turkish doctor in charge of the World Health Organization (WHO) anti-malarial campaign up in Kunduz, some 150 miles north of Kabul, happened to be in the capital. Mehmed dropped in on him and his wife: 'Come and see us when you reach Kunduz.' At the British Embassy the Military Attaché, a typical ex-RAF officer, but without the appropriate moustache, provided good tips about the road conditions up north, and what to look out for.

The police had said that visas to travel up north would be ready by early afternoon. Police headquarters were in a huddle of buildings in a large compound, the visa office in a little shack by the main gate, manned by a grumpy functionary. Only Mehmed's visa was ready. The British, for political and historical reasons, were anyhow not at all popular in Afghanistan. It also turned out that our travellers' by now much-thumbed general visas for Afghanistan had all expired a few days previously. The final decision concerning Nigel and Tony rested with the Foreign Minister or even the Prime Minister, who was the real stoker of anti-British feeling in the country. No one could get to see either of them anyway. Maybe the British Embassy could take the matter up? The Turks, however, who were pretty well in with the Afghans by comparison, were not so sure that it would come off at all. So nobody would get to Mazar and Balkh in the north, which, according to travellers from the past, was easily the most interesting part of Afghanistan.

Over early evening drinks or 'sundowners' the British Ambassador, with commendable frankness and lucidity, described how the reasons for anti-British feeling in Afghanistan were three-fold; firstly, for the historical reasons of the three Afghan Wars; secondly, for the fact that in the old days when Britain was in India, she gave aid to Afghanistan, but now she couldn't afford it, or anyhow was quite prepared to let America give money instead; and thirdly, there was the Pakistan border problem. You could blame it all on the British – so perhaps

Nigel and Tony were being made useful scapegoats. Mehmed now went off on his own to see the unhelpful, obnoxious character in the visa section. Armed with an Expedition prospectus and a copy of the local newspaper with everyone's faces smudged in it, and suppressing bloody-minded instincts, he set off. Time dragged. Two hours later he was back. It was the same old story, neither a definite 'no' nor 'yes', but 'come back this afternoon'. As a last resort David Hannay at the British Embassy was roped in to try and get an official diplomatic letter. It seemed Nigel and Tony were the first Brits to have suffered thus that year. It was frustrating – the great Hindu Kush right up in the north of the country beckoned. Mehmed subsequently returned empty-handed from another excursion to the police who now could not make up their minds whether everybody's current visas had in fact run out or not. Mists of obscurity were closing in.

Kabul, up on the high plateau, ringed with mountain fastnesses, was so different from the rest of Afghanistan. Turbaned Pathans, a blanket swinging nonchalantly from one shoulder, clashed visually with their countrymen in Western dress. Large foreign cars, mainly American and Russian, hooted their way through clusters of *gharies*. Women, enfolded inside their *chadors* as in a chrysalis, shopping at fruit stalls, and schoolgirls in their black uniforms and white headscarves, exemplified the changing face of Afghanistan. The Kabul River, which flows through the whole city, was put to every possible use; camels, donkeys and humans drank from it; people washed themselves and their clothes in it; they urinated and defecated in it; they washed their lorries and plates in it; and they even swam in it when the melting snows and spring rains had filled it up.

There was a reason why women wore coats and headscarves, if not shrouded in a *chador*. Two years earlier when the liberation decree came out, women who took off their *chadors* were often attacked. So another decree was issued saying that they could not be touched if they wore a headscarf and a coat – that is, in public. Reports from Kandahar said that hundreds of people or more – the reported figures varied wildly – were killed in the ensuing riots. The girls' school was burnt down and martial law proclaimed. In their own homes women could take everything off, if they wanted to. In public they wrapped up. Under the hem of the *chador* you could sometimes catch a furtive glimpse of the modern Western clothes of the wearer, short skirt, nylons and high heels.

In Kabul some school kids were educated in privileged surroundings. At the rather impressive Najat Lycée German was the lingua franca for the teenagers. The director, Hamidollah Enayat Seraj, happily showed off the classrooms, reading-rooms and library. The school had about 1,650 pupils and the student–master relationship and the standard of work were most impressive, even if everyone seemed to shake hands everywhere all the time, and classes stood up when visitors entered – just as they would do in Germany.

Another good example was the Malali Girls School, the largest girls' school in the country, situated securely opposite the Ministry of Interior. The Directress, a strikingly good-looking woman, clearly in command, entertained Nigel and Tony in her spacious study. Everyone talked in French in their enthusiastic descriptions of the school, the subjects it taught and the general history of girls' schools in Kabul. This was followed by a visit to various classrooms where lessons were in progress. Most impressive was the nursery and playroom for the teachers' children, so that married women could return to their old profession. Tony could not help thinking that such supportive social practices could be profitably followed in England. Over coffee, cake and wonderful Afghan delicacies the Directress and some of her teachers almost palpably enthused about what they were doing.

Both these examples showed how, against many odds, education in Afghanistan could flourish. Some of the money might have been foreign: but Afghans were doing the job.

Not that education necessarily brought just rewards. Over tea and biscuits, Professor Mohammed Ali, one of the foremost Afghan historians and a lecturer at the university, provided some insight. His daughter was the first woman doctor in Afghanistan, having qualified in obstetrics and gynaecology in Pakistan and America. However, she had met a great deal of opposition before being able to finally set up practice. She earned only 1,500 Afghanis a month, while her father received 6,000 a month, and her brother, a newly qualified pilot, already got 5,000 a month. Such was the unimportance given to the qualified women doctors in Afghanistan, although there was an acute shortage of the medical profession in the country.

A nervous if rickety Afghan state toyed with vigilance. One day a Dr Dupree came to offer lunch at his house. He was an American archaeologist and anthropologist who had been in Afghanistan for the previous ten years with his wife. They related how in the Afghan police-state all servants of foreigners had to submit a report to the police about their employers' movements, etc. The Duprees tried to treat this as a joke; Dr Dupree offered his waste-paper basket to his servants with all his old correspondence in it.

Meanwhile, Afghan people went about their everyday lives – including the business of getting themselves and their goods from A to Z. Throughout Afghanistan, even more so than in Iran or Turkey, the stranger paying his first visit to this country was forcibly struck by the gaudily painted buses and lorries. Mehmed was used to similar means of transport in his native Turkey. Nigel and Tony not only admired these ancient and colourful contraptions, but also marvelled at the enormous amount of goods and the number of passengers they carried at one time. Had they followed one for a while, they would probably soon have witnessed one of the numerous breakdowns that plagued these conveyances.

The police seemed little more, if at all, committed to their roles as guardians of public order than did those in Iran. While the Kombi was obediently stationary at some traffic lights which were still red, a local car shot by at speed. The policeman on duty vainly blew his whistle, the motorist not paying the slightest attention, so the policeman shrugged his shoulders and resigned himself to relieving himself behind his little red and white striped hut. Yet the Kombi was stopped a dozen times and its inmates quite rudely questioned about what on earth their strange German *Zollnummer* plates were all about.

It was time to take a broader look at this complex country. Drinks with the Turkish Ambassador provided deeper insight into Afghanistan in general, the political, economic, cultural and educational fields, as well as perhaps the most important sphere of all, religion, which still seemed to dominate so many questions in the country's life. He had seen two looming developments in the north of Afghanistan: the discovery of oil by the Russians, and their plan of opening five or six experimental farms. He told the story of how the Afghan government had sabotaged a United Nations plan to improve water supplies to the people. Water was controlled by the government. If an uprising occurred it could easily cut the supply and the insurgents would be unable to resist for long. The UN was told to mind its own business.

The Ambassador talked of the heterogeneous character of Afghanistan. Understanding the tribal bedrock was the key to decoding the country. Out of a population of 8 million, 4–5 million were of Pashtu-Afghan origin and they ruled the roost most of the time. Constitutional lawyers were trying rather feebly to 'fix' tribal groups' status by religious, social and other methods. The Turkmen, Hazaras and other Shi'a were in any case barred from high office. Most of the kings had come from a few tribes around the Kandahar area. The social structure and politics of Afghanistan, in spite of economic development, and with intellectuals studying abroad, brooked no communication of political ideas or sizeable opposition. It was an autocratic kingdom offering no alternative to this kind of rule. In 10 to 20 years' time, said Mr Benler, with better communication, things might improve. They changed all right – but not for the better.

As for foreign policy, the government's pro-Pashtu emphasis was not only dictated by the dominance of the 4–5 million Pashtu-speaking peoples in Afghanistan but by the existence of another 7 million Pashtu over the frontier in Pakistan. It was a 'national' problem; the only thing artificial about it was the porous Afghan-Pakistan frontier – the Durand line, named after the British official who in 1893 traced it straight through the heart of Pashtu country. The policy of balancing one power against another on the backs of the Pashtu harked back to the British 'Great Game' against Russia. Once the British left India, the Afghans felt quite alone, and tried to establish the foundations of their own foreign policy. In 1952, they asked the West for arms and economic aid. Russia, meanwhile, continued looking down from the north for an appropriate occasion to get in. With neighbours Iran and Pakistan developing, Afghanistan could not remain an island of poverty and ignorance. The West ignored the arms and aid request, despite initial US responses. Faced with no guarantee of Western aid, Premier Mohammed Daud Khan said Afghanistan would take aid from any quarter, even Russia, knowing full well the consequences. So the Russians moved in.

The Afghans still wanted Western aid. The government did not want to deal with just one power – they wanted both. When the Afghans launched their second Five-Year Plan, the Russians offered to foot the whole bill. The Afghan government refused and split it in two – half from the Russians and half from the Americans, the Germans and the West in general. The Afghans clearly wanted the presence of the West to guarantee their political independence and non-alignment.

Russia, said the Ambassador, had three advantages over the West: proximity; their sort of regime; and their way of giving aid through short- and long-term policies combined and adaptable to the conditions of the country. The Americans gave $40 million in aid, but spent $10 million on their ex-pat personnel; thus the Americans lived in relative luxury compared to the modest standards of ex-pat Russians. The Afghans noticed this and were not impressed.

The Russians had kept to their bargain, so far – an intelligent policy. At that time they sought not to impose, to avoid being overbearing. They bided their time and did not force the pace because everything was going their way. Afghanistan was a convenient shop-window of a benign Soviet Union. In time they would become more strident and risk upsetting this comfortable relationship only if they felt a threat from the Afghans themselves, or from others using Afghan territory and politics to upset their security interests, above in their sensitive Central Asian underbelly. For the time being the Russians perceived no such threat – only opportunity.

The big issue was Russian military aid, both the supply of arms and training. The Afghans would take such aid from anyone as long as the border problem with Pakistan remained unresolved (persistently both countries claim each other's territory). Though much of their equipment was out of date, the Russians had supplied MIGs and were training the airforce. The Russians were also trying to get into education through the back door by military training. They had tried more straightforward methods, from offering to send teachers for an art school to actually building it (the Afghan government turned that offer down too). The Poles and Czechoslovakians also had teams on the ground. But Eastern Bloc teams clashed, as did the Western ones, through inadequate co-ordination of aid programmes. 'The Helmand Valley scheme' was a particular fiasco. The geological survey underestimated salty soil and bad drainage. The Russians made a quick impression with their kind of visible aid. American aid was longer-term but fewer people noticed.

Afghanistan, concluded the Ambassador, would not be lost to the West unless the West did something extremely stupid. And, he added, one had to bear in mind, both in internal and external affairs, the influence of the *mullahs*.

Subsequent events would bear out this analysis.

Autumn arrived very suddenly in Kabul, and when it did, it was breathtakingly beautiful. The reds, yellows and golds of the leaves stood out in sharp outline against the azure blue sky. Before long the first fingers of winter would stroke the city's streets and hardened Afghan men would go nonchalantly in sock-less slippers through the snow in minus 15 degrees centigrade. But for the moment it was bliss.

The autumn sun warmed the stonework of the Kabul Museum, probably the best in Central Asia. The museum drew on a natural treasure ground of remarkable artefacts left by the civilizations that had dwelt in Afghanistan over the centuries. The upper storey had almost finished being redecorated and the various *objets d'art* were being recased with new lighting and were extremely well laid out. Much of the credit for this had to go to French archaeologists who were also digging, and had recently unearthed some wonderfully preserved old Buddhas, lots of pottery, urns and coins. Much of this wealth was to be plundered in the years ahead.

There was yet another frustrating visit to the police station; it now seemed highly improbable that Nigel and Tony would ever get visas. So Mehmed would go up on his own to Kunduz and Mazar. Hence at least one of the party would get there, and Mehmed could take plenty of photographs, and write his impressions when he returned.

Early on Monday, 23 October at the civil airport workmen were still hammering away at the new air terminal. In the background a new Russian cement factory blew out clouds of dust, which slowly rose into the clear blue sky above a semi-circle of mountains. While the companions were waiting in the chill morning air for Mehmed's departure, five Russian planes touched down, presumably part of the daily airlift of grapes out of the country ... Soon afterwards Mehmed climbed aboard. With a roar of its twin engines the DC3 workhorse slowly lifted into the air and banked towards Kunduz and the north. With luck, Mehmed would be back a week later.

So to the police station for the umpteenth time. 'No news – ring me up tomorrow.'

After the Kombi had been dumped at the garage for its 12,500-mile service, it was a good opportunity to stretch legs along the banks of the Kabul River, pausing at various shops to sample the merchandise, before turning down a narrow alley into the cotton and cloth market, where numerous small boys sidled up and whispered, 'You want to change money, dollars?' So on, past rows of shops where merchants were busy making hats and coats to measure, as far as the Russian Embassy. It appeared to be the only embassy in Kabul that kept its doors shut and barred; and certainly the only embassy with a woman doorkeeper, a big, well-proportioned, red-lipped Muscovite. Nigel wanted, eclectically and not without *chutzpah*, to read the unabridged version of the report of the much-vaunted 'turning point' 22nd Communist Party Congress held a month earlier in October in Moscow, after the Expedition had left. There, Khrushchev launched his plan to build 'Communism in 20 years', ditched the slogan of 'dictatorship of the proletariat', sealed the USSR's break with China, and contrived the removal of Stalin's corpse from the mausoleum in Red Square. Full reports of this controversial Congress were slow to emerge and a complete report on the proceedings of this Congress would not be made fully public until a decade later. Not everyone in Moscow was enchanted with the Congress results – Stalin's spirit lingered on. No wonder that the red-lipped Muscovite was cautious about these unseemly visitors to the Soviet Embassy in Kabul. After a certain amount of questioning, Nigel and Tony were ushered into a dull little reading room and given copies of the two latest official papers on the subject. These sparse sheets set out the reasons that compelled Khrushchev to look after the peace-loving nations of the world by exploding his 22nd atomic bomb; and reading about the Berlin crisis. Maybe one day East and West, one thought, would see eye to eye, but it won't be yet awhile.

On 26 October, while Nigel and Tony were busy cleaning the Kombi and clearing the veranda for an impending party, the Turkish Ambassador told them he had just received a telegram from Baghlan to the effect that Mehmed was being held in custody. There was nothing anyone could do. Mr Benler said he would find out what he could.

Meanwhile there were diversions.

Ron Stegall, the 23-year-old head of the administration for the Institute of Education, a big, balding fellow, full of ideas and with an immense appetite for hospitality, invited Nigel and Tony to an Institute picnic at a place called Istalif. Nigel would see a lot of Ron in later years in the USA. This was now a golden opportunity for getting out of the city for the first time in over two weeks. Istalif was a short way off the Bamiyan road, where Kuchi nomads were migrating towards Pakistan. Some were on the move towards Kabul with their camels and donkeys fully laden, while others were encamped in their black tents by the sides of the road. Estimates said there were as many as 2 million of them, but no one knew their exact numbers. Soon there was a glimpse in the distance of the whitewashed buildings of the ancient city of Istalif itself, set on a hillside overlooking the plateau below. The colours of the trees and bushes were breathtaking, binding in leafy wreaths all the possible hues of red to gold, orange, yellow and almond. At the hotel, set on a knoll overlooking Istalif, some ancient gardens were shaded by trees reputed to be 800 years old. From here, etched against the sky to the north, the distant view of the freshly snow-clad Hindu Kush range dominated the horizon. It was a surrealistically beautiful setting for lounging on carpets for a veritable feast of kebab, rice, *pilao*, fruit and tea.

Istalif boasted famous kilns for the delicate blue pottery of Afghanistan. At first sight this part of the town seemed like a ghost-village, virtually deserted except for the few people working in the potteries. The centuries-old industry was still carried on in its original crude form, hence possibly the terribly cheap cost of the products, priced at way below their true value for beauty, in the shops in the bazaar below narrow, twisting lanes, where booths and homes clung higgledy-piggledy and precariously to the hillside.

From here, too, the towering mountain wall of the wonderful Hindu Kush beckoned almost teasingly from its snow-covered peaks inaccessible to most human beings. Fingers of ice etched their artistry up the flanks in spears of white, silver, green and grey to where they touched sparse clouds vying for attention with the dazzling sun. Nigel and Tony gazed at those great mountains, almost as if in a trance. They were determined by hook or by crook (probably the latter …) to cross its snowy redoubt. The Hindu Kush turned out to be more powerful than them.

As they drove slowly away from this quaint old town, the sky turned almost blood-red, casting a reddish-tinged light over the whole valley and the surrounding mountains. This effect lasted only a few moments, but not before the red had diffused the pregnant snow-clouds, which were threatening to burst and shake out their white flakes.

Nigel and Tony decided to defy the powers that be, and set out next day for Bamiyan without permits. As they were leaving the town, a blue Mercedes overtook them and parked about 50 yards ahead. This rigmarole was repeated several more times, with more or less obvious excuses offered by the driver such as stopping to buy a melon. After an hour or so he disappeared. The automatic reaction was that he was a policeman sent to tail Nigel and Tony after their virtual 'confinement' in Kabul.

As far as Charikar, 40 miles north of Kabul, the country had been the dry and sandy landscape of the plain, with its great curtain-drop of mountains. Now the road turned westwards into a long valley with vineyards and poplars and wandering streams, awaiting their fill from the winter snows. Side valleys opened with terraced fields and almond orchards, herds of cattle and fat-tailed sheep. Some of the homes had trailing vines on their verandas. It could almost have been northern Italy. Narrow cultivated strips along the river valley gave way abruptly to steep, rocky mountains. The sun set over the Shibar Pass, yielding a glorious view over the lower mountains in the evening sun. It began to get

One of the sixth-century
giant Buddhas at Bamiyan,
on one of the old Silk
Routes in the Hindu Kush,
north of Kabul.

cold – it was 10,000 feet after all. Bamiyan itself was reached in the pitch black
and freezing cold. The hotel, once the governor's palace, was a gaunt building
perched on a spur over the valley.

The next morning Nigel went to fetch water, and had a tough job breaking
the ice from around the tap. The hotel window looked out on the two colossal
Buddhas carved out of the sandstone cliffs across the valley. Almost 2,000 years
ago merchants who travelled between China and India stopped there to rest
before crossing the mountains. Monks lived and meditated there; they had left
their traces in the caves that still honeycombed the area. It was they who built
the great stone statues, the smaller one 120 feet high and the larger 175 feet.
Bamiyan remained prosperous in spite of various wars until the time of Genghis

TO ASIA'S HEARTLAND

There were five linked
lakes near to Bamiyan.
The rich blue colour
comes from the
travertine walls of the
lakes.

Khan, 700 years before, when his grandson was killed in the valley. Thirsting for
revenge, he ordered that every living being there, animal or human, should be
killed.

The terrain was harsh
near the Band-e-Amir
lakes.

In March 2001, more contemporary vandals would wreak their wanton violence
as the Taliban, with their fervent, religious hatred of what to them was the
'brazen image' of offence to the Creator, fell upon this unique site and destroyed
the Buddhas.

A few miles further the road dropped down through harsh terrain to the
amazingly blue waters of Band-e-Amir. Its five lakes form a chain, separated
from each other by natural dams. The water was so clear that one could see fish
swimming 15 to 20 feet below the surface.

Two punctures punctuated the drive back to Kabul in the dark. Nigel and Tony
pumped furiously every few miles to get to Kabul in the early hours of the
morning. The engine 'pinked' badly from the low-grade Russian petrol, like little

hammers knocking against the pistons. Before the Pakistan border was closed, high-grade American petrol was sold in Kabul. Now, with no tankers coming through Pakistan, the Russians were sending tankers down over the Hindu Kush.

The following day, lunchtime was drawing on, and heads were clearing after a wild party at Ron's house. Suddenly, through the gateway of the Turkish Embassy appeared Mehmed, carrying his holdall and a basket full of grapes. After a much-needed shower and meal he told his story.

13

TO THE OXUS

How Mehmed Pushed His Luck

It was 23 October and Mehmed's plane was soon climbing over the Salang Pass. With their primitive equipment, the old World War II DC3s always took this course, quite low near the peaks, giving the passengers an unrivalled view of the snow-covered tops of the Hindu Kush. Far below the Russians were building a phenomenal road with a three-mile tunnel right through the mountains. For nearly 15 minutes the plane plodded along, at times dangerously close to the icy tops. Then it descended gradually to land at Kunduz, a small town with a large cotton factory and an airport project. The Americans were going to build a control tower and a 2,000-foot-long tarmac runway. So far there was only a short, dusty patch with two *Aryana* – Afghanistan's national airline – vehicles waiting at one end for the disembarking passengers. A barefoot child squatted, playing in the dust.

Dr Kardesh, the Turkish doctor in charge of the WHO anti-malarial campaign in Kunduz, was an old friend of Mehmed's family, and his wife was an excellent cook. WHO headquarters were at the Cotton Company's hospital, and their hostel served as a hotel for foreign travellers. Kunduz was important strategically. The road to the north led to the Soviet Union, only 40 miles away, and had only recently been completed with Russian financial and technical help. Once predominantly Uzbek, the population now seemed at least half-Afghan – that is, Pashtu-speaking people from the south, who had been resettled here. Kunduz was not exciting, but the Kardeshes seemed quite happy. 'At least we have electricity and water,' they said. 'In many WHO malaria regions conditions are much worse.'

The Oxus, or as it is called locally, the Amu Darya, is the longest and by far the most important river in Central Asia. It stretches for 1,000 miles and constitutes a natural boundary between Afghanistan and the Soviet Union for about 400 miles. Foreigners were not even permitted to set eyes on it. Andrew Wilson (author of *North From Kabul*, which Expedition members had all read avidly before their

TO ASIA'S HEARTLAND

Barefoot child in Kunduz,
northern Afghanistan.
There was a wide mix
of ethnic groups here
including Tajiks, Pashtuns,
Hazaras, Uzbeks and
even Arabs.

Some were better shod.

departure) had written, 'I watched for some sight of the Oxus – that elusive great river which gave its name to the country over which I travelled, but which every device of security had prevented me from seeing'. This presented Mehmed with a challenge, to which more flames were added when the Kardeshes told him of the strict security measures and the skill with which the Afghans kept all foreigners in their sight.

Mehmed learned that lorries to Kizil Kala, the border town in the Kataghan Province, left early in the mornings. So he told the hotel manager he would be getting up early to go to Khanabad, sister town of Kunduz, only 15 miles away, and home of the best *bushkazi* team. Dressing discreetly, he slipped out of the front door before dawn. The policeman who had been detailed to watch his every movement lay fast asleep on a chair in the foyer. The idea was that, as a Turk, and after all 'Turks and Afghans are brothers', the 'mistake' would be treated

Mehmed, on the left,
photographed at the
start of his unauthorized
trip north to the River
Oxus.

lightly, especially because of Dr Kardesh and the Turkish Ambassador in Kabul. About 100 yards up the road was an international licence-plated tanker with a non-Uzbek co-driver who was supervising the *giriskar* ('grease monkey'), as a lowly mechanic was nicknamed. This was ideal, as Mehmed could thus speak in Farsi with an Afghan and so have a second 'excuse'. Luckily, he spoke bad Farsi. 'Bandar in half an hour!' he shouted. 'Bandar' means frontier in Persian, and thus the fact that Kizil Kala was not mentioned was even more pleasing. Hoping that the *giriskar* would do his job quickly, Mehmed jumped into the lorry. Two policemen were standing around, so he looked the other way, quietly cursing under his breath. The *giriskar* and the co-driver then began to quarrel over new supplies of grease. The *giriskar* demanded more; the co-driver refused. Eventually the co-driver gave in, and 15 minutes later they were off. Fifteen minutes of wondering when they would catch up, for surely the officer in the hotel had woken up by now.

The road was good and looked fairly new. Suddenly, the fertile cotton fields stopped and gave way to a bleak, unrelieved wilderness which the Afghans call *dasht*. A vast, dead plain without skyline or horizon, in which nothing lived or moved but the smoking dust. After nearly two hours, the lorry topped a small hill and there below were the cotton-growing plains of the Oxus. In the background stood the big depots storing Russian petrol, and other buildings of Kizil Kala, and further still rows of hills. But where was that elusive river, the Oxus? The driver had not talked much the whole way, but alternated instead between bouts of song and pinches of *naswar* to keep himself going. The truck passed safely through the customs post.

Mehmed's idea was just to look at the river and then give himself up to the chief of the frontier police. Everyone kept looking at him, so he hurried in the direction of the watchtower from where he hoped to see the Oxus. Two minutes later and there it was. There was no one around: absolute silence. All that could be heard was the gentle lapping of the water on the bank below. Across the snaking blue waters lay the USSR. Apart from a barbed-wire fence, and a site way over to the west where the Afghans were having a port built, there was nothing. A Russian ship steamed slowly upstream against the current as Mehmed unwillingly walked the ten yards into the compound of the frontier guards. The first part had been successful. What would happen now?

Mehmed, with one eye still on the river, asked to see the *Komiser* (chief). Bedlam broke loose in the camp as people woke up from their siestas. Finally the *Komiser* arrived, looking very puzzled. He was short and fat, looking more like a cook than a *Komiser* in his ill-fitting, dark brown uniform. After they had politely asked after each other's health, Mehmed, smiling stupidly, explained in Farsi that he had got on the wrong lorry and arrived in Kizil Kala instead of Khanabad. Would the *Komiser* use his authority to get him away as soon as possible as he had no right to be there?

They began walking back together down the hill towards the shops and *chaikhanes*. There was a lorry pointing in the direction of Kunduz. The *Komiser* told the driver and his cleaner, both Uzbeks, to take Mehmed straight to the *Komandan* (chief of police) in Kunduz, and said farewell. But elation was to be short-lived. Just outside the city boundary at Kunduz the lorry was stopped by the pock-marked officer who had been left fast asleep in the hotel a few hours previously. He was furious, and said he had been waiting for two hours. The *Komandan* was run to earth in his shabby office, dressed in a smart uniform reminiscent of pre-war Italy. He was talking on the telephone to the *Komandan* of Baghlan, the provincial capital, about the captive upon whom it soon dawned that he was no longer the popular 'Turkish brother'. They looked all prepared to take hell out on him, for it was quite a serious slip-up for a foreigner to have 'lost' his way to Kizil Kala.

The *Komandan* started questioning in Farsi. Mehmed pretended not to understand. The chief's face became red with anger, and almost unable to speak, he sank back into his chair while an Uzbek translated what he had just said. The whole procedure was becoming a farce, everyone talking at once, and the *Komandan* talking on the telephone to Kizil Kala, haranguing the *Komiser* for his stupidity and demanding that the driver be found and locked up; then, more respectfully, to Baghlan, to keep the *Komandan* there informed of the latest happenings. Finally they decided to put some questions written in English which, in turn, would be translated by the hotel manager into Farsi.

Mehmed's request to have Dr Kardesh as interpreter was granted, and the party moved across to the hotel. *En route* to see the *Komandan* he called on the governor, who said that if he had wanted to visit Kizil Kala he should have asked permission. As it was he had acted contrary to Afghan laws and so was subject to punishment. For the umpteenth time they asked, 'Why didn't you enquire from the police which road you should have taken for Khanabad?' and 'Why did you say you were going to Khanabad, and then go to Kizil Kala instead?' Mehmed replied warily, 'As soon as I found out my terrible mistake, I immediately gave myself up to the *Komiser* and urged him to get me transport out of town.'

This sort of procedure could have gone on for hours, but luckily Dr Kardesh arrived and told the police that his wife had prepared dinner for the three of them. The whole thing could be settled the following day. After a good night's sleep, Mehmed woke to find that he had been 'jailed' in the hotel. Towards midday the pock-marked officer turned up with the chief clerk and the driver of the lorry to Kizil Kala who had spent the night in custody. 'Why didn't you ask the driver if he was going to Khanabad?' the chief clerk asked. 'I assumed that only buses and lorries for Khanabad would leave from that point,' Mehmed replied. The chief clerk looked rather pleased with himself at this weak excuse and walked off.

After lunch Mehmed was packed off to Baghlan by the same lorry that had taken him to the Oxus. Accompanying him this time was a shoddily clad private acting as bodyguard, who kept a grip on Mehmed's passport and a thick envelope containing all the questions and answers from the interrogation session in his grubby hand. A pistol, especially given him for the occasion, hung conspicuously down from his belt.

Three hours later they pulled up behind a Russian Jeep parked outside the *Komandan*'s office in Baghlan. 'Is the *Komandan* in?' shouted the private in an important manner. 'No,' said one of the sentries. An inquisitive crowd gathered to look at the 'spy'. Seconds later the *Komandan* arrived. He smiled in a friendly fashion and read a letter from the Ministry of Education in Kabul that Mehmed handed him. 'Where are you going?' he asked. 'Mazar,' said Mehmed hopefully. 'You can join the *Komandan* of Aibak who is going up there in the morning,' he said and walked away. He paid no attention to the envelope which the bodyguard was hesitatingly pushing forward. Mehmed grabbed his passport from the puzzled private, picked up his holdall, and jumped in next to the *Komandan* of Aibak in his Russian Jeep.

None of the gauges worked. The water stood at 110 degrees centigrade, the petrol-tank read dry, and the current read 20 amperes. It was a miracle it kept going. The night was spent at the Baghlan sugar factory club. Dinner was a delicious plate of Afghan *pilao* and chicken, with fresh salad. Shir Mehmed, a friend of the *Komandan*, waited until everyone else had finished then grabbed the remaining plates and finished them off, washing it all down with a jug of water, followed by six apples and three very large slices of melon. It was still bitterly cold when they all left the next morning.

The narrow road twisted and turned back upon itself at times, and for the last few miles the Jeep crawled upwards in first gear. Ahead lay the plain of Aibak, dominated on one side by a solitary snow-covered peak, very reminiscent of Mount Ararat in eastern Turkey. After a fine lunch in Aibak, Mehmed left the *Komandan* and Shir Mehmed as he wanted to push on to Mazar. He had heard that there was to be a game of *bushkazi* the following afternoon.

There was a tension and bleakness about Mazar which its proximity to the Soviet border did nothing to diminish. Its blue mosque and shrine, containing the relics of the Fourth Caliph of Islam, made it a holy city, which for generations had been a symbol of Muslim resistance to Russian encroachments from the north. Under the existing government it had become a centre of Russian

149

Local transport – a *ghari*.

technical and military aid operations. Three big highways came right down to the Afghan border on the Russian side, and the Russians were building roads in Afghanistan to link up with cities like Tashkent, Samarkand and Stalinabad (now reverted to Dushanbe, as part of Khrushchev's de-Stalinization process late in 1961). How close Russia felt.

(Opposite, top)
Impromptu *chai* and a
lie-down outside the blue
mosque in Mazar.

(Opposite, bottom) Street
barber in Mazar.

The game of *bushkazi* was cancelled as the ground was too hard. A game was going to be played with donkeys instead. It was hardly worth watching this prostituted version. A better option was to visit Balkh, the 'Mother of Cities' and birthplace of the Aryan civilization. Once it held the same status as Rome and rivalled Babylon in prominence.

Here he met a gentleman called Bahadur Khan, a name reminiscent of old Mogul lineage, a contact that Mehmed had been given in Kabul. Later in Mazar, Bahadur would tell how he and his family had got through the fence by the Oxus and crossed those icy waters on large pieces of wood back in the 1930s. They were some of the last refugees to escape from Soviet Turkestan. Now they hired a Russian Jeep and from the bazaar drove up a track into an enormous saucer of dust. These were not 'ruins' in the classical sense: no broken arches or towers or graves, just this great dust saucer surrounded by a continuous, jagged, crumbling wall. But Balkh was no disappointment. The Timurid mosque was covered with deep blue tiles, half on the dome, half scattered on the ground. All you had to do was pick yourself a specimen of these valuable tiles, dating back to the fifteenth century. Afghan restorers were hard at work with new and revolting colours, and slowly the dome was losing some of its shape.

Back in Mazar, Bahadur Khan was a kind host. He was in the import-export business, and was the Pye Electrics agent in Afghanistan. His nephew, Lutfullah, a young Uzbek of 19, appointed himself guide and interpreter of Farsi. At a grand dinner, *pilao* was served. Two months earlier Mehmed and Nigel had had this delicious Uzbek national dish in Tashkent, the capital of Uzbekistan. There it was washed down with wine; here green tea had to suffice. In Tashkent talk ranged over world politics, nuclear physics, and economic ideologies; in Mazar, not so far away, the only topics of conversation were religion and the Expedition – even the street barber apparently had got to know about it. In Tashkent, everyone in the house had received higher education; in Mazar, none had gone beyond primary school.

Mehmed visited the new girls' high school, and sat in on a lesson. 'Do you speak English?' he asked the young teacher from Kabul. 'No,' she said. Later she was introduced as the English teacher. She made the children read extracts from *Aladdin's Lamp*. They paid scant respect to punctuation marks and had appalling pronunciation, a clear indication that they did not understand more than half of what they were reading. This the teacher later admitted. Asked if they understood the words, the teacher replied, 'Not yet'.

The mosque in the holy
city of Mazar-i-Sharif.

Mehmed had reluctantly to leave Mazar sooner than expected. Instead of hiring a Jeep to Kabul, which would cost 300 Afghanis, he preferred the overloaded Chevrolet *servis* bus to Pul-i-Khumri. The only seat available on the bus was at the back by the door. You had to pull your feet right underneath the seat while people climbed in and out, otherwise they just trod on you. The seat was small; the door had no windows, so dust was blowing into his face. At the first petrol stop he decided to get up onto the roof and travel *havakhurri* ('eating air') as the

Persians say. Clambering over people's legs and shoulders, he pushed his way to the front to see better.

Afghan buses had sides built on the roof, about 50 centimetres high like a truck, to stop people from falling off, but at the front and back there was nothing. The seat was on top of the tool-box, a slightly precarious position, with nothing to hold on to. Sitting cross-legged, gripping the edges tightly with both hands, Mehmed prayed that the driver would not suddenly brake. From Mazar to Pul-i-Khumri his travelling companions were young Uzbeks and Turkmen on their way to do military training. They were a cheerful bunch, and welcomed Mehmed as a 'brother'. Despite wearing three sweaters, two pairs of trousers, a pair of pyjamas and a sleeping bag, he nearly froze to death during that 17-hour drive. It was only the raucous singing of the friendly, ill-clad conscripts, and the occasional cup of tea and bowl of rice that enabled him to survive.

On reaching Pul-i-Khumri, Mehmed shook hands with his fellow passengers and caught a *ghari* to the Nassaji Club, the second-best hotel in Afghanistan. A sentry with a rifle and a tired-looking clerk made up the reception committee. Desperately tired, Mehmed ate all the eggs in stock, took a hot shower (ten Afghanis extra) and retired to bed to wake up 13 hours later. The club stood above the river, overlooking a terraced garden of roses and snap-dragons, illuminated at night by coloured lights. Pul-i-Khumri was decidedly the most pleasant place Mehmed had visited north of Kabul, excluding the architecturally interesting parts of Mazar and Balkh. The river ran through a narrow valley overlooked on both sides by mountains. The riverbanks were lined with trees in fine autumn colours.

The last few miles of the long journey back to Kabul were in relative luxury, on Russian paved roads, despite being on the top of a tanker. The smoothness of the surface helped Mehmed reflect on the last seven days. North of the Hindu Kush was an entirely different world, and an entirely different country – Turkestan. Everything was different, race, language, habits, culture. Artificial boundaries had been created and Turkestan was divided into four parts: Russian, Persian, Chinese

(Opposite) Selling watermelons by the roadside, Hindu Kush.

and Afghan Turkic areas. Resettlement plans had changed the appearance of the parts. Just as Russian Turkestan was unmistakably Russian, Afghan Turkestan was so typically Afghan. With all the new road links with Russia, Mehmed wondered how much Russian influence would entrench itself in the northern provinces. The southern border with Pakistan was closed; the northern one was very active.

The noise of the traffic in Kabul rudely pulled Mehmed out of his reverie. Ambassador Benler was most relieved at Mehmed's safe return, and he and his wife invited everyone in for drinks that evening to celebrate his release, and so Mehmed could tell his story.

Reunited, Tony, Nigel and Mehmed later drove into town for a last meal at the cafeteria, and were later joined by their student friend, Ali, who gave his views on the different ways different countries had of giving aid to Afghanistan. So much had been seen or heard of the American and Russian 'approaches' on this subject that it was good to hear an Afghan's views. 'It is true,' he began, 'that the total foreign currency value of Soviet aid is greater than that of the United States. It is also true that their projects have made a greater initial impact on our people than have those of the US.' He paused. 'But,' he continued, 'this is not necessarily going to be a long-term evaluation. In Russia itself, so I'm led to believe, they seem to stress quantity rather than quality in their work. But, I admit, the Russians score immediately on their kind of aid,' he emphasized in a matter-of-fact tone of voice. 'A silo, cement factories, arms, air-lifts, paved roads. While the Americans embark on more long-term policy projects which do not show so quickly: education, irrigation schemes such as in the Helmand Valley, and roads which are out of town! For Afghanistan neutrality is an attractive and well-paying way to draw economic and military aid from both "blocs",' he added with a quick grin.

(Opposite, top) The road over the Hindu Kush, northern Afghanistan.

(Opposite, bottom) Fruit stall and local tribesmen from north of the Hindu Kush.

Mehmed, meanwhile, wondered what had happened in Kabul so that, instead of having life made very unpleasant for him – apart from a few thumps – he had been given VIP treatment in Baghlan. Dr Kardesh, it appeared, had sent a cable in Turkish to Ambassador Benler; two words only: 'Demirer nezarette' ('Demirer in custody'). At the very moment when he was being taken to Baghlan from Kunduz under arrest, four high-ranking Afghan Air Force officers were waiting for visas from the Turkish Embassy. Their plane was due to leave Kabul airport the same afternoon. Mr Benler, guessing that Mehmed must have done something stupid but nothing criminal, called the Afghan Foreign Ministry and told them, 'Unless Demirer is released immediately and shown traditional Afghan hospitality, the visas will not be issued.' That was how Mehmed's luck had changed so dramatically in Baghlan.

Passing through Bamiyan on the last bit of his journey back, Mehmed had bought a basket full of beautiful grapes which he presented to Mrs Benler, who had a weak spot for him. Grapes or no grapes, Mr Benler first listened to Mehmed's story and, after taking him aside to give him a telling-off, said, 'Get out of Afghanistan as soon as possible ...'

They did.

The next day Mehmed, Nigel and Tony set off for the Khyber Pass. They had now completed the first stage of their Expedition, and had covered 13,000 miles.

*

During the afternoon of 13 January 1842, an exhausted man and horse rode up to the walls of Jalalabad. Dr William Brydon, ancestor of Bob's wife, was the sole survivor of the British expeditionary column. Behind him lay 4,500 soldiers and 12,000 civilian camp followers who perished during seven days of non-stop ambush in the perilous defiles descending over the Khyber to the plains below.

Over a century had passed, and on 15 February 1989, General Boris Gromov, Soviet commander, was the last man to cross the Termez Bridge out of Afghanistan. Ten years of Soviet invasion were over at the cost of tens of thousands of Soviet and Afghan lives. Mujaheddin, clans and warlords, then the Taliban wreaked their own tolls on the country. Now a US-led coalition bitterly wonders how it was lured there in the first place and wriggles to get out. In 1961, a traveller could already sense the fragility of Afghanistan, caught up in the battle for influence between the West and Russia, pitched against the Pashtu people astride an artificial frontier line with a touchy Pakistan, beset with its own strains and contradictions. The failed non-state of Afghanistan remains a vital and volatile geopolitical turntable for regional security – or anarchy.

*

The number of Kuchis increased as the Kombi chugged closer to the border. Some of their womenfolk were striding barefoot down the road, weighed down with ornamental bands of silver coins around their gaily embroidered blouses, in brilliant flowing bloomers, and heavily braceleted on wrists and ankles. They were often beautiful and always unveiled. Donkeys and camels were loaded with pots and pans, children, squawking chickens, tent poles and the felt sides of tents. Dogs, like heavy, bristling wolves, loped alongside. The men in brightly coloured garments, all in tatters, rode gaily caparisoned horses, sat regally on camelback, or in less dignified fashion on the backs of donkeys, their legs outstretched so as not to touch the ground.

One hundred thousand or more Kuchis faced starvation along the border. As they had done each winter, these Kuchis were returning from their summer grazing grounds in Afghanistan towards the plains where they passed more than half the year. This time, however, they were stopped at the Pakistan border. They were asked for passports and visas and valid international health documents for themselves and their great herds of cattle – demands for things that meant nothing to them. So the bulk of them were now stranded on the border. There was nothing for them to return to, as their summer lands were under snow. In the high passes where they had been blocked, the nights were already freezing cold, and every day saw the snow line on the hills come lower, while their herds demolished the thin grass along the trail, and their own supplies for their interrupted march dwindled. The Kuchis were a warrior tribe, and when the choice became absolute they could not be expected to choose starvation rather than fight, although the fight had to be a losing one. Though the Kuchis migrated primarily for fodder for their herds, they turned their hands also to the hardest manual labour. Pakistan would feel their absence that year. Already in some districts the sugar cane stood late in the fields because the Kuchis were not there to cut it. Gunfire had broken out in one incident, and Kuchis had been killed. As the cold and their dying flocks made them increasingly desperate, many more such clashes threatened.

That night was spent at Jalalabad, a historic border town famous as a lush winter resort for royalty but often turbulent and contested by warring tribes. After a quick cold shower, punctuated by Nigel's choice of oaths, the three left the modern, newly built Ningerhar Hotel and headed further out towards the border. Just before reaching the edge of the town, they visited the police station, having first gone to the Russian consulate by mistake. Their exit visas had expired the day before, so by rights they should have been out of the country by then. No one seemed to worry much. But it was better to drive through the Khyber Pass by daylight, hence the stop for the night at Jalalabad. The bazaar had an oriental atmosphere, heightened by the textile shops, rich with silk and imported rayon turban cloth, and owned by the Sikhs who for generations had made their homes there. The *chaikhanes* were vulgarly bright, with colour prints of saucy ladies from Delhi. The wireless blared music from Indian records. Beyond the last grocer's shop, with its splash of red capsicums strung up to dry in the sun, the bazaar ended, and there was the inevitable open wasteland where houses had been demolished to make way for a projected New Town. The line of demolition hugged balconied mud houses, with lines of drying washing and an air of fiesta. Mehmed went off to see the Governor's Secretary to see if he could be persuaded to help. Nigel and Tony sat drinking awful tea with the clean-shaven, stern-looking, but kindly chief-of-police.

Soon Mehmed returned – his visit to the big man had worked. Everything was apparently OK, everyone shook hands, piled into the Kombi and drove towards Pakistan as quickly as the Kombi would move, just in case anyone should change their mind; and this even after the chief-of-police had offered them lunch. A few kilometres before the actual border there was a passport check, but no one mentioned that the visas were out of date. The number of Kuchis encamped by the roadside had gradually increased as the border drew nearer, their black tents firmly dug into the ground, and their camels and donkeys cropping the sparse grass around the encampments. The Kuchis would certainly not have understood what all this trouble over visas and jabs was about. The Pakistanis were certainly going to miss their salt, timber and carpets, which the nomads normally sold before their long march back across the Hindu Kush.

The border was deserted and as silent as a graveyard, with empty lorries pulled up by the roadside. All the desks in the customs office were closed, except one. A thin layer of dust had formed on the woodwork, and an air of silence reigned throughout the whole building. No Afghan or Pakistani was allowed to cross, so all the bus services stopped here, ejecting their disgruntled passengers, who milled around the frontier-post, just to make sure the border really was closed.

Only tourists and those people who travelled on diplomatic passports were allowed through. It took a while to persuade the customs officials that a *carnet* was not needed for the Kombi, before they dropped the heavy barrier chain. On 7 November, the Expedition slowly crossed the 100 yards of no man's land into Pakistan.

SOUTH TO SERENDIPITY

14

BEYOND THE INDUS

Afghanistan receded and, immediately on entering Pakistan, a change came over everything – people, scenery, buildings, the lot. The customs officials insisted on tea and biscuits with them before Mehmed, Nigel and Tony set off, on 7 November, through the Khyber Pass. An essential part of the old Silk Route into today's Pakistan, this was indeed a wonderful pass. It twisted and turned ever downwards, while the dark, satanic mountains loomed up out of the gathering dusk on both sides. The view back into Afghanistan was magnificent, falling far into the distance between two ranges of mountains. Dotted around on the tops of most of the hills were forts, relics of tribal warfare – the Pashtunistan problem again – under British rule in India. Now they were back in use, this time as watchtowers. The Pashtun people on both sides of the border wanted to be unified. The Durand Line Agreement in 1893, however, had carved out the new North-West Frontier Province (NWFP) in what was then India. Several exchanges of gunfire had recently burst forth from these forts. Many nationalist tribesmen had made raids 'for the cause', with no little loss of life on both sides. One could imagine hordes of tribesmen with their homemade *jezail* muskets and blades pouring down on the British from the surrounding hillsides. The Expedition descended from the hills to the plains and, thank goodness, to asphalt roads, and on to Peshawar.

Lodging was found at the youth hostel adjoining the new University of Peshawar, which happened to be hosting a conference of school inspectors staying at the same place. This was a good and unexpected opportunity to chat with them and catch up with education work.

Peshawar, with its turbulent history of competing political appetites, only ten miles from the entrance to the Khyber Pass, went back to about 100 AD. Peopled mainly by proud Pathans, it was the principal town of the North-West Frontier Province. Peshawar was really two places. The old city, walled and fortified, was the great southern market for Central Asia. The newer 'cantonment' area from British India times boasted pleasant, tree-lined roads, and still held a garrison, shops and a cinema or two for foreign films. The Hindu Kush range to the north towered over them both. The mighty Indus flowed nearby, emerging from the mountains towards Rawalpindi.

Driving through the
Khyber Pass, an essential
part of the old Silk Road,
into Pakistan.

The original protective wall, with 16 gates, had been partially knocked down to allow for expansion. The cantonment was the military headquarters on Pakistan's western frontier, its proximity to the Khyber Pass making it a place of strategic importance throughout the ages, none more so than under the Ghazni and earlier Mogul dynasties, the centre of whose power straddled the border ranges between Afghanistan and the Punjab. Kushan Kings, Hindus, Sikhs, Moguls and later the British all made it their home, and each fought over it in turn.

Powindahs, Afghan nomads and travelling merchants once led their caravans every autumn to Peshawar from Kabul, Bokhara and Samarkand, bringing horses, wool, dyes, fruits, carpets and sheepskin clothing to what was still a major trading centre with industries of textiles, copper utensils and leather goods. Pathan tribes from Afghanistan had held sway, giving major headaches to the Mogul emperors. In the early nineteenth century, Ranjit Singh crossed the Indus and after much hard fighting firmly established Sikh authority. That Peshawar contains no architectural monuments of any value is due mainly to the devastation he inflicted on it. In 1849, the British seized the city. Like the Sikhs before them they strove to make it once more a city of gardens, though with a distinctly English suburban taste. In the years before the formation of Pakistan, in 1947, the Peshawar Valley was shaken by the 'Red Shirt' movement, whose founder Abdul Ghaffar Khan subsequently led the Pathan separatist movement and the agitation for a Pashtu province in newly independent Pakistan until arrested.

The Expedition now came face to face with the personification of that turbulent history. Daud Kamal, a friend from Cambridge, was a senior lecturer in English at the University of Peshawar, son of the Advocate-General of Peshawar. He introduced Mehmed, Nigel and Tony to Ghani Khan, Pathan poet and painter, and son of the legendary Abdul Ghaffar Khan, popularly known too as the 'frontier-Gandhi'. Ghani lived in a rambling old building (incongruously like an old English country farmhouse), set in extensive, well-kept grounds with flowering shrubs and trees. The place was full of valuable pictures and paintings, antique vases, bowls, carpets and cushions. Ghani was a far cry from his father. Wonderfully relaxed, and although no longer young, he dreamt of a year in Paris to learn more about painting. Everyone reclined on cushions on the floor while a local Indian refugee musician softly played Pathan and Indian music. Ghani regaled his audience with stories from his fascinating life, which he kept up non-stop throughout the buffet-banquet.

An ancient gateway led into the old city, which originated from Mogul times, three to four centuries earlier, although most of the oldest buildings had gone. The walls were extremely thick but crumbling in many places with grass growing thickly around their feet. They enclosed a labyrinth of narrow alleys. Buildings were simple reproductions in carved wood of an excellent tradition in Muslim architecture. Unfortunately, as Sir Olaf Caroe (author of *The Pathans*) said, 'they have been repaired by hybrids which paid no account to the old crafts and failed to absorb the new'. Ornately carved wooden balconies of shops and houses overhung the roadway. Houses were built of sunburnt brick in wooden frames, of three or more storeys in height. The shops, occupying the lower storey of the high houses, were full of life and bustle: dried fruits and nuts, bread, meat, sandals, saddles, bales of cloth, pots and pans and books were displayed, each in its own quarter.

Daud took his Cambridge visitors to the alley of the silversmiths and up to a mosque. From the top of one of the minarets one saw the whole of the old city spread out below, with its crazy wooden structures perched precariously on the top of the brick foundations, leaning over the thronged, noisy, busy streets below. Afridi and Shinwari tribesmen passed by with laden camel caravans, bullocks and donkeys, all bound for the market-place, while creaking water buffalo carts jostled to move past the vendors of cheap cloth, sugar cane and nuts, who somehow managed to scrape a living together. Over the rooftops one saw the poverty in which some of the Peshawaris lived. Daud maintained they were not as badly off as they looked. Peshawar had a distinctly softer South-Asian atmosphere, with its thronged, noisy, narrow, busy streets, in contrast to the harder patina of Central Asia and the mountains. Few women could be seen, their long white veils a reminder of the strict Muslim *purdah* enforced here.

In its Arabian Nights atmosphere Qissa Khwani Bazaar was a compelling place. Renowned from days of old as the 'story-tellers" bazaar, the flavour still lingered with fortune-tellers and hawkers, stalls piled high with apples, melons, plums, oranges and bananas, and cook-shops with their rich sweetmeats. On the way 'home' a certain Farok and other Pathan friends of Daud called everyone over to join them at an outdoor café to enjoy a kebab, roasted and savoury over pungent charcoal.

Old Peshawar was very much as Mountstuart Elphinstone, the British envoy, found it in 1809 when he was received by Shah Shuja. 'Peshawar-Khar', or the City, as the Pathans call it, 'was no longer a capital', sighed Farok as he thoughtfully sipped his green tea.

At the university Mehmed attended an engineering lecture, and Nigel one on history. Tony was whisked away to the law faculty to meet Mr Naway, the lecturer in International Law. It was a new subject in 1961; the lecturer himself had only been studying it for a year. It emerged he knew Tony's International Law lecturer in Cambridge. Tony sat in on a lecture on the UN and was impressed by the number of bright students. They all gathered afterwards, over a cup of tea, to debate international law in general. The faculty was still getting onto its feet. Tony paid a quick visit to the law library and found it hopelessly under-stocked. There was little the Expedition could do to help. Tony's own 'collection' of law books was limited. Their legal system, though based on English law, was not identical and the books they needed were not necessarily in English.

SOUTH TO SERENDIPITY

A trip the following morning to a garage to see if they could discover the source of a horrible noise in the Kombi's engine elucidated a cracked exhaust pipe. A minor problem – the by now venerable lady could live with that. The Expedition decided just to carry on with the noise as it was.

Once Asia's Switzerland

The way to Swat first lay along the road to Rawalpindi, with glimpses of the great Indus flowing alongside. The road was packed with people, all leading water buffaloes, oxen, cows and sheep away from a cattle-market just outside the town. How the Kombi failed to hit anyone or anything was anybody's guess. From Nowshera a smaller road turned north towards Swat. The fields on either side were full of sugarcane, and the creaking carts being pulled along by lumbering water buffaloes were piled high with the cut stalks. Many nomads *en route*, herding their cattle southwards: the women dressed in black cloaks and carrying the family's pots and pans on their heads, while the men, with their swarthy, bearded faces, carried a rifle slung casually over their shoulders. These nomads were the equivalent of the Afghan Kuchis, while the rest were Powindahs, who originally came from Tashkent with rugs and carpets.

In Saidu-Sharif, capital of Swat, an independent state up in the tribal areas of the old North-West Frontier, it was already dark. Jahanzeb College was easy to find. The Principal apparently was a good friend of Cambridge people. A still sleepy gatekeeper led the way to the Principal's house. Everyone was soon old friends and, over numerous cups of welcome tea, Principal Khwaja Mohammed Ashraf told stories of his many years in the field of education. He promised an introduction to the *Wali*, the Ruler of Swat, the next day, and he graciously offered dinner and beds in one of the hostels of the college for the night.

Saidu Sharif was impressive with its palace, schools, college, hospital and an unmistakable dark yellow colour to its walls and stonework. Mingora, the commercial town a few miles further north, had busy streets and a snappier pace. An earthquake subsequently destroyed it.

At a famous shrine called Pir Baba, devotees came from hundreds of miles to pray. The unmarried prayed for marriage; the poor prayed for wealth; and those who were childless and scorned family planning prayed for children. But such was the irony of fate that the children born after the intercession of this Saint Pir Baba were invariably unhinged – well, that's what the legend said. This, added

Accommodation was
provided at Jahanzeb
College, Mingora;
since destroyed by an
earthquake.

some wags, accounted for the allegedly large number of lunatics in this part of
Pakistan. Another persistent legend had it that only those pure of heart returned
safely from this pilgrimage. People like our Cambridge travellers would tumble
into ravines, as had a bus-load of 'wicked' pilgrims a short time before.

There was an ancient legend relating to the siege and capture of the royal Hindu
fort (its remains were still to be seen in the village of Udigram) by a Muslim
prince. In spite of repeated assaults, the proud and impregnable fort defied
the strength and strategy of the Muslim warriors. But the incredibly beautiful
daughter of Raja Giri had fallen violently in love with the Muslim conqueror.
In the darkness of the night she opened the gates to her lover who carried her
off, and vanquished his enemies in one stormy attack. But, alas! She was a fairy

The Kombi was well protected
by 'pistol wallahs' provided by the
governor of Swat.

princess as beautiful as the rainbow, and as soft as butter; a delicate creature who had never seen the light of day; as she rode behind her happy lover in the blazing sun, she melted out of sight.

Swat boasted fine arts and crafts including brilliantly coloured curtain cloth woven on hand-looms, soft *pattu* (woollen cloth), primitive wood-carvings, embroidery and ornate silver ornaments. Vestiges of the Ghandara civilization left traces in crude attempts at artistic creations. Bears, panthers, antelopes and monkeys loitered in Swat's forests. Trout were cultivated in the upper reaches of the Swat River and other fish abounded.

Young girl on bed,
Mingora.

The *Wali* spared a few minutes of his valuable time to answer questions about education in Swat. Unlike other parts of Pakistan, the students here paid no fees. With new schools opening at a rapid rate, Swat provided an excellent example of what could be done by goodwill, hard work and learning.

Swat acceded to Pakistan soon after the partition of India in 1947, and some of the powers of the Ruler had been transferred to a partly elected, and partly nominated, council. However, apart from foreign affairs, the *Wali* and his Council of 25 ran Swat as a semi-independent state.

The *Wali* kindly supplied the use of a Land Rover to go to the nearby *Marghazar* (Sanctuary of Birds), where his father, the former and first Ruler of Swat, had a summer palace of white marble. Enclosed by steep, wooded hills, it was a veritable sanctuary, with birds singing in the bushes, and the autumn leaves changing into reds, oranges, yellows and gold. The palace gave a wonderful view of the valley, the hillsides neatly terraced to grow crops of rice, wheat, maize and barley, the high mountains beyond freshly clad in a white mantle of snow.

The *Wali* also supplied his assistant private secretary as a guide – probably to keep the companions out of trouble. Mahmood Khan, a law graduate of Lahore University, turned out to be a boon and charming company. Before setting off he said, 'Let's have some lunch first: you can't travel on an empty stomach.' Finally setting off in the middle of the afternoon, Mahmood had insisted on taking his 'pistol-wallah' along as well, as guard and extra guide. So there were now six hefty men and a pistol packed into the groaning Kombi as it wheezed up the mountain roads. Up the valley beside the blue waters of the River Swat, farmers were busy ploughing the fields, still using the same methods as their forefathers. Further up, the river became a rushing torrent as it forced its way down the narrowing valley. Sawn-up logs were being swept downstream to the mills. Timber was one of the few exports, and woodcutters were busy trying to free those logs that had become stuck, otherwise they would have had to wait till the rains came.

It was cold on arrival higher up in Kalam, for the sun had already gone down. But one could still make out the peak of Falakser Mountain peering through the clouds. Above the rest-house, where bed and board were provided courtesy of the *Wali*, towered a whole range of snow-clad mountains, while the village nestled by the river at the foot of the cliff several hundred feet below. Myriads of stars twinkled in the heavens as everyone sat round a blazing wood fire in the 'hospital', talking to the doctor and his six-year-old bare-foot daughter. Mehmed, Nigel and Tony were spared the monotony of their normal frugal meal – spaghetti and dehydrated meat, without sauce – when Mahmood produced a steaming bowl of curry, rice and chapattis, followed by fruit and tea.

(Opposite, top) Driving further north up the Swat valley, pausing 15 miles from Kalam, before driving on to Gabral, some 7,300 feet above sea level, mainly with the Kombi in first gear.

(Opposite, bottom) Well north of Mingora in the Swat valley, northern Pakistan, was this curious but wary child.

SOUTH TO SERENDIPITY

Driving in the Swat valley.

At 6 o'clock the next morning the sky was beautifully clear and blue. The mist and clouds which had shrouded the 19,415 feet of the distant Falakser had been swept away and it was clearly outlined against the azure sky through a narrow valley between two tree-covered mountains. Mahmood walked around completely swathed in a blanket; until the first rays of the sun began to flood the valley, it was decidedly chilly. He thought only another nine miles' driving up the Utrot valley would be possible. The narrow road was even more beautiful than before, as it wound through the forests of dark green pine trees. Below, the river roared down in a torrent. Logs acted as swaying bridges. What it must have been like when the spring snows melted one hated to imagine.

With the Kombi climbing slowly up the valley in first gear Utrot was reached at 7,300 feet. The people here were completely different, often with fair hair and blue eyes, and they spoke an entirely different language – Kohistani – from the Pashtu-speaking Yousufzais of the valley below. Mahmood said that

174

these people, the Torwais and Garhwis, rarely travelled down to Saidu Sharif or Peshawar. At Utrot it turned out that one could push further up the valley, as a new 'road' to the little village of Gabral had just been completed. This proved to be a real stroke of luck. The valley grew wider, the river faster and the mountains higher. Small, pretty chalets dotted the green pastures; cattle contentedly chewed the cud under a vivid 'Cambridge blue' sky. The Alpine appearance gave Mehmed the idea of calling it 'Asia's Switzerland'. This really was the end of the valley – from here only horses could climb up the steep passes to Chitral. Everyone sat reminiscing in the utter peace and solitude that the surrounding mountains imposed. Even the rifle-carrying villagers and their bare-footed children just sat in silence. Finally everyone snapped out of their reverie, and the locals were only too pleased to be photographed beside the Kombi.

*

In spring 2009, *Dawn* in Islamabad together with *Al Jazeera* recorded the descent into hell of the Swat Valley in Pakistan's North-West Frontier Province. The tourism magnet with its alpine scenery became a valley stained with blood as radical cleric Maulana Fazalullah rampaged and destroyed people and property. Pakistan's rulers pathetically looked on as nearly a third of Swat's 1.5 million people fled, adding to the number of Pakistanis with zero faith in the institutions of their own country. The risk that a collapsing Pakistan faced with an ebullient India might plunge the whole region into nuclear disaster bubbles beneath the surface.

*

Reluctantly, 'paradise' was left behind for the return journey to Peshawar. The local women, their inquisitiveness having overcome their shyness, scuttled back into their doorways, silver earrings, bracelets and bangles glinting in the fading sunlight. The clouds gathered, transforming the beauty of the valley, as the Kombi drove slowly down towards the Malakand Pass. In 1897, the Malakand Field Force, including a cavalry second lieutenant called Winston Churchill, waged violence against tribal warriors. Peace prevailed afterwards. It still did.

Back at Saidu Sharif, Mahmood provided a lavish 'late lunch' in his garden, on a hill overlooking the town, as the sun slowly set over the surrounding hills. Mr Ashraf, the Principal of the Boys' College, wished everyone *Khuda Hafiz*

('May God be your protector'). That was more than enough at the time. The long drive to Lahore lay ahead.

The Road to Delhi

'Too much work, much too much work,' muttered the customs official as the Expedition drifted, on 20 November, through the customs post outside Lahore, at the border between Pakistan and India. Well advertised by the three-inch lettering – Cambridge Afro-Asian Expedition – on the side of the Kombi, the ordeal was over more quickly than expected, and a fast, well-paved road led down to Amritsar, to the Golden Temple. The idea had been to get to Chandigarh before dark, after a quick look at the Temple. But it had taken longer than bargained for.

It was the eve of the birthday of the Fifth Guru of Sikhism, and celebrations were in full swing. Banners flew from the house-tops, buses jammed the narrow streets, fife and drum bands shrieked in one's ears amid strenuous efforts to push a way through to the Temple. A courtyard, crowded with Sikhs preparing for worship, lay in front. 'Will you step this way please?' A voice from the side broke the reverie of bewilderment. An impressively bearded Temple custodian took charge, ensured that shoes were removed, and gave everyone a yellow cloth like a duster to cover their heads. Looking like pantomime pirates, they walked around the Temple, gazing in wonder at its extraordinary situation and beauty. The afternoon sun softened the blinding incandescence of the roof, casting subtle reflections into the shimmering water that surrounded the building. It looked unworldly and yet the constant flow of worshippers in and out reminded one of its deep-rooted reality.

Open at all times and on all sides, this Temple symbolized the tolerance and accessibility of the Sikh religion, said the guide. The giant-sized kitchen for feeding hundreds of people a day was another product of their philanthropy.

(Opposite, top) The custodian at the Golden Temple at Amritsar in India provided suitable clothing before entering the temple.

(Opposite, bottom) Sikh service in the Golden Temple.

One of many university
buildings in Chandigarh,
a shrine of modern
architecture.

A small enclosure was the site where Tara Singh made his protest-fast in a bid for Punjabi separatism. He had been invited to represent Sikhs after World War II and argued fiercely against the Muslim League's demands to partition India. Inside the temple, bedecked with flowers and bemused with incense, holy men, seated cross-legged before their books, intoned the scriptures for the benefit of the faithful.

Enthralling as everything was in this Mecca of the Sikhs, it was time to move on to Chandigarh, the shrine of modern architecture. Midnight, despite the Expedition's by now ingrown habits of nocturnal arrival at a place to stay, was not the best time to turn up anywhere. This applied especially to Chandigarh. Quite lost in the intricate maze of sectors and zones, they came upon the university completely by chance; but in spite of the late hour, they were given a room in the guesthouse.

The next morning they gladly accepted the offer of some students to show them round, and several of the students piled into the already over-loaded Kombi, which was by now used to this sort of thing. The French architect, Le Corbusier, who some say lived in a 'wonderland of imagination', drafted the plans for this remarkable new capital since 1953 of the Punjab State. From the terrible problem of partition of India and Pakistan thus rose one of the world's most modern capitals. The philosophy behind the capital was to make manifest the solidarity of Punjab India and to provide and set a new standard of living. Prime Minister Nehru himself had put it perfectly: 'It is symbolic of the freedom of India unfettered by the traditions of the past.' But even so, not everyone was enamoured of such modern design.

One of the highlights of this dominating architecture was the great eight-storey government building – the Secretariat. Fascinating in its intricacy, overwhelming in its totality, this building was for many the most impressive. The jigsaw puzzle of the sun-breakers on the façade presented a continually changing pattern. From its spacious rooftop garden there was an expansive view of residential areas and shopping centres shimmering in the heat, and people hugging such shade as there was. In summer Chandigarh was like an oven; but this problem had allowed the architects considerable scope for ingenuity, and even the inhabitants seemed to like the results. In front of this high vantage point reared the then unfinished Assembly Hall with its vast, spiralling superstructure which provided ventilation for the interior. In front of the open 'Forum' stood the High Court, which was in full operation. Corbusier's solution here for reducing the effects of the terrific heat was a vast roof form which was virtually a giant sunshade.

In the city's many sectors administration and dwelling blended. Great scope was allowed for the needs of the inhabitants – as well as the imagination of the architect. Socialist ideas were not apparent in the different categories of housing. The difference between the grandest and the simplest was a reminder of India's tenacious class and caste system. Each sector was a little town in itself, with its health clinic, schools, post-office, shopping centre, Sikh temple, restaurant, cinema and recreational green – a rectangle about three-quarters of a mile square – in which up to 15,000 could be housed. And buildings were still going up. Women with baskets of sand on their heads laboured away too in the construction work. One of the students took everyone off for a drink to the

'Aroma Restaurant', which he had nicknamed the 'belly-worshipping temple', because of its modern band and Western-style layout. A tour of the university followed.

The university was established in October 1947, following the partition of the Punjab. India's great millennial centre of learning, Lahore, was now Pakistan's second city and intellectual capital. Chandigarh filled the gaping intellectual hole left in the Punjab of the new India, its jurisdiction extending over the Punjab and Himachal Pradesh. All the teaching departments, except journalism, were located there. By 1961, it was already attracting many students from other countries, mainly Malaya and Burma, and in Africa. English was the language of instruction except in classical and modern Indian language classes. As part of the policy of replacing English by Hindi and Punjabi, MA examinations were conducted in the language concerned.

Lunch was enjoyed in one of the male student hostels attached to each affiliated college. No student was admitted until he had fixed up his lodgings; every student not living with parents or guardians had to reside during term-time at an approved hostel or lodging. The campus at Chandigarh had four hostels, each accommodating 1,320 students, all exactly similar in shape and design, and they were all next door to each other. Except, that is, for the women's hostel, which was a little way away, the inmates being virtually hidden away behind lattice-work grills. Tony found that rather disappointing. But each student had his own room, many with a small balcony looking out over the grounds. Cambridge, where many a first-year undergraduate then slummed it in dingy digs off Parker's Piece and elsewhere, could not boast better.

A young and charming university lecturer, Amin, constrained everyone to stay one more night. He wanted very much to go to England to do postgraduate work. Chandigarh was such a young university – compared with Lahore, Allahabad, Patna and Bombay. It was a matter of broadening his outlook. 'Books and lectures don't make a university!' For him the cultural atmosphere in Chandigarh was limited, which was why so many wanted to go to the United Kingdom. And, indeed, in those days, many did from India.

He talked of the difficulties that the city had suffered. At first there was no main road, an insufficient water supply and desperate living conditions. All that had obviously changed. 'But here was a battleground of social issues,' he said. Should housing be graded according to income? Chandigarh had said 'yes'. But when these questions were put under the harsh spotlight of social justice, answers were scarce. Was it valid to sectionalize a city's population? And what would be the long-term reaction? The architecture of the city in general could not fail to impress. But to many Indians Chandigarh was a monumental reminder of the manner in which 'a foreigner, however expert, could not possibly understand the genuine requirements of a people to whose ways he was a stranger,' said Amin. This was not perhaps Corbusier's finest achievement, even for his admirers.

Speeding on to Delhi, the Expedition camped on the apartment floor of Stephen Barber, the *Daily Telegraph* correspondent for Asia, a source of much wisdom and many good contacts, including some in Kathmandu, as it soon turned out.

The stay in Delhi was too short for serious comparative education observation. The Expedition had not planned any substantial studying of education in India. To do so in this big and populous country would have been a major enterprise in itself and added months to the Expedition's life. A reasonable length of time was wanted in Nepal. And getting a place for the Kombi on the monthly ship from Bombay to Mombasa had already posed problems enough. Missing one sailing already was to give time for a visit to Ceylon.

Meanwhile, a surprise awaited in the Turkish Embassy in Delhi, in the form of the strong man of the 1960 Turkish military coup – Colonel Alparslan Türkeş. He too finally had joined the cohort of colonels who had been exiled, just like Colonel Akkoyunlu in Kabul. His invitation to lunch was the opportunity for a big talk about Central Asia, in which he was keenly interested and towards which he felt a certain Turkic 'pull', and then the military coup of May 1960. He had played his cards in such a way that in November 1960 he and the 13 other Turks were sent abroad to various embassies in exile as 'consultants'. He was of course convinced that the military take-over was justified at the time, but was against the hanging of Menderes, Zorlu and Polatkan; indeed, all that had happened after he was exiled. Türkeş blamed everything that had happened on the Republican People's Party founded by Atatürk, then run by Ismet Inönü, Atatürk's heir. 'Ismet Pasha had eventually,' said Türkeş, 'simply told the members of the so-called National Unity Committee [of which he, Türkeş, had been an influential member] what to do.' Colonel Türkeş now invited Mehmed to join the political party he was going to found – it was to become celebrated for its cover of the notorious 'Grey Wolves' and would inseminate much violence into Turkish politics. The offer was politely refused.

SOUTH TO SERENDIPITY

Another chance meeting was with Father Zulu at a drinks reception at a hotel in Delhi, where the priest was attending a gathering of Anglicans. In August 1960, Mehmed had travelled by night train from Johannesburg to Durban to meet Alan Paton, whose book *Cry the Beloved Country*, with its protest against *apartheid*, had been widely read at the time. Alan Paton's son was at Cambridge, where Mehmed had met him. He had arranged the meeting with his father. Mehmed was so interested in South Africa in 1960 that he had ventured on this 12-hour train journey. This was during *apartheid* and Mehmed was of course in the section of the train reserved for whites. He had met Father Zulu at the station before the train's departure and they had got talking about religion, usually neither Mehmed's pet subject nor speciality. But somehow he was keenly interested to talk with this man of religion. Since Father Zulu was black, he told Mehmed that they could not continue the conversation in the train but he would be pleased if Mehmed would visit him in the Anglican Church of Durban.

He did not know how obstinate Mehmed was.

After the train left Johannesburg, Mehmed left the 'Whites Only' section and walked back to the 'Blacks Only' compartments, where he found Father Zulu sitting in one by himself. 'Although he could not come to where I should be travelling,' said Mehmed, 'no one stopped me sitting in his compartment and we talked until the early hours of the next day. We talked about religion, Christianity, Islam, etc.'

The next day, after talking and lunching with Alan Paton, Mehmed had been to Father Zulu's church where the priest had made him give a short talk, about his religion and Turkey. Although Mehmed had a lot to say about Turkey, he started stammering when he had to speak about Islam. High school education in the 1950s in Turkey did not make experts on Islam.

The Delhi University Students' Union staged a reception for Major Yuri Gagarin – the world's first cosmonaut. Somehow the Expedition was still joined by a thin umbilical cord to Russia where it had all really started.

From Delhi the road led to Agra and the Taj Mahal with its sublime, ethereal beauty. It was dedicated to the wife of Mogul Emperor, Shah Jahan – Mumtaz Mahal. Nowadays, this sounds like mere tourist routine. It was not so in the 1960s. Completed in 1653, it took 22 years to build. His son, Aurangzeb, deposed Shah Jahan and put him under house arrest in the nearby Agra Fort. Upon Shah Jahan's death Aurangzeb buried him in the mausoleum next to his

Dancing monkey at
Fatehpur Sikri.

wife. By the late nineteenth century, parts of the buildings had fallen badly into
disrepair. During the Indian rebellion of 1857, the Taj Mahal was defaced by
British soldiers and government officials, who chiselled out precious stones from
its walls. At the end of the nineteenth century, the British Viceroy – Lord Curzon
– ordered a massive restoration project. He also commissioned the large lamp in
the interior chamber, modelled after one in a Cairo mosque. The gardens were
now remodelled with British-style lawns.

The next day the Expedition made a detour to Fatehpur Sikri, the red sandstone
city near Agra, world-renowned for its wondrous Mogul architecture fringed
with ivy on every corner. Akbar, greatest of all the Mogul Emperors who ruled
India, ascended the throne in 1556, at the tender age of 14. As soon as he had

A typical street in
Benares (now Varanasi),
the centre of Hinduism
in India.

consolidated his power, Akbar built an impressive imperial capital – the Agra Fort – which was a great asset militarily, as well as serving as the royal residence. In due course, Akbar decided to shift his capital to Fatehpur Sikri. The city took 15 years to build, and it grew into a magnificent township larger than contemporary London. The failure of the water supply to support the growing population forced them to abandon Fatehpur Sikri a mere 14 years later. The temple was still there, jealously guarded by its custodian.

(Opposite) Custodian of
the temple at Fatehpur
Sikri.

Bathing in the Ganges,
which is meant to be pure
despite the ashes from
funeral pyres.

Back in Delhi, the Kombi was sounding quite sick. There were no proper VW
dealers or service stations in India. But there was a Mercedes dealer who, possibly
out of loyalty to German engineering, was extremely helpful and mended it. Thus
back in form the refreshed Kombi took the Expedition a week later to Benares
(now Varanasi), in time to celebrate Mehmed's 22nd birthday on 12 December.

Benares had been a cultural and religious centre for several thousand years. The
most sacred city in India, it was the centre of Hinduism and Sanskrit learning.

The streets down to the holy Ganges were lined with crippled beggars – all wanting, and getting, alms – and wandering cows, which had the absolute right of way. Benares was at the confluence of three rivers. Its waters, despite the ashes from the frequent funeral pyres at the *ghats*, were meant to be pure.

It was now time to head for Kathmandu.

15

THE LONG, HIGH VALLEYS OF NEPAL

Nepal's border was reached on 14 December. Across an icy pass and there was Kathmandu, 4,500 feet up. Tired and hungry, Mehmed, Nigel and Tony spent their first night shivering in a student's room. Their luck changed the next day. Stephen Barber in Delhi had given them a letter of introduction to Field-Marshall Kaiser, a member of the Rana dynasty. The Ranas had served as the hereditary prime ministers of Nepal. The revolution of November 1950 brought an end to the aristocratic Rana regime that had ruled the country since 1846. Nepal then saw the dawn of democracy. The Field-Marshall prospered still and lived in an old palace, with lots of bedrooms. He said he had no room – perhaps because his incredibly attractive wife, who had appeared on the cover of Harper's Bazaar, and had been voted one of the ten most beautiful women in the world at the time, was standing next to him and being ogled at by three young men. Instead he paid for them to stay at the best hotel in Kathmandu – the Hotel Royal – for ten days, and gave them £30 to spend on food to boot. Six waiters could not serve the hungry travellers quickly enough as they emptied their plates in the hotel's restaurant.

The Kingdom of Nepal, a narrow strip of mountain-bound land between India and Tibet, had been inhabited for centuries. But no outsiders got there before the 1950s. Most Nepalese lived in scattered settlements herding flocks on the plunging slopes of the Himalayas or farming fields that ranged from poor and rocky plots to fertile plains. The Kathmandu Valley was the fertile centre-piece in a string of Middle Himalayan valleys stretching east and west through the 500-mile length of the kingdom. Northward, the mountains rose and thickened to a great white wall that includes nine of the world's 14 highest peaks. To the south, the way was barred by rugged hills, forested and choked with 15-foot elephant grass, jungles made dangerous by tigers, and swampland running along India's northern border. Access to the inner kingdom was so rugged and precipitous that for centuries the only goods to reach or leave Kathmandu were carried on the backs of porters.

Short and tan-skinned, the people of these cities dwelt among soaring temples and monoliths, locked into their villages in the valleys by the compass of

Buddhist votive offerings.

mountains around them. They adhered to the Buddhist and Hindu faiths, many of them practising both in common rites. Now both sides were busy placating their gods to try to avert the anticipated disaster on 4 February when it was said that nine planets would be in conjunction – as in 1934 when the same thing happened and Nepal experienced the most devastating earthquake of modern times. The people painstakingly observed an intricate caste system, based on traditional family trades and crafts, but for all the strictures of caste, they were tolerant of exceptions and social climbing. A life rich in ceremony and a society satisfying in its firm order sustained them as the modern world impinged on ancient Nepal. The houses showed the original form of the pagoda, with their sloping roofs and projecting eaves. The wooden pillars and house fronts were elaborately carved with animals, birds, flowers, figures from Hindu mythology and grotesques of various characters. These carvings were all of *Newar* origin – that is, of the original and still thriving tribe of the valley. There were a number

SOUTH TO SERENDIPITY

A Hindu temple
photographed late in the
day in Kathmandu.

(Opposite, top) Street
sellers.

(Opposite, bottom)
Friends playing.

of pagoda-style temples, all heavily ornamented and many with erotic tantric carvings.

Shaped like a maple leaf and surrounded by mountains almost a mile high, the Valleys of Nepal contained 209 square miles of fertile land and more than 400,000 people crowded together. Farming was the basic work of the valley, carried on intensively by the large, clan-like families that were the basic unit of the valley society. Every day members of a farming family went out to work their plot, which was usually rented and often as small as one-tenth of an acre. The other members remained at home and plied the traditional trade or craft that long ago determined their caste. Farmers' thatched-roofed homes were tucked into the scores of hamlets dotting the rice fields.

The valley's three cities – Kathmandu, Patan and Bhatgaon (all over 1,000 years old) – lay within walking distance of the fields. Many people were city dwellers as well as farmers. Inside the cities, the complex interchange of goods and services that helped to create them in the first place went on in a caste-prescribed way. In the open on the streets of Kathmandu, the dense population did their everyday chores. The pottery makers worked in their workshops and the priests officiated in their temples. Innumerable religious holidays, always marked by lavish ceremonies, the costs of which sometimes kept people in debt for a year, supplemented the bustle of commerce. The Kathmandu 'Orchestra' was more photogenic than musical to judge from the noise emerging from its instruments. The three cities had long since outgrown the walls built to defend them in the eighteenth-century twilight of fierce chieftains, when each city was a kingdom at war with the others. Nepal was less a nation than an aggregation of more or less self-sufficient villages.

At least ten broad ethnic groups and many smaller ones inhabited Nepal, each with its own combinations of physical traits and cultural characteristics. Showing Tibetan influences, the northern border peoples – like Tamang and Sherpa – were generally short, yellow-skinned and Buddhist, and spoke Tibeto-Burmese dialects. Under Indian influences, the Nepalese along the southern border were tall, dark-skinned and Hindu, speaking Indo-Aryan dialects. Between the two bands the tides of migration produced a great mixture with spectacular results in the Kathmandu Valley. The most important language spoken in Nepal – and the only one with any body of writing – was *Newari*, that of the Newars, whose ancestors first developed the valley. Their culture had survived in spite of suppression by the ruling Ghurkhas, a warrior caste famed as fighters far beyond Nepal. The Newars still bore marks of Mongolian origin, both physically and in their customs, which

Kathmandu 'Orchestra';
they were more
photogenic than musical!

were similar to those of other races akin to the Mongols. Probably the Newars had originated in Tibet, or even China, and had acquired Indian blood, habits and religion, through invasion and immigration. The joint or extended family unit, its members all related on the male descent side and living together in one home, existed at all caste levels in the Kathmandu Valley.

Nepal brought into the modern world a staggering catalogue of problems – as old, varied and complex as the civilization of the Kathmandu Valley. The homes of more than 3 million Nepalese along the southern border were at times disastrously flooded. The rate of literacy was low – somewhere between 2 and 9 per cent. King Mahendra had made a model of monogamy, but polygamy still existed. Pockets of slavery persisted. Bartering was still the main method of trade and payment. Bits of railway and paved roads were so recent that the first wheel seen in Nepal, besides those used for making pottery, appeared on an aeroplane, as late as 1950, flown in from India to relieve a local shortage of rice. The cost of living was high, with an average per capita income of about $30 a year, and the standard of living wretchedly low. Only slightly more than 10 per cent, or some 6,500 square miles of Nepal's total area, was under cultivation, but this was practically every inch of the rugged country's arable land. The Nepalese took extreme measures to utilize the land, terracing hillsides, using hand tools, to a height of 10,000 feet above sea level. Increasing population had produced subdivision and re-division of the land, about two-thirds of which was cultivated by tenant farmers. Farms of half an acre were self-sufficient and farms of over two acres produced a marketable surplus. But while great landlords owned up to a million acres, private or rented holdings of less than half an acre were still the rule, despite attempted land reform. The economy stagnated because there was no middle class to moderate the extremes of wealth and poverty.

Only after the mid-1950s could foreigners access the Kathmandu Valley. Tourists could visit Kathmandu, but then it still required special government permission to travel outside the valley. In 1956, the valley was finally connected by a paved road to India. Americans were installing telecommunications, building roads and airstrips; Indians worked on educational and health programmes, huge power and flood-control projects; Russians were building a cigarette factory and a hydroelectric installation; the Chinese built cement and paper factories and a road to Kathmandu from Lhasa. Many people feared the Chinese would persuade the Nepalese to become Communist. In due course, they nearly succeeded.

Nepal faced an acute refugee problem. Since 1959, Tibetans had been crossing over the border into Nepal to escape the clutches of the Chinese Communists. They lived in settlements, especially round Buddhist temples, scraping a meagre living by making Tibetan works of art and selling them to tourists in Kathmandu.

The Red Cross did a great deal for the Tibetan refugees, both in Nepal and in India. But refugee numbers increased daily and over 40,000 had already poured into these two countries. The Red Cross had even tried settling small colonies

(Opposite) The enthusiatic young soloist of the orchestra.

Busy life on the streets.

of them in foreign countries, such as America. Despite their sufferings, they always had a ready smile on their round, ruddy faces. The Dalai Lama's personal representative for Nepal, Lopsang Gailen, told the Expedition about Chinese atrocities in Tibet, particularly the treatment of the monks – how they were not allowed to keep their heads shaved and were imprisoned if found praying.

Since 1956, Nepal had done much in the educational field, particularly making education entirely free, rationalizing textbooks, printing and distributing them widely in the country. Education was no longer only for the privileged classes and the high illiteracy rate was rapidly decreasing. Nepali-written textbooks were replacing those from abroad with every hope that a Nepali culture would flourish and the country become more united. More schools and colleges were opening, as was a new university. Over two-thirds of the costs had been met by the people themselves, a sign of how strongly the need for education was felt in Nepal. Previously there were few schools in Nepal, and classes did not go beyond the age of 13. A commission appointed to study these problems and develop a national education policy reported in 1956 and 1961. It emphasized vocational training, but this was an expensive option needing help from experts. America responded by financing and training teachers.

The natural difficulties of change, compounded by the endless differences among Nepalese politicians about how to do it, slowed progress. Some criticized locations chosen for US aid projects. Yet American steel for many footbridges rusted in the hills while the government debated where the next one should be located. Very much aware of their strategic position between India and the Red Chinese in Tibet, the Nepalese veered before each political wind, trying to stick to their avowed course of neutralism. To show their independence of India they kept the Nepalese clock ten minutes ahead of Indian time. Yet they were enthusiastic and eager to please every nation working to help them. Their civilization – that of the Kathmandu Valley – was a strange relic, but it had survived; perhaps because of, rather than despite, the waves of migration and invasion that had swept over the land since pre-history. Assimilating new peoples into the valley society had perhaps kept it from the rigidity that characterized some of the world's defunct civilizations. The Nepalese perhaps would absorb – rather than be absorbed by – modern technology.

In the Kathmandu Valley, overhung by the 20,000-foot peaks of the Himalayas, the capital city was surrounded by irrigated fields. In the old quarters most of the city's 100,000 or so people lived crowded together in shapeless squares and narrow streets among the magnificent, golden-roofed temples. For centuries trade in and out of the Kathmandu Valley depended on the sure step and strong backs of the Nepalese porters, some of whom could carry 160-pound loads, consisting of anything from rice to pianos, and parts of cars. Patan, the oldest city in the valley, just outside Kathmandu, reached its prominence as a Buddhist city, though its outward appearance and most of its 40,000 people were Hindu. The strategic position of Nepal, sandwiched between Tibet to the north and India to the south, made it politically vulnerable in twentieth-century politics. But the mountainous country was so drastically cut up that it took three weeks to travel from the capital city of Kathmandu to the end of the Kingdom.

Before leaving Kathmandu a climb up to the British Embassy's bungalow at Kakani, at just over 7,000 feet, provided a phenomenal sight of dawn breaking. The whole snow-clad panorama of the Himalayas was spread out from Annapurna to Everest. A sea of mist hung over the terraced hills and clusters of huts towards Kathmandu.

SOUTH TO SERENDIPITY

The British Embassy
bungalow at Kakani was
said to have some of
the best views of the
Himalayas.

On Christmas Eve the Expedition got underway again after a great Christmas lunch with John and Brenda from the British Council, and sharing a bottle of whisky at the Public Works Department hostel. Arriving at the border at midnight, the Kombi crossed back into India without stopping – no formalities or signing of papers. This apparent bonus was to cause headaches for Mehmed a month later.

16

A WOULD-BE PARADISE

Ceylon

Driving back to Delhi by the route it had come, the Expedition carried on with all haste to Bombay, where it arrived on New Year's Eve and stayed in comfort with the Turkish Consul. It emerged here that the travel agents, even after three months, had still not finalized the papers for shipping the Kombi to East Africa, thanks to a sloppy customs broker. Ceylon, today's Sri Lanka, beckoned. It was decided that the Kombi needed a rest and that the long journey to Ceylon and back could be more effectively done by various means of public transport, and without all the Expedition's gear. Shipping the Kombi from Colombo to Mombasa was impracticable. Hence the Kombi was garaged at the ever-patient Turkish Consulate for its well-earned holiday. Off everyone went on a long, tiring, 27-hour train journey to Madras – third class, wooden seats, people everywhere, the smell of stale food and stale sweat.

From Madras a plane completed the journey to Colombo – but not before facing the consequences of that earlier crossing back from Nepal into India without stopping, completing formalities or signing papers. At Madras Airport, the passport policeman told Mehmed: 'I cannot let you out because you are not in. If your story is correct, go back to Patna and enter India properly. Then come back, and then I can let you out.' He, of course, showed no interest as to how Mehmed would, or could, make the over 4,000-mile trip there and back. Fortunately, Mehmed had written an article which had appeared in the best Madras newspaper. The editor of the paper came to the airport, showed the passport police the article, and thanks to him Mehmed was allowed out – without an entrance stamp.

The Vickers Viscount aircraft flew over a perpetual sea of clouds from Madras. Suddenly it dropped through a gap, and there below us was the glinting sea and Colombo, capital of Ceylon – *Serendip* as it was called way back in old Persian, before Western seafarers discovered its charms.

SOUTH TO SERENDIPITY

Visits were made to
several schools in
Colombo.

Ceylon was going through an awkward period. Import and foreign exchange
restrictions, dock, post and bank strikes, and strict censorship of the press
made life difficult for many people. Yet to Tony, whose cruiser, HMS *Gambia*,
had docked there for a while during his National Service in the Royal Navy,
life in Colombo seemed to carry on much as usual. The traffic was still terrible
– crowds of people jostled each other on the footpaths. An incessant stream
of creaking bullock carts, bicycles and cars rumbled and screeched along
the roads. Pedestrians obviously considered they had the absolute right of
way, for they criss-crossed the road at every angle, with no undue haste, and
often without even a glance at the approaching traffic. Sweat poured off the
rickshaw boys as they padded along on their bare feet.

An almost carefree three-week stay in Ceylon revealed a country of multiple beauties and some serious educational insights. An enormous, beaten-up, old Chevrolet was coaxed into service for a journey up to the tea plantations, from which Ceylon derived two-thirds of its export revenues. Out through the ever-expanding suburbs of Colombo, and into rural areas, the narrow, winding road snaked between jigsaw-shaped paddy-fields, with intermittent villages of small, mud cottages thatched with *cadjan* (a by-product of the coconut tree). Stolid water buffaloes roamed at will along the roads, their dark grey hides spattered with mud.

At Bogawantalawa, right in the heart of the tea-country, lines of bushes stretched out into the distance wherever one looked. They stretched up the sides of mountains, leaving unconquered only the crests where the jungle ruled undisturbed. The lines of tea bushes spread across the valleys in geometric patterns broken only by pale ribbons of roads. Groups of female Tamil tea-pluckers smiled shyly as one passed, revealing betel-stained teeth. Their baskets were strapped on their backs to leave both hands free, and their hands and arms moved rhythmically over their shoulders then down to the bushes.

From the bungalow where they were guests of Mrs Gordon – with whom Tony had stayed three years earlier when on a rugby tour during his National Service ('how nice to see you back dear boy!') – Tony and friends could see the distinctive hump-backed shape of Ceylon's most famous mountain, the 7,500-foot Adam's Peak, considered a most sacred place by Buddhists, Christians, Hindus and Muslims. Getting up very early, they lumbered up to this holy peak in the snorting Chevrolet, then climbed 4,000 feet, under twinkling lights, past hordes of devout, chanting pilgrims, all going to see the sacred footprint of the Buddha on *Sri Pada*, as Adam's Peak was known to the people of the country. The sunrise seen from the top was spectacular. A magical shadow seemed to be projected upon the clouds, instead of lying on the forest below. The ocean shone some 60 miles away.

Coming back down they drove to Kandy, the last stronghold of the Sinhalese Kings, and visited the Temple of the Sacred Tooth of Buddha, brought to Ceylon, says legend, in the fourth century AD from India, by a princess of Kalinga, as the Indian state of Orissa was then called. From a bridge over the moat around the stronghold one could see hundreds of turtles swimming round in slow circles in the sluggish, brown-grey water. More steps led under a stone archway into a paved, covered courtyard with carved stone pillars. It was the hour of the famous Temple drummers thundering out their rhythms. Saffron-robed, shaven-headed priests walked by pensively. Flower sellers sat against glowing murals,

SOUTH TO SERENDIPITY

Climbing towards Adam's
Peak.

and worshippers bought white blossoms to offer in front of the Buddha images. Candles were lit on silver tables, and pilgrims bowed to the ground in front of the door to the sanctuary, which contained the Sacred Tooth of the Buddha.

Next day started with a beautiful morning and a departure in high spirits, not dampened by Tony's diversion of the Chevrolet into a gulley. The road was extremely narrow down between the tea-bushes, with a ditch on both sides. Tony, with much cursing, managed to slip one wheel into the ditch and the Chevy slid along until a friendly rock stopped its further progress. Everyone piled out and stared rather cluelessly. Just then there was a stirring in the tea-bushes and crowds of Tamils tore down through the plantation to see what had happened. One of the overseers quickly organized them on all sides of the car, and with much shouting and shoving, the vehicle was set back up on the road again. It started, the only damage being a dented petrol tank, and an offside door which wouldn't open. After this little interlude they drove into Kandy.

There followed a sort of *blitz* day at the university. The University of Ceylon was in the final stages of being rebuilt at Peradeniya, near Kandy. The original buildings in Colombo were an imposing block in Cinnamon Gardens, a wealthy and affluent suburb in Colombo, though there were no longer any signs of the spice plantations from which it got its name. The university dated from 1870 when the medical school was founded. In 1921, University College, modelled on the University of London, was built to encompass a broader curriculum. Then, in 1942, the two combined to form the University of Ceylon under the Vice-Chancellorship of the celebrated educator, Professor (by now Sir) Ivor Jennings – incidentally an ex-St Catharine's man. Peculiar to this university was the fact that it charged no tuition, examination, or degree fees for citizens of Ceylon, where free education started in 1944.

In 1962, the medium of teaching was English, but it was in the process of changing to one of Ceylon's own *Sirabasha* languages (Sinhalese and Tamil), with English as the second language. Despite the British colonial heritage, the few foreigners on the staff were mainly American.

A lot of Ceylonese students had previously been abroad to university in England, America or Australia, and the numbers increased under the British Commonwealth-inspired 'Colombo Plan' for economic and social development in Asia and the Pacific. New Ceylon government rules allowed students to go abroad if the subject was not available in Ceylon itself – e.g. Spanish and French, Archaeology and Anthropology, Biochemistry or … Spanish Dancing!

The day started with an early interview with Professor Jayasuriya, Chairman of the National Education Commission. He said what the Expedition was to hear repeated many times – 'nearly all students want to do white-collar jobs rather than manual ones'. Alas, there were many more vacancies for manual labourers, with the consequence that many of the students were unemployed or under-employed despite the degrees or school certificates in their pockets.

Mehmed and Tony talked to Mr Nesiah, a lecturer in comparative education and a Tamil. The tensions were already growling under the porous surface. Mr Nesiah wandered seamlessly from politics to education. For him Sirimavo Bandaranaike, the celebrated world's first woman prime minister, had a mass appeal to the people of Ceylon. But he also wanted to 'turn the clock back to the situation Ceylon was in before the British came; one race, one people and one religion'. There were a million Tamil tea-workers in the country, but their children were prevented from attending any schools other than those provided on the estates.

The schools on these estates were just primary schools, so the Government was deliberately depriving these children of secondary education. Perhaps because Mr Nesiah was a follower of Mahatma Gandhi's teachings, he kept quite calm when he spoke of 'One of the biggest armies of Ceylonese modern history' in reference to the Tamils.

All this was before long to plunge Sri Lanka into tragedy. Sri Lanka, once a land of much promise, has been whittled away by a devastating and pitiless civil war between Sinhalese and Tamils. The war is over, but the new struggle back to peace and prosperity is bleak.

Dr Sorath Chandra, a proctor and lecturer in Sinhalese, was also an active playwright, one of the few writing in Sinhalese. Students in Asia, he said, seemed much more politically conscious than their counterparts in the West – mainly because of the more unstable situation of their countries. A talk, started over the meal table, was continued in one of the student's rooms. With ever-increasing numbers, students were forced to share the rather small and austere rooms that only supplied the bare necessities – a hard bed, wooden table and chairs and a small wardrobe. But it was 'home' and at least they did have a wash-basin. They were a lively crowd and the discussion ranged from Communism to jiving, yet the perennial trouble at the university, rearing its ugly head like a malignant growth, was the lack of jobs for graduates – arts graduates in particular – which Professor Jayasuriya had talked about. Dr Gunasehere, Head of the Economics Department, thought that given Ceylon's economic depression, the people ought to tighten their belts and do without certain things, so as to save. 'People,' he complained, 'are doing the exact opposite, thereby driving up inflation.'

Woken up the next day at the ungodly hour of 4.30 am, and after a hasty breakfast, Mehmed, Nigel and Tony piled their luggage into the Chevy and set off towards Ruhunu (or Yala) National Park. At Hikkaduwa they stopped to have a second breakfast and a swim at a newly constructed rest-house set on a promontory, jutting out into the sea. Further on lay Galle, said by some historians to be the *Tarshish* mentioned in the bible. King Solomon is said to have sent his ships there to buy gems for the Queen of Sheba, and to load cargoes of grapes and peacocks when he was building his temple in Jerusalem. Whether this was true or not, Galle was a fascinating town. For nearly a thousand years it was known throughout the Eastern world as a prosperous trading post. Ships from India, China, Egypt, Arabia, Persia and Java all called to buy silks, jewels and spices (especially cinnamon), and Greek and Roman merchants were known to have traded there.

Huge elephant about to
charge in Yala National Park,
Ceylon (now Sri Lanka).

Ceylon had changed hands often. The Portuguese arrived early in the sixteenth century, and they found Moorish traders loading elephants and bales of cinnamon in Galle harbour. They built a robust fort there, only to lose it 50 years later to the Dutch, who built the present fortifications and held Galle for 150 years until the British grabbed it. In ancient times Galle owed its prosperity to the splendid natural harbour. The British were less lucky; nearly 20 of their ships were wrecked in monsoon storms and on rocky shores. By 1875, Colombo, a safer harbour, had become Ceylon's main port.

To walk through Galle was to turn back the pages of history. Reminders of the Portuguese and Dutch occupations were everywhere. An old Dutch canal ran into the sea across a main road. Close one eye, use a little imagination,

SOUTH TO SERENDIPITY

Escaping from the
elephant, they returned to
Colombo in more tranquil
surroundings.

and Amsterdam hove into sight. Over the gateway of the fortress was a shield dated 1669, with a crest of lions and cocks and the letters V.O.I.C. (*Vereenigde Oust Indische Compagnie* – United East India Co.). The old Dutch church was paved with tombstones and its walls were covered with relics of the seventeenth and eighteenth centuries and records of burials and marriages. The burghers, descendants of the invaders – those of Portuguese or Dutch ancestry – had built themselves houses with distinctive white pillared facades set back from the narrow streets. All around stood the circle of dark walls and ramparts, many feet thick, which were built by order of the Dutch and Portuguese so long ago.

A peaceful lunch by a lakeside rest-house was followed by a drive into the Yala National Park, 50 square miles of game reserve with nearly every form of wildlife to be seen in Ceylon. Just before dusk around the dusty tracks at Buttume they surprised a crocodile drying on a slab of rock by a pool, his jaws wide open, and a bird meticulously picking his teeth for him. Dozens of peacocks strutted through the grass – some of the superbly coloured males displaying their feathers, trying to entice the plainer females in their love dance. Often the female would spurn her suitor, and disdainfully walk off into the undergrowth, while the plaintive cry of the male echoed through the trees. Lonely elephants were seen melting into the foliage, or contentedly munching away on the plains somewhere; herds of water buffalo cropped the grass or wallowed in the shiny mud; spotted deer shyly peered at the intruders before bounding away through the bushes; a solitary eagle perched motionless on an outcrop of rock; and wild pig snorted across the roadway. Around a headland jutting out to sea the waves lapped on the wide beaches and the dark jungle disappeared into the background. Just the noise of the sea, and the deep-throated croak of the bull-frog, the flashing of the fire-flies and the beam of the lighthouses out to sea.

Up at dawn the next day but it was still too late for many of the animals, nocturnal hunters who, after their early morning drink, had retired to sleep off their night's activities. Even so, there were several elephants, including a 'rogue' one – an outcast from a herd – who decided to charge the Chevy, after several cunning subterfuges to get as close as possible before his attack. They were wonderful creatures, so graceful despite their large, ungainly-looking, grey bulk. Several mongooses skulked around, many more peacocks performed their mating rites, herds of spotted deer passed nobly by and a herd of wild boar trotted along, their newly born litter scampering after them. A swim, followed by a run along the beach, disturbed some *samba* (elk), which grunted, and bounded back over the sand-dunes into the jungle. You could sometimes see them at night, swimming in the sea, as salt water helped to remove ticks which got into their skin.

A call on Thurston College provided the opportunity to listen in on a five-day Seminar of Principals of Schools. The Chairman introduced the Expedition and this was met with slight, polite applause. A discussion was underway about school supplies. Headmasters were complaining about the delay in delivery of supplies, and their poor quality when they did arrive. One man commented, 'Though it's possible to turn the goods back if we don't like them, we don't do so, as we know that if we did, it would be another year before we got a new supply!' Criticism of the Government's education policy abounded – it paid too much attention to insignificant matters, passing over important topics. 'This question of the typewriter keyboards has become an important topic at cabinet level!' one frustrated principal shouted. Teaching staff merited little trust in the eyes of their principals, many of whom were themselves arguing about minor details.

At a school outside Colombo, Mr Cooray, a very enlightened Principal, showed the various buildings and several classes that were in progress. For him the Sinhalese language question 'was all an emotional one, not an educational one'. Nigel and Tony listened in later on a Rural In-Service Training class. About 20 teachers, mainly women, were sitting round listening to one woman teacher holding forth on a basic English lesson, to a dozen or so small children. These teachers all came from rural schools. None of them had had schooling above school certificate level. Certainly none had had teacher-training as such. It was like becoming a teacher in England immediately after passing G.C.E. 'O' level. Most of them seemed too shy to speak – mainly because of the foreign visitors. As the discussion went on this shyness dissipated.

The last day in Colombo dawned bright and too early, but bags had to be packed and farewells said. Driving to the station with five minutes to spare, there was just time to dump baggage into the 2nd class berths – complete with toilet and washbasin – before the train started to steam slowly forward. Although it was only 8.30 pm, everyone retired almost immediately, partly to meditate on the three weeks' stay in Ceylon and partly because Mehmed was feeling the effects of a previous night's Herculean effort of writing up his notes, his diary and drafting an article as well as feasting – a handsome if demanding combination.

The train got to the ferry-point before dawn and everyone sat around on the platform in the pitch dark while customs and currency were organized. There was a three-hour queue in customs, while they searched every single bag, box, jar and packet, even going to the extremes of emptying out boxes of nuts all over the table and floor. Quite the worst and longest Customs procedure our travellers had ever seen, or heard of. Yet, when their turn eventually came, the 'Chief', having been shown the Expedition prospectus, let them through with no trouble at all, and without paying a penny of duty on the presents of tea they were carrying. During a chat the 1st Officer came up with the 'inside' news about smuggling in this area.

It took just over two hours to churn across the smooth water of the Palk Strait. The ship moored at the end of a long jetty, stretching out from the flat, bare expanse of sand that was Dhanushkodi. *En route* Mehmed, Nigel and Tony managed to get yelled at for snoozing in the 1st class refreshment room.

The train was waiting on the jetty. There were no buildings except for a few sheds and shacks. A rush through customs, a bit of bribing – after all what is a few rupees between friends for relative comfort – and they were safely ensconced behind the locked doors of 2nd class berths for the overnight haul to Madras.

Friends met them in the morning at Madras Egmore station. After an enormous lunch in an air-conditioned restaurant they visited the *Hindu*, the top newspaper in Madras and one of the most respected throughout the whole of India. The paper agreed to take almost as many articles as they could write for them – even after returning to England – so perhaps that would help pay off some Indian debts as they had had to borrow from local Cambridge friends in order to continue the journey.

They had breakfast at the station, before catching the morning train for the last leg of the 27-hour ordeal. Away they steamed, with black smuts of soot pouring through the barred windows of the 3rd class compartment as the train passed through the suburbs of Madras. Their Indian travel companions sat cross-legged on the hard wooden benches, stoically scratching their feet. The one female in the assembled company of eight was talking roughly 8,000 words to the minute. Everyone hoped she would exhaust herself quickly. Twenty-seven hours of purgatory, but still it would be good for the soul after the past few weeks of having it too soft and good in Ceylon. One bore crouched in the corner seat talked purely and solely about railways – 1st, 2nd and 3rd class, the fares and distances and times taken from town to town. Women with bared breasts suckled their babies. Every so often one could buy food at station restaurants. Everyone settled down to sleep all right, despite the lights being on all night and the sounds of deep snoring coming from adjoining compartments. Tired, but thankful, they arrived back in Bombay dead on midday, after three nights and four days of actual travelling from Colombo. Back to the Turkish Consulate, a hot shower, a change of clothes and a good, filling, Chinese meal.

The Kombi, fresh and relaxed after its brief holiday, had been left at the docks in the hope that it would be loaded safely on board ship while a last evening in India was spent frantically writing letters, packing and doing last-minute washing. At last all the papers were in order and the precious vehicle was hoisted up on to the deck.

*

SOUTH TO SERENDIPITY

India has roared ahead economically and politically to emerge in the new millennium in the BRIC (Brazil, India, China and – undeservedly – Russia) group at the world's top table, much at the expense of an ailing Europe. Indian democracy has proved to be remarkably resilient. India should now be able to feed itself. It competes internationally in much industry and technology as testimony to its skills and potential. But its security, despite huge arms spending, remains fragile. And great inequalities threaten a society where bright young things prosper in Bombay and Bangalore while Maoist rebels in Kerala and Calcutta feed on groaning rural and urban poverty.

TASTING INDEPENDENCE

17
INTO AFRICA

A rush down to the Alexandria Docks, No. 16, and there she was – S.S. *Achilleus*, all 7,000 tons of her – the chartered ship to take the place of the *State of Bombay*, which was having a refit. Spirits dropped at the sight of her, and even more so when told she would not stop at the Seychelles. She was normally a pilgrims' ship, i.e. taking Muslims to the holy shrine at Mecca. There were 'only' 600 other passengers this time. Normally for the pilgrims run they crammed in 2,000. Still, the busy round of customs, police, currency controls and other formalities kept all occupied until eventually everyone was on board. Mehmed, Nigel and Tony travelled 4th ('bunk') class, which meant being herded in a hold with hundreds of other passengers. But it was quite cheap, so who could complain? All were squashed together in a mass of humanity; children screaming, using the deck as a toilet, and whatever else took their fancy. So the answer was to keep kit below decks and sleep on camp-beds on deck every night. Just before 1 pm the ship slipped her moorings and the tugs pulled her into the lock. Suddenly, people started throwing coconuts and flowers and nuts over the side of the ship. It seemed it was a Hindu custom – those friends and relatives staying behind gave these things to the embarking passengers as a sign of love and friendship. Once the ship sailed, the passengers threw them all back over the side, as a sign of reciprocating these feelings. The tug boat's crew, not being quite so religiously minded, quickly got out poles with long nets and fished out as many of the coconuts as they could reach. At last the ship had actually set sail.

The ship slowly steamed out of the bay, passing the Gateway to India and the Taj Mahal Hotel on the starboard side. Tony, as a former Royal Navy seaman, was not feeling too happy about the ship in general. And there was the possibility of having to eat rice for nine days to boot. So when Indian music came blaring forth over the loudspeakers all over the ship a few hours later, a certain amount of swearing broke loose. But when sleeping on deck, listening to the rush of the sea against the side of the ship, and looking up at the myriads of twinkling stars in the clear sky, life seemed much better.

Everyone awoke to the noise of seamen scrubbing the deck at 6 am; a reminder to go to bed earlier the next night. Children were screaming and the lights stayed on all night in the hold. So even though it was a bit windy, it was probably more restful than otherwise down below. Sitting in deckchairs watching the dawn slowly fill the sky with diffused reddish-yellowy light provided a more tender awakening. Meals were taken on tables in the starboard well. The food was very filling, and really quite good, all things considered; the threat of a diet of rice receded. Soon after breakfast-time the ship came in sight of land, and an hour later anchored off Porbandar, the first and last port of call before heading across the Arabian Sea into the Indian Ocean and on to Mombasa. Here several hundred Gujaratis, who form the bulk of Indians in East Africa, came on board. The anchor was soon hauled up and the eight-day trip got properly underway. The days were terribly hot, yet the nights were cool, which made sleeping on deck very pleasant.

Mehmed, Nigel and Tony were in a sort of tired vacuum, which they hoped would disappear soon, relaxing at sea. While the ship rolled its way across the almost flat ocean they typed and wrote articles for the *Hindu* and tried to catch up on unwritten diaries. Mehmed and Tony established a regular beer-drinking time just as the sun went down, when they would sit on deck and talk of plans for the future. How many of their carefully thought-out plans for the next five years would come to fruition they had no idea – all they needed was some cash to get started, so the planned book, photos and report would have to be highly successful.

It didn't quite turn out that way.

Sunday, 4 February 1962 was the Day of Destiny. This day, the eight planets would fall in conjunction, and many Buddhists and Hindus thought that it would be the end of the world. However, the sun rose as beautifully and peacefully as it had done for the past few days, so there was no cause for undue alarm. The 3rd Officer, Sebastian Rodriguez, a Roman Catholic from Goa, recounted a little about the ship. She was normally on the Jeddah run, taking hundreds of pilgrims up the Red Sea to within a few miles of Mecca – which was why the way down to the bunks was called the 'Pilgrims Way'. This cargo-passenger boat kept up an average speed of about 13 knots, so was expected to arrive in Mombasa on the 11th. Down below decks the sight was almost indescribable – Sikhs, Hindus, Muslims and RCs all crowded together, with washing hanging up to dry and children crying and crawling all over the floor. It was very hot down there – so goodness knows why more people didn't just come up at night and sleep on deck. Everyone was very friendly, and particularly Yusuf Jiwaji, an Ismaili Indian from Nairobi, who had just done a three-month tour of the Middle East by

213

TASTING INDEPENDENCE

Volkswagen, having gone up through North Africa the same way the Expedition hoped to go. Another good shipboard friend was a swarthy bearded Sikh, a professional photographer, and his beautiful wife. The Expedition's 'office' was right next to the table-tennis table. A tournament started – some of the Indians loved taking charge of the organization. The weather was getting warmer and as the evening breeze blew, a new warmth from the land nibbled away at the coolness.

The officers were mainly from Goa (India), and were very obliging. And educative. On arrival at Mombasa on 11 February, the captain's mate dangled a live chicken on a piece of rope down into the cargo hold to check the quality of the air – they often carried vegetables which sometimes 'went off'. If the chicken died, the crew did not unload that day, but waited till the fetid air had cleared.

Arrival coincided with the end of Ramadan, the time when Muslims fast during the hours between sunrise and sunset. Most Muslims rose before dawn, and prepared an early meal. Fasting in the month of Ramadan was compulsory for every Muslim adult.

Yusuf, as already mentioned, was an Ismaili Muslim whose family lived in East Africa. Ismailis had a particular story to tell in the many-faceted world of Islam. They broke away from the main body of Shi'a Islam in the ninth century AD. In 1818, one of them was granted the title of Aga Khan by the then Shah of Persia. In 1840, after an abortive uprising against the next Shah, this first Aga Khan fled to India. There he and his descendants remained leaders of the several million-strong Ismaili community, which spread to Syria, Iran, Pakistan and East Africa. The Aga Khan, born in 1936, was only the fourth in the line, and became Imam (spiritual leader) in 1957, at the tender age of 20. His charitable record was at least as good as his success with horse-racing and as a socialite. He is still the Aga Khan today.

Approaching East Africa was exciting – and for Nigel it was a new continent. One was quickly struck by a sense of so much noise, energy and life in the people, even if at times the intensity could be vaguely frightening. The old town of Mombasa – Island of War – was Kenya's second town and the main port of East Africa. With its carved Arab doorways, narrow alleyways, coffee vendors and carpet dealers, it had all the glamour of the East. It met the West and rubbed shoulders with it at places like Kilindini Road and Port Tudor – modern, Western-style Mombasa.

But first of all something had to be done about the Kombi – it needed a new engine, and money to pay for one. The route would be roundabout but Nairobi was the only place to get a new engine.

The Kombi arrived in Nairobi having been towed by a mad, fast Indian driver the last 50 miles or so. Starting from Mombasa only three gears had functioned, the fourth gear having packed up a long way back in Nepal. The poor Kombi finally ground protestingly to a halt outside Kiu station. 'Help' was an Indian gentleman driving a commercial vehicle, obviously in a hurry to reach Nairobi as quickly as possible. He produced a fairly short towing rope, tied it to the bumper, and started driving at 50 miles per hour, so that each time he slowed down there was the risk of collision. The arrival in Nairobi after this hairy drive found the companions in low spirits. Driving directly to the Volkswagen garage, Mehmed was relieved to find the German manager he had known from his previous trip to Africa. A Sikh mechanic examined the engine and confirmed that 'it was completely knackered – a new engine will cost you £400'. Nigel sent a cable to his long-suffering father for further funds. Tony and Mehmed unpacked the Kombi, leaving most of the kit with the family of Yusuf, the Ismaili student they had met on the boat. This offered an opportunity to tour Kenya, Tanganyika and Uganda without too heavy a load after the Kombi had recuperated in the VW 'clinic'. From Nairobi the road now went back south again via Ngorongoro to Dar.

It was now that Mehmed had some good news from home. As we saw, his father had been arrested two days after the Turkish coup in 1960 and had been kept on Yassıada Island outside Istanbul for 16 months. The judges had then acquitted him. So, in theory, the Turkish legal system owed him 16 months. Early February 1962, while Mehmed was on the ship between Bombay and Mombasa, they arrested his father again for an obscure and trivial charge: that he had illegally distributed imported radio batteries before the 1957 general elections, while he was the Minister of Communications; and that the Post Office had actually imported the batteries. The charge apparently merited six months' imprisonment. There was a brief piece of news about it in the *Ceylon Daily Mirror*. The paper was inspired to mention it because it had published an article written by Mehmed only a few days earlier. So when she saw 'Demirer arrested again' on the front page, a friend in Ceylon, Cynthia de Mel, sent the cutting to Mehmed in Nairobi. Obviously disturbed, and with no other means of checking, Mehmed sent a cable to Ankara, to his mother. It turned out that his father's smart lawyer got him out only a few hours after he was put in jail again. He argued that as the charge was six months, and Mehmed's father had already had served 16, they owed him some. He was released.

TASTING INDEPENDENCE

The cable about the release came just before a visit to Ngorongoro Crater, the natural sanctuary for thousands of animals and many species of insects and birds. Lush highlands surrounded the crater, falling away to the tawny plains and the alkaline lakes of the Great Rift Valley.

Dar-es-Salaam (the 'Haven of Peace'), the capital of Tanganyika (now Tanzania), was a more or less circular natural harbour filled with astonishingly blue water, trimmed round its edges with palms, red acacias, white sands, coloured stones and shells. Arab dhows manoeuvred tranquilly to and from the islands at the entrance to the bay. The beginnings of the town were established in 1866 by a Sultan of Zanzibar, but it was the Germans, during their occupation, who built the town to its present plan.

In December 1961, Tanganyika had become a self-governing member of the Commonwealth and a completely sovereign power. For the first time, its multi-racial society began to mould its own destiny. Its population was then just over 9 million (now four times as many), thinly distributed over an area about four times that of the UK. It was one of the oldest places of human inhabitation in the world.

Nearly all the African population of Tanganyika was Bantu. A blend of the Hamitic and Negro races, they were essentially an agricultural and pastoral people. When the British took over the administration of Tanganyika in 1919, not – so they said – as self-interested colonists, but as subordinate trustees of the League of Nations, the country was in great difficulties. Disease was rife. So was ignorance. Self-government by Africans was from the very start a British objective in Tanganyika; education as equipment to rule was thus a burning necessity. The one education officer appointed in 1926 by the British found that the Germans had built 99 schools and enrolled 6,000 Africans at them. Many of them could read and write Swahili. Everything was badly needed: elementary schools where children could be taught to read and write in Swahili, secondary schools, teacher training centres, and technical schools. And they had to be staffed as far as possible by locally trained African teachers. Here the Christian missions came into their own. Anglicans, Roman Catholics, Lutherans and Baptists – British, American, German, Swiss and Italian, all helped. In 1962, Tanganyika had 64 secondary schools, 3,192 primary and middle schools, and 33 teacher training centres. For higher education Tanganyikans had had to go to Makerere College in Uganda, the University College of East Africa; but a site had been chosen at Morogoro for a university college in Tanganyika itself. Still, only 44 per cent of school-age children were at school. Few of these continued study after the age of 11. The only way to induce foreign teachers to come and work in Tanganyika was to pay them much more than they got in the USA or the UK.

Heading back north again from Dar the tortuous month's stay in East Africa now involved a weary arrival in Moshi at nearly 3 am. The Moshi campsite was, unsurprisingly, locked. What was left of the night was spent under the stars with Mount Kibo rising up like a ghost in the background. At the very respectable hour of 10 am breakfast was coaxed from a dying stove. Then on to Arusha, today a centre of multi-cultural population and diplomacy, headquarters of the newly reanimated East African Community, and of the International Criminal Tribunal for Rwanda. At that time it was more modestly famed as a good base for visiting Mount Kilimanjaro – at 19,000 feet the highest mountain in Africa, with its impressive, volcanic, snow-covered peak. This was Tony's second visit to Kilimanjaro, which he had climbed with the Marines during his Royal Navy days. Then on to Serengeti National Park – Tanganyika's oldest and most popular national park, a World Heritage Site, acclaimed by many as the Seventh Wonder of the World.

In Arusha, Masai boys trotted by with spears, earrings and corks through their ears. With them were young girls, wire beads around their necks, all painted red for a ceremony, singing and chanting with babies slung on their backs like papooses. The YMCA supplied a welcome shower and a meal. Then – memories of Iranpur in the Türkmen Sahra – a relaxing visit to the cinema to see *The Honeymoon Machine* with Steve McQueen, which was all about sailors. An attempt to camp on the Royal College playing fields was politely but firmly rebuffed. Camp for the night ended up by the roadside.

Another puncture – mending tyres – vulcanizing tyres; this was part and parcel of the Expedition. A cheap lunch at the YMCA set everyone in the right mood for the drive first towards Nairobi before heading for Kampala along a welcome, asphalt road. The route went into Kikuyu country, seemingly peaceful enough at the time among the very pleasant, highly fertile hills. Just before Gilgil, Lake Naivasha loomed on the left, its calm waters looking very inviting, its flamingos a mass of pink and white. The very modern and clean market at Nakuru sat at the nub of flower- and tree-lined streets. Then to ranch country and pine forests. At over 6,000 feet the scenery stretched beautifully beyond sight – *The Green Hills of Africa*. Dusk and the birds in the forest were sleepily calling and the crickets had started chirping. The Equator was crossed in complete and utter darkness. Down came the rain and the moisture rose in clouds from the *murram* (all-

TASTING INDEPENDENCE

Near Arusha, in Tanganyika (now Tanzania), a Masai 'standing guard' over the Kombi.

weather) road. And so into Uganda, where kindly policemen supplied an escort to the golf course in Jinja and an ideal if impromptu campsite. It poured all night. How on earth the tent held out defied all reason.

Kombi admirers in
Uganda.

Kampala, reached in the early afternoon, was the capital of Uganda – perhaps then the most advanced of the three East African territories. And tranquil. The pain and turmoil of Uganda from Idi Amin, to tribal infighting, to the Lord's Resistance and to the Rwandan tension, was still away in the future.

At 3,789 feet, allegedly built on seven hills, Kampala was impeccably laid out. Makerere College, on the top of one of the hills, was very modern, with pleasant, long halls of residence. During the search for somewhere to be put up on the college campus, the warden of one of the halls offered welcome drinks.

At the palace of the Kabaka, king of the important region of Buganda, from which he ruled his 1.8 million loyal subjects out of the then total Ugandan population of over 6.5 million, a parade was celebrating the Bugandan Independence Agreement. Full independence for all of Uganda was to come in October. The Kabaka himself sat proudly in his military uniform on his throne while a very smart band played 'Colonel Bogey' out of tune. In the background some sort of army stood in battledress, with battle ribbons, whilst further down the line ragged conscripts stood at ease in an odd assortment of baggy suits, pink and yellow shirts and even one or two warriors with shields and spears. Mehmed and company were privileged to sit with the elite and 'high society' on chairs (even if they were school ones) in the front row, just a few seats from the Kabaka, while several thousand more people crouched, sat or stood round the football pitch. The city of Kampala spread out below. Then came some slow marches, with the band of 32 reaching the whole length of the field. The tempo quickened and they marched in single file to form a square, before reforming in front of the flagpole. The drum major strutted up and down the pitch – one sock up, one down – before rejoining his men with their jackets, maroon and white shorts and yellow belts. In the finale the band formed the letter 'K' for the Kabaka, followed by the letter 'Y' for Yekka (the monarchist political party) before disappearing behind the crowd, still valiantly playing, then returning followed by a platoon of fezzed and bayoneted guards. The last post was played as all stood to attention while the flag was slowly lowered, the sergeant pulling it down with a terrific rush at the last moment, having started off too early. The final march past was conducted with easy-going gusto and improvisation. Then came tribal shouting and drumming.

After two days of rain and low, ugly, fast-scudding clouds, the next day dawned pleasant with bright sunshine lighting up the whole campus. Mehmed and Nigel talked to someone from the Institute of Social Research; Tony went to see the editor of the *Argus* to arrange for two articles on education and later attended a talk by Mr Bell, the Permanent Secretary of the Ministry of Education, entitled 'The Educational Needs of Uganda'.

Dinner was taken in one of the halls. The food was markedly English. There were over 900 students here, of which only 92 were women – almost as bad as Cambridge at that time. This figure included 150 American teaching staff. The pupil-teacher ratio was indeed generous. But there were limits. One teacher noted to us that there was no extra reading for pleasure, and no intellectual stimulus once away from the university. The working morning started with a visit to the Warden, a tour of the campus, the fixing up of interviews and appointments. Another tour followed lunch in the Hall before Nigel and Tony succumbed to the temptation of a beer. Mehmed abstained – he was observing a rather notional one-day fast during the month of Ramadan 'for the good of my soul'. A sudden consumer impulse led to the purchase of some enormous Ugandan drums. How these were to fit into the already confined and loaded spaces of the Kombi, together with all the rest of the gear, seemed to preoccupy no one.

After a series of discussions and further insights into the very real educational efforts being made in Uganda, a one-day drive brought the Expedition from Makerere College back to Nairobi, in preparation for continuing further north, and a first campsite by the roadside just outside the city.

Sixty years earlier the land on which Nairobi now stands was the border between Masai-land and the Kikuyu, teeming with game of all kinds. When the Uganda Railways were driven inland from the coast in 1900, Nairobi became a railway construction camp. From that modest beginning grew the capital of Kenya and the commercial hub of all Eastern and Central Africa, and one of the continent's biggest.

The next morning, a bearded head appeared in the tent doorway. It was another Tony who, with a certain Debbie, was part of a university tiddly-winks team from the UK. Only a British university, seemingly, could mount such a strenuous sport. But apparently it had takers in Africa. They were originally eight, and came down through the Sudan, but ran out of money, so he was now in a film unit and she was teaching. They kindly offered to let the campers sleep at their bungalow until they left for Ethiopia. Everyone stayed up very late talking – not about tiddly-winks.

An interview was obtained with the Executive Officer of the KANU party, Mr Mwai Kibaki. In view of his subsequent rise to the top of Kenyan politics and the country's presidency, this was quite a catch. He was a very ebullient, easy-to-get-on-with, direct-talking guy, a former warden of Livingstone Hall, Makerere College. He said that Kenyan Internal Independence would definitely happen in 1962 – and total independence possibly by the end of the year, or early 1963. Indeed, *Mzee* Jomo Kenyatta was subsequently elected Premier in Kenya's first general election in May 1963. Kibaki then went on to talk about education. In many districts there was something approaching universal primary education – at least for boys – and about 50 per cent for girls, but then came the bottleneck – the lack of secondary schools. It was mainly a shortage of money. The Kenyans hoped to economize by integrating schools. Kibaki considered the curriculum, especially in the secondary schools, should be broadened to give more choice to students. At that time exactly the same narrow range of subjects was being taught to everybody – farming, accountancy, etc. 'And Kenyans want to retain Swahili as their main language.'

While Mehmed and Nigel visited some African schools, Tony went to the Faculty of Special Professional Studies, Royal College, Nairobi, and met the Dean –

TASTING INDEPENDENCE

Enthusiastic students at a
school in East Africa.

Mr Ellmer. He reminded Tony that there were 44 different tribes in Kenya, so
it was very difficult to develop a national identity rather than tribalism. The
country had no mineral wealth and relied primarily on agriculture and foreign
investment. In the climate of uncertainties before independence there was great
strain and worry among the staff – for Europeans in particular, but for Kenyans
also, especially for those with young children. There was also a fear of the
resurgence of the *Mau Mau* – who had rebelled against British colonial rule
between 1952 and 1960. Like Peter Wright, a former Ceylon tea planter met at
the Long Bar of the New Stanley Hotel, Mr Ellmer thought that 'if people could
hold out for four or five years, everything would be fine'. The way ahead turned
out to be rockier.

✳

The Expedition's visit coincided with the final phase of British rule in East Africa. Many early hopes for these newly independent countries were soon dashed. Federation ideas toyed with by the British crystallized in June 1963 when the leaders of Kenya, Tanzania and Uganda in their Nairobi Declaration created the East African Community. Fourteen years later the project collapsed amid acrimony, structural imbalances, different ideological choices and jealousies about fair shares of the benefit cake. Three decades on, the three original countries, plus Rwanda and Burundi, have come full circle, to envisage a full-blown East African Federation by 2013.

*

Before they left Nairobi on 10 March there was a debate about whether it was possible to drive up through the NFP (Northern Frontier Province) of Kenya into Ethiopia, without a four-wheel drive. Mehmed, Nigel and Tony said 'yes' – and were later to wonder about the wisdom of that decision. At first, no problem. The road went through scrub, sisal country, and then more agricultural land. Kikuyu women carried babies slung on their backs, and huge loads held by a strap round their foreheads. After crossing one of the frequent police checkpoints the question was – where is the District Commissioner's bungalow? After going the wrong way, while backing in the dark, Nigel tipped the Kombi and its contents into a ditch at rather a dangerous angle. Being very tired, the party left it and marched to the DC's bungalow. This was Nanyuki, 180 miles from Nairobi.

The following morning, at the accident site, everything had to be unloaded from the Kombi and stacked haphazardly on the surrounding grass. But it was all so peaceful. A ridge of mountains to the left, a vast scrub-desert plain to the right. Ostriches and giraffes trotted past as the Kombi crew lunched by the side of the road. This was Samburu and Turkana country, and the tribespeople could not but impress with their spears, bows and ornaments. The hour before sunset was probably the most beautiful time of the day. Out of the dusk emerged a first African elephant – with big ears flapping and long tusks.

So on to Isiolo, gateway to Kenya's still untamed north. Just before Isiolo, in the distance, was the snowy spire of the 17,040-foot Mount Kenya shining in the moonlight like a cathedral tower. Lake Rudolf stretched away across the plain which, with its outcrop of hillocks, looked rather like the surface of the moon. Isiolo was an outpost of the National Forest Programme. It consisted of a collection of corrugated iron-roofed shacks, and was the gathering place for different tribes – bare-breasted Turkana women, men with spears and floppy hats,

TASTING INDEPENDENCE

North from Nairobi,
Kenya, *en route* to
Ethiopia, passing these
harvesters ...

Somali women with colourful shawls. This was the frontier of neo-civilization –
from here the road headed for the uncertainties of the desert.

Marsabit National Park, an almost perfect cone in the middle of a lava plain, was
wild and remote, with a savage mixture of mountain ranges, volcanoes, forests,
several deserts and rivers fringed with palm trees. Finely striped and graceful
Grevy's zebra and a reticulated giraffe with its intricately patterned coat slipped
coyly away. Herds of greater kudu were nipped at by colourful desert birds. More
nomadic tribes, the Rendille and Samburu, crossed the plains with donkeys laden

… and one learning
to play the drums in
northern Kenya.

with their worldly possessions, the women's wrists and arms covered with wire amulets. The Samburu 'houses' were simple, dome-like structures covered with skins or dung. The road was basically volcanic rock and one just had to hope and pray that the tyres would hold out. Daylight rose, however, over the welcome sight of a very comfortable guesthouse on the top of the cone, run by a British manager. As the road circled up the cone, it went through a number of different climatic zones, each with its distinctive vegetation.

Thick mist and cool morning air met the sleep-bedraggled travellers. It slowly cleared as the morning unfolded. Now came the difficult part of the road – the last 155 miles to the Ethiopian border – little more than a narrow, twisting, bumpy track. The Kombi would jump right into the air, fly through space for a second or two, then land smack on its stomach, leaving Nigel worrying about odd things like the differential, axles, and so on. It was amazing how such changes of road could affect the general spirits of the Expedition. Conversations would then suddenly acquire a new character and substance. These phases rarely lasted very long. After a while everyone went back to his own assessment of life, leaving the others alone with theirs. Especially at night one had ample time to think. Time to think like never before – and probably never again after.

Over lava rocks at 2–3 miles per hour. Fantastically wild and rugged country. Past a volcano on the right, with hawks floating motionless over the crater. Rolling hills were covered with sparse scrub and bushes, the plains spreading into the distant horizon. At the bottom of the crater was Lake Rudolf, a huge pool, with a few herds of cattle grazing nearby. Otherwise, sheer desolation. A sea of lava stones, herds of camels, mountains looming out of the heat haze on the horizon like icebergs from the sea. 'What's the road like ahead?' –'Oh tarmac all the way,' said an Asian lorry driver. Jackals and wild dogs gambolled in the headlamps. With rain the road turned into a mud skating rink. As usual, it was dark before getting to Moyale, where there was an effective curfew as travel at night was frowned on. The Kombi and its occupants, however, carried on in ignorance until they were suddenly confronted by an African police sentry yelling *Usimama*! (stop!) and taking aim with his old .303 British army issue rifle. Tony came out of the Kombi with his hands up, and fortunately the sentry's superior appeared and calmed him down. A camping patch was soon found and everyone thankfully crashed out behind the police station.

Time in the morning was spent chatting to the British frontier officer. A lugubrious soul, he was not particularly encouraging about the road ahead. 'Have

Sunset in East Africa.

you ever been on the Ethiopian side?' 'No, never.' 'Do you know how the roads are?' 'Very bad, very bad indeed …'

This proved to be very true and the first taste of it was the next few yards to the Ethiopian frontier post – a hair-raising drop down a cliff face, as it seemed, and then to the customs post. Formalities were few – they were mostly interested in guns, and this time everyone's visas seemed to be in order. Customs took an hour, but it did give Nigel a chance to blow the dust off his Italian. Pressing on to Mega it was soon obvious that there was actually no road at all – just a riverbed, which was passable when dry but hell when wet. The rains had just begun. Each day at about 2 pm it would start to rain. Driving in these conditions was impossible so one had to make the best of the few hours in the morning to make much progress. It then turned out that Mehmed had left his £20 light meter in the riverbed where they had got stuck in the sand and mud – three times – once very badly. So to Mega, up the final very steep hill. The road climbed up a series of steps which needed to be negotiated with accelerator and hand-brake. Tony and Mehmed at one point got out and walked.

Mega was a one-horse town. It was market day with goods, bags and wads of cash flurrying everywhere. A fair number of people seemed to be drunk. At the British Council it appeared that the representative was away. Some other foreign travellers on the road had advised checking in with the Norwegian missionaries who had come to Ethiopia in 1949 after being thrown out of China. Mehmed, Nigel and Tony thus ended up at the Norwegian Mission, where the pastor put them up in the Lutheran chapel. The mission compound itself was built like a stockade, with wooden posts all the way round. The Norwegians had mission stations in most of the larger villages along the road. Their help was invaluable as they knew every detail of the road, which frequently saved travellers from getting stuck by taking the wrong fork, where the road split into several branches to avoid some obstacle or other. Mega was built in a cleft in the hills, half-way up, and looking upwards one saw more mountains, and looking downwards a plain, covered with thorn scrub bushes. Apparently it had taken a new diesel Mercedes lorry five days to get from Moyale to Mega – a distance of only 72 miles.

18
NORTH TO THE NILE

A blustery, windy morning shook sleep from the eyes and brain. Clouds scudded across the sky, threatening the rain everyone so badly did not want. Ethiopia had been reached just two days before the border was closed to traffic – 'because of "the rains"'. It would be a very eventful five days before completing the 200 miles to Dilla, creeping and slithering almost every inch of the way. Every day there was no option but to unload, shift and then reload the Kombi when it got stuck in the mud.

The Norwegian Mission compound faded into the distance to the strains of children singing in the chapel. The main street of the next township to the north was just a mud track, lined by mud huts. It took half an hour getting petrol out of oil drums before a session of shuffling paper at the medieval police station. Lots of people were wearing black patches as a sign of mourning for Emperor Haile Selassie's queen who had in fact died quite a while back. Lightning and thunder in the distance soon unleashed torrential rains. There was no option but to skid to a halt in some bushes, forced to stop for the night some 30 miles from the next small town.

The next day the rain still poured. Stories heard of people stuck in the mud for two and a half months started to become very real. Despite the real threat of actually getting stuck – especially not having a four-wheel drive – the dawn chorus of birds was fantastic music to the ears. Skidding on for almost a mile, the Kombi finally ground to a halt up a slight slope. The only thing to do was to wait and hope that in a few hours the ground would dry out a little. There was supposed to be a police post about nine miles away, so Nigel and Mehmed went to try and reach it, hoping to send a telegram to the Norwegian Mission at Alghe; or maybe even the police themselves might help.

Tony found himself with at least six hours to wait in the middle of nowhere. So, legs and feet covered in mud, with flies crawling all over him, bull-frogs croaking in the bushes and the cries of birds seeming to mock him, he decided to try again and again to get the reluctant Kombi to move. Being alone didn't worry him, but if it were to be for some days, the sense of utter desolation would begin to tell. He finally manoeuvred the Kombi out, coaxing it to slither back on to the track. All seemed OK except for one place where he cut himself to ribbons hacking thorn bushes out of the way. Then Mehmed and Nigel came walking back. What a relief.

They had walked on to the next village, hoping to rent some muscle to push the Kombi out. They were far from fit for this kind of exercise from sitting in the vehicle so long and with no proper shoes. Eventually they reached a village, where – as usual – Nigel asked if anyone spoke Italian, the lingua franca on the road left over from colonization by Rome. This time people only spoke Amharic but seemed to understand some Italian. One way or another, Mehmed and Nigel seemed to get their point across and the headman, impressively dressed in a British Officer's Warm Greatcoat, assigned three lads to go with them for an agreed price. The lads seemed to think this was a great lark and having thrown a few stones and shouted ribald remarks to a girl who was fetching water, they started to walk with purpose. This was the country of the great Ethiopian athlete, Ghebre Selassie, where people walk enormous distances at an amazing pace. Mehmed and Nigel feared that if this went on at such a pace for the entire distance back to where they had left the Kombi, they would be exhausted. Fortunately, Tony had managed to get the Kombi across the ford and up the other side. They were mightily relieved to see it coming up the road and not to have to walk much further.

They drove past beautiful young girls tending herds of cows – long, curly hair in hundreds of short plaits. The girls stopped them, then ran alongside the Kombi. Baboons were swinging around and chattering in the jungle. The track was good for over six miles. Two toucans appeared. Out of the jungly forest all of a sudden stretched a beautiful plain, completely surrounded by forest – a sort of oasis. Camel and donkey trains soldiered past. The Kombi just made the hills up to Alghe. The Norwegian Mission there offered them water and bread, and they ate lunch with lots of small children lying on the grass watching. Driving on they hoped, God willing, to reach Dilla the next day. On the way, at Hagere Maryam, the local missionary was extremely helpful. But a local police chief took exception to the dates of their visas. It seems that either they should not have been in Ethiopia at all, or they should have left by then as – according to him – the visas had expired. Eventually they were allowed to continue, but the time it took to argue their way out meant that the rain was about to start when they wanted to leave. There was nothing for it but to slog their way back to the mission – up at 6,000 feet – for the night.

A warm welcome was
given at the Norwegian
mission in Alge.

A welcome invitation came for breakfast with the missionary and his wife. Prayers and songs were both in Norwegian. It was all very moving, considering the problems these remarkable people had to go through, living in the back of beyond to spread the Gospel, far from their native fjords.

The British Consul from Mega happened by chance to be on the road – 'very bad road – four lorries stuck,' he reported. There was nothing for it but to force one's way on for a further 25 miles. And then down came the rains again. A camel train trudged up on the 'main road'; all the drivers were bare-foot. Everyone stopped for a 'chat' and Nigel gave the camel drivers cigarettes. At one stage, a dry riverbed-cum-road turned into a raging river, and it was a close call to having to be rescued from being carried down with the rainwater.

TASTING INDEPENDENCE

There was more than a
little trouble *en route* from
the Kenyan border to Dilla
just across the border in
Ethiopia; four-wheel drive
was normally considered
essential, but the Kombi
struggled through.

Meeting the camel train …

The hills became steeper and more frequent. Sometimes the two who were not driving dismounted and walked. But by and large they continued to make progress and felt that they had a chance of getting through to Dilla, where they thought the road had been properly built. That soon turned out to be an illusion. In front of them was a seriously steep and long hill and the Kombi was really struggling to get up the slope. They had been climbing gradually but were getting close to 6,000 feet and less oxygen which might have affected the Kombi's performance combined with the poor, low-octane fuel. Night had fallen already and everything had come to a complete standstill – but fortunately within sight of the top of the hill.

Nothing for it – camp beds off the roof; Mehmed was to stay with the Kombi and Tony and Nigel set off up the hill to see what they could find. In those parts, it seemed there was a police post and a bar on top of every hill, so they were confident of at least finding some shelter. Just as they set off, it looked as if a vehicle's lights on

the other side of the hill had loomed up and then gone out, but it was hard to say. There were no stars. The rain clouds had not dispersed and it was pitch dark. It was about half a mile to the top of the hill and with considerable relief they put the camp beds down and went into the bar. A big man in military uniform was sitting talking to the head of the police post. The policeman was saying *Ishi* at frequent intervals with the utmost deference, so this was clearly someone important. Nigel started trying to explain the situation in rudimentary Italian, when the big man said with a Southern drawl, 'Do either of you guys speak English?'

He turned out to be the Training Commander of the Ethiopian Air Force and was called Wing Commander Abera Woldemariam. He was on leave after a stint in the United States and spoke perfect English with that Dixie drawl. He had been hunting. But, unfortunately, he had killed a lioness, leaving two young cubs without their food provider. So he had got them in his Jeep and was taking them back to his home in Asmara, in northern Ethiopia. Nigel and Tony explained their problems and he was sympathetic since his own progress to this point had been difficult even in a Land Rover. He turned to the police officer and began issuing instructions, accompanied by a stream of *Ishis* from the policeman. A market was being held in the next village the following day. Visitors to the market who would pass the Kombi would take a piece of our kit from it and bring it to the police post where it would be safe. The Kombi would then be virtually empty and could make it to the next village where 4 x 4 transport could be hired. The kit would be loaded on the 4 x 4 and taken probably to Dilla, where there was a larger mission station and where the road improved. The Kombi would then have to negotiate the same road to Dilla, but had a sporting chance unloaded. This was just amazing, hardly believable luck. The commander then disappeared to his vehicle and came back with some things not seen for weeks: whisky, Western cheese and butter, American crackers. In the morning he was already down by the Kombi making sure that his plan was put into effect and sure enough, all the kit started arriving at the police post.

Tony set off to look for 4 x 4 transport in the next village, found some and went back to the police post to load up. The unloaded Kombi got then to Yirga Chefe,

(Opposite, top) … they eventually arrived on this extremely muddy main road in Dilla …

(Opposite, bottom) … and there was not another vehicle in sight.

well known as the place where coffee was first discovered growing wild and still a major producing area – the origin of the famous Abyssinian coffee. Apparently, Yirga Chefe means 'Let it remain a swamp'. They stopped there because of the rain and spent the night in the Kombi. The following morning Nigel was up early, stretching his legs after a cramped night, when a man emerged from the side of the road, dressed in European clothes, and said in Italian, 'Come and have some breakfast'. He led the way to a *tukul* (circular thatched hut) where there was a woman sitting by a fire dispensing coffee into very small cups from a coal black pot. The coffee was incredibly strong. The man was very hospitable and insisted on several shots of *anise* grappa – a combination which made him very talkative. They parted the best of friends. Then came the toughest stretch of the road to be tackled.

The main lorries on the roads were huge Fiat trucks with cross-country tyres which tore great trenches in the road bed. The Kombi simply did not have the clearance to drive in these tracks so one had to drive with one side on the central divide and the other on the edge of the road. This sometimes worked but sometimes did not. The going got more and more difficult, but people on the road came to help until the Kombi got really stuck. The road ahead looked absolutely impassable. It happened that a 4 x 4 taxi had caught up by now. One of the passengers, previously met at one of the Mission stations, was a teacher and spoke excellent English. He began recruiting helpers to get the travellers through to the next section. One, in particular, was a dynamic Somali who basically took charge. He might have noticed Mehmed's medallion with its verses from the Koran, and wanted to impress a fellow Muslim (not that that was Mehmed's strong point). The Somali soon drummed up willing helpers and the Kombi was virtually manhandled to the point where it might deign to be driven again.

Just before Dilla the road was so bad the Kombi had to be towed by a lorry for some way. In Dilla they found the Mission Station and were reunited with their kit. The Kombi needed some minor repairs, and these were expertly done by one of the Italian mechanics who seemed to be there to keep the trucks on the road. Two to three days were happily spent in Dilla with the missionaries before setting off for Addis Ababa along a now better road.

Addis Ababa was reached on 21 March. This was another world. Addis stood at 8,250 feet, among some of the most friendly people in the world, and in the heart of wild, rugged country. One of the Expedition patrons, His Highness the Dejazmatch Asserati Kassa, President of the Senate, arranged an audience with the Emperor, HIM (His Imperial Majesty) Haile Selassie I, the Conquering Lion of the Tribe of Judah, Elect of God, King of Ethiopia.

The ADC opened the door of the Audience Chamber, the Minister of the Court made beckoning gestures and Mehmed, Nigel and Tony walked ceremoniously and respectfully through to bow to the diminutive figure of Haile Selassie I. Selassie effectively began to rule Ethiopia in 1916. Since then, apart from the short interval of the Italian occupation, he had been governing his country by a unique combination of personal power and feudal authority.

The audience started with the court interpreter going from Amharic to English, but soon Haile Selassie got so excited by the conversation that he binned the protocol of imperial audiences and dismissed the interpreter. His English was good. He had learnt it in Bath in his exile years, from 1936 to 1941, during the Second Italo-Abyssinian War, when Italian conquest was born out of Mussolini's desire to bolster his domestic situation through the establishment of an Italian East African Empire. He also wanted to avenge Italy for the previous humiliation and defeat of a madcap Italian colonial venture by the Ethiopian forces at Adowa way back in 1896. At the end of the audience Mehmed, Nigel and Tony were given gold medals. During the audience Mehmed had borrowed a pen, and after they had bowed their way out and were going down the palace steps, the Chief of the Guards rushed up and asked them to stop. Mehmed thought he was about to be arrested for pinching the pen, but 'no' – the Emperor only wanted them to shake paws with his lions, which were chained up at the bottom of the steps. Following this audience, they were written up in a local paper as 'Agricultural students'.

Later they met Afewerk Tekle, an immensely talented artist who, amongst other things, created the stained-glass windows in Africa Hall in Addis Ababa, and also those in Marseille Cathedral. Africa Hall was presented by the Emperor to the United Nations Commission as its permanent office. Tekle was probably the first court painter modern Africa had produced. He was about to do the first ever portrait of Haile Selassie. The previous year the Ghanaians commissioned him to paint Nkrumah for the African summit that had met in Addis Ababa, now becoming a nodal meeting point for African and other summits. Tekle spent three weeks as Nkrumah's guest, complete with personal bodyguard.

Tekle was a product of London's Slade School of Fine Art. It was through the Slade, paradoxically, that he discovered Ethiopian painting. One day his professor took him to the British Museum to see the hoard of Ethiopian manuscripts which

TASTING INDEPENDENCE

General Napier had brought to London 100 years previously. Before going to the Slade Tekle had been, as a protégé of the Emperor, to an English boarding school. Before that he had spent five years (until he was eight) in hiding with his father, who was fighting in the Ethiopian anti-Italian resistance. Tekle himself was subsequently wounded nine times and even then had a large gash from a bomb splinter on one cheek. He went back to Ethiopia in 1958 and plunged into a series of works commissioned by the state. The biggest of these was a 60-foot-long stained-glass panel showing the colonial dragon being slain by African knights, led by an Ethiopian carrying a huge torch of liberty.

Tekle was by no means a retiring man. He had a Jaguar XK 150 embellished with his coat of arms (a streak of lightning, a sword and a painter's palette on a shield). He had a country cottage in the gum-tree woods near Addis airport, with the coat of arms on the front door and the front gate. On formal occasions he dressed in a court uniform designed by himself, and on slightly less formal ones in a dark suit whose jacket was held together by magnets instead of buttons. Until Ethiopia had more painters, Tekle would continue to turn his hand to everything from murals to statues and stamps. He used to hang his designs for stamps in his flat, like pictures.

The British Ambassador put the Expedition in touch with the headmaster of one of the top local schools (an Experimental High School). The headmaster, Bob Last, was a bearded LSE (London School of Economics) graduate, and they stayed with him and his wife in their house for the rest of their time in Addis Ababa. In the cultural field the most remarkable advance had been the foundation of the Haile Selassie University. In 1943, there was only one secondary school in the capital. In 1962, there were many, some having been gifts of foreign states eager to show their goodwill for African progress. English was the first language in all the government schools.

The university, which opened in 1962, grew out of a university college which was established, with generous foreign help, in 1950, and had developed faculties of arts and sciences. Plans were being made to open a medical faculty – an urgent need. In 1943, only one Ethiopian had a full medical qualification – and he did not even practice his medicine. By 1962, there were still only some 30 qualified doctors, for a population estimated at 20 million.

Education, first and foremost, was not merely a prestige word in Ethiopia, but an act of faith to which enormous efforts were being devoted with a simple and touching fervour. Every Ethiopian youth studying abroad was commanded to appear before his imperial master upon his departure and on his return. Of course, there were still too few schools but their number was increasing. Church schools had maintained at least a modicum of literacy. The university was then housed in the old Imperial Palace – in which some rebels had attempted a *coup d'état* in 1960.

Ethiopia in 1962 was one of the most astonishing contrasts in Africa, or indeed in the world. Its clashes of ostentatious riches and stark poverty in the towns were untenable. A land bigger than France, Italy, Holland and Belgium combined, it was one of the world's least-developed countries, with a very high illiteracy rate. Despite the fact that more than a fifth of the national budget was being spent on education, only just over 2 per cent of children actually attended school. And it was visibly poor – the shanty towns on the outskirts of Addis were eye-openers – yet Abyssinian leaders were conscious of their superior status as members of an ancient empire. With this in mind they liked to think of themselves as among the leaders of modern Africa, despite the fact that their autocratic, royalist and economically backward regime was, one would have thought, completely contradictory to the declared aims of the newly independent countries of Africa. The question that everyone asked was 'what would happen after the Lion of Judah went?' Some people thought that the component parts of the Ethiopian Federation would fly apart once the Emperor's strong hand was removed. Probably the answer would be decided by the mood of the Army at the time of his death, for it was they who, as in Spain, would control the situation. After all, Ethiopia had the largest and most efficient armed forces in sub-Saharan Africa.

Addis itself was a sprawling city where prime buildings like the £1 million Africa Hall rubbed shoulders with tin-roofed shacks and grey stone villas of the early 1900s. By day, blinding sunlight at high altitude gave Addis a colour-drained, deceptive modernity. At night, it reasserted itself. The sun went down in an orgy of crimson; the air turned as cold as an English December, and the city spread a forest of neon-lit signs in English and Amharic, and the soft red lights of a thousand tiny brothels. These brothels were something of a cross between Japanese geisha houses and Wild West Saloons – at least, that's what they said. Yet there were signs that, with other trappings, like the exotic ceremonies of Imperial banquets, they would soon be swept away in a change of attitudes.

Was there enough time left during the Emperor's reign for the development of a constitutional monarchy blended with the country's ancient heritage? In spite of the foreboding of Communist subversion, the Soviet Union never had any serious hopes in Ethiopia. In 1962, the influence of the Queen of Sheba remained more real and more potent than that of Karl Marx – or even of Mr Khrushchev.

*

With its 80 million people, today the country has been scarred by turbulence. Ten years after the Expedition's audience with him, Haile Selassie and his dynasty were overthrown. In 1962, Eritrea broke away and its struggle with Ethiopia has poisoned the bloodstream of the two countries ever since. A Soviet-backed brute called Mengistu Haile Mariam replaced Selassie. Coups, revolts, drought, war, refugees, deportations, forced starvation of opponents left over a million dead. In 1998, Ethiopia held its first multi-party elections. Ethiopia today is a regional economic and military powerhouse, but is politically stressed. *The Economist*'s Democracy Index has called Ethiopia a 'hybrid regime' somewhere between a 'flawed democracy' and 'authoritarian'. By its sheer size and weight Ethiopia remains a key force for good and bad throughout the horn of Africa and beyond.

*

It took three days to reach Asmara – now the capital of Eritrea. The good, Italian-built roads ran along the edge of the Great Rift Valley, giving magnificent views. At no stage in the 625-mile drive did the road drop below 7,000 feet. In Asmara Wing Commander Abera, his wife and the two lion cubs were the Expedition's hosts. He flew them down to the Red Sea at Massawa, where they stayed in the naval base. A torpedo boat took them out to an island in the Dahlak Archipelago and a marine park in the Red Sea, where an Israeli expedition was studying sea life, as part of the Marine Biological Year. The 20 Israelis on the island had been born in 14 different countries. Several of them originated from the Soviet Union.

The resident Norwegian officers, who were training the Royal Ethiopian Navy in Massawa, offered breakfast one day – beer.

Returning to Asmara, the road climbed 7,500 feet in 35 miles. Along the way Wing Commander Abera introduced the Enav brothers who ran a canned meat factory, and gave the Expedition 48 tins of canned beef and 24 of stewing steak. Fifty of those tins were eventually and usefully sold in Khartoum and Cairo.

Heading north, the Kombi arrived in Kassala, on the Ethiopian-Sudanese border, on Tony's birthday, 11 April. In Kassala it had to wait until a convoy was available to guide it across the desert, as there was no such thing as a road to

Khartoum. Mehmed was surprised at the changes during the two years since he was last there. Sudan was a very different country from Ethiopia. It was under military rule, but terribly friendly. It would have cost £60 for them and the Kombi to get up to the Aswan Dam, by train and boat. A word with a minister met at a party elicited generosity in the form of them getting their fares paid, as guests of the government, plus a welcome £50 towards the expenses of the Expedition. And this was in addition to the free accommodation provided by Khartoum University.

While Tony repacked the mess in the Kombi, the government flew Mehmed and Nigel to Gezira to see the famous irrigation project. The brown Sudanese wilderness abruptly gave way to smiling fields. As far as the eye could see, rectangles of cotton fields, divided by tiny canals, showed how fruition had been brought to this new agricultural land, not so long ago a barren desert.

Beans and millet were harvested in December. The cotton harvest started in January and went through to late April. In May, the cotton bushes were torn out of the ground and burned. The fields had to be cleaned up by the end of May when the long, harsh months of drought set in. One and a half million impressive acres were now under irrigation. Originally started to yield a cotton cash crop for export, the area had become the backbone of the finances of Sudan, providing half the country's revenue. Two British commercial companies were partners in the scheme with the state. Tenant farmers did the agricultural labour. With the nationalization of the scheme, social services were introduced in the way of clinics, water supplies, education, agricultural instruction and research centres. This whole enterprise both changed the lives of former nomadic tribes and financed the country with such success that the cotton had been called 'white gold', and with reason. This was before the discovery of oil, the 'black' gold, in Sudan.

*

Sudan in 1961 was already in the grip of an endless civil war pitching northern Arabs and Nubians against southern Christians and animist Nilotic peoples. Colonel Omar al-Bashir grabbed power in 1989. The north–south conflict was formally resolved in the first decade of this century. Meanwhile, another conflict festers in Darfur where Arabs fight Africans. Sudan, part of that sad club of mono-commodity economies stricken with the curse of oil, lapses repeatedly into conflicts fired by ethnic ambitions, greed and underdevelopment. In 1962, the Expedition glimpsed the agricultural potential of Sudan. The Saudis indeed saw

The government flew
Mehmed and Nigel to
Gezira – an area between
the White and Blue Niles,
which was a successful,
major cotton-producing
project.

(Opposite, top) At the
border town of Kassala, there
was a wait for a convoy
to assemble, as there was
no discernable road to
Khartoum!

(Opposite, bottom) Finally
arriving in Khartoum. This
was the main shopping
street.

it as their future granary across the Red Sea. Little has come of that. Oil has won the battle against food.

*

Gezira means 'island' and as such it was formed between the two arms of the White and Blue Niles. This flat land sloped slightly from north to south, just enough to irrigate it without the aid of pumping stations. In 1929, Egypt and the Sudan signed an agreement regarding the usage of Nile water. Gezira and the Sudan could only use the water from 15 July until 1 January each year. Egypt used the water for the rest of the time. The problem of water use in the region increasingly comes to a political head today.

The Expedition left Khartoum on 20 April for Egypt – first by train up through the vast Nubian Desert, then by Nile steamer from Wadi Halfa. To relieve the monotony of the long journey, Tony managed to have a 24-hour romance with an Italian girl, whose father ran the second biggest hotel in the Sudan. Mehmed and Tony slept in the Kombi, which was on a flat-car at the end of the carriages. It was quite fun in the morning, washing in front of the Kombi, while the train whistled on through the never-ending sea of sand. From Wadi Halfa they passed Abu Simbel before arriving in Aswan. The *feluccas* (traditional wooden sailing boats) moved imperceptibly on the old river under their swaying lateen sails. The companions took a ride in one late of an evening as an ideal setting to sink a bottle of whisky they had been given in Khartoum. The ice cubes were full of straw.

On to Luxor, ancient Thebes, and a walk at midday through the Valley of the Kings – with its marvellous tombs. Tony got sunstroke and took to his bed to moan quietly. It was a calming place with a marvellous light and a perfect pace to its daily life. Impressive too was the sight of new schools being built in most of the villages on the way.

Without the Nile, Egypt is nothing. Apart from the scattered oases in the western desert, and the coastal areas along the Mediterranean and Red Seas, the Nile Valley was the only habitable area of the country. For centuries the river had provided Egypt's entire water supply, its chief means of internal communication, its only source of power, and the basis of its complex and vital pattern of agricultural development. Until the nineteenth century this pattern had remained virtually unchanged since the days of the Pharaohs. The floodwaters of the Nile, which reach Egypt in the summer, after the rainy season in the highlands of

Traditional Egypt – one
man and his camel.

Ethiopia, were diverted by irrigation canals on to as much land as possible. When
the flood subsided, the peasants gathered their single crop for the year, and lived
on it until the yearly miracle was repeated. Occasionally Nature failed them and
there was famine; or the flood was excessive and washed away their mud villages
and drowned their livestock. Either way the Egyptians accepted, with resignation,
an apparently unchangeable, beneficent natural cycle.

Reforms in government and modest improvements in the standard of living of the
peasants, especially in health, boosted the birth rate and the population exploded.
In the first 50 years of the twentieth century the population of Egypt doubled.
But the country's resources remained practically unchanged, and the benefits
of improvements in irrigation and agricultural techniques were dwarfed by the
number of new mouths that had to be fed. This was the situation that confronted
the group of young and completely inexperienced army officers who, in the

revolution of 1952, destroyed a corrupt monarchy and seized power. At first they thought that basic problems could be solved by reforming the social structure, destroying the hold of a few rich landowners on Egypt's immense agricultural resources, and providing the incentive for peasant owners to co-operate in the production and marketing of their crops. Cotton, which had been introduced with great success in the nineteenth century, yielded – by 1952 – some 80 per cent of Egypt's foreign exchange earnings. But the cotton trade was largely in the hands of foreigners and wealthy Egyptian entrepreneurs. The young officers thought that controlling or dispossessing the foreigners and entrepreneurs would do the trick.

It didn't. Even the scheme of land reform which the officers put into effect soon after their seizure of power affected no more than 5 per cent of the total cultivated area and a little over 100,000 farmers. It had value as an expression of the new regime's social policy – but its economic impact was negligible. A radical policy change was needed, some altogether new approach to finding food and employment for a population which increased by almost half a million each year.

The obvious answer was industrialization – obvious, that is, as economic theory, but immensely difficult to put into practice in the reality of Egypt's resources, both of raw materials and of human traditions and attitudes, and most difficult of all in view of Egypt's fragile international situation. In 1952, there was still a British army of occupation in Egypt. The first aim of the revolutionary government – taking precedence even over its ambition to raise the standard of living of the Egyptian people – was to make Egypt genuinely free and independent, putting an end to centuries of foreign domination and exploitation. It was easier said than done.

Egypt's independence struggle retarded economic advancement. Politics dominated. No sooner than, in the summer of 1956, the last British troops had gone, did the Egyptians turn to schemes for industrialization and economic growth. They were then embroiled in the Suez crisis. The spark for that crisis was precisely the most ambitious of all these schemes – the Aswan High Dam project.

Before 1956, projects were ill co-ordinated and money was short. But economic development was needed to combat poverty, ignorance and disease. Four inheritances from the Suez crisis freed the Egyptians from this vicious circle: the revenues of the Suez Canal, more than £50 million a year; expropriation of foreign concerns providing a stock of capital and plant for future expansion;

The journey onward was
by train, with the Kombi
on a flat car, to Wadi
Halfa in Egypt. Then by
boat to Aswan to see the
Pharaohs, which had to
be moved when the dam
was built later.

Russian money to build the High Dam; pressure from the international
blockade in 1956 and 1957, making Eyptians think seriously about their
economic future.

Time in noisy, bustling, fascinating Cairo was short; little educational work
had been planned. At a 'souvenir' shop money was changed at black market
rates. Spare food was sold, so that only soup, the interminable spaghetti and
dehydrated meat, Oxo cubes, salt, jam and cooking fat were left. At a real
antique shop Mehmed ascertained that his icon from Moscow (obligingly

TASTING INDEPENDENCE

The face of Egypt.

smuggled out of the Soviet Union by Tony) was genuine. A climb up the highest Pyramid provided a ringside seat for a *Son et Lumière* in French, with the Sphinx lit up. In 'Sahara City', a tented nightclub in the desert, they saw the famous belly-dancers perform.

But there was more. For 1,000 years the greatest school of Islam had been Cairo's Al Azhar University – one of the world's oldest universities. In 1962, Egypt's colleges produced probably more secular teachers, doctors, lawyers and technicians than all the rest of the Arab world put together. Al Azhar still is an intellectual beacon of the Arab world, and not only because of its religious authority.

The veil for women had, in the early 1960s, almost disappeared from the Arab countries bordering the Mediterranean. In the big cities only the poor and the middle-aged wore it. Among the *Bedu* of the countryside the veil had never been customary. Only in small towns and the then diminishing areas of religious conservation did it persist – a sign to most Arabs of provincialism and backwardness. In Turkey, Atatürk had condemned the veil. Arab countries were moving forward, not so much through changes in the law, but by small day-by-day adjustment of public opinion.

Alexandria since the revolution probably lacked the particular atmosphere that had captured Lawrence Durrell – fashionable reading for British undergraduates at the time. The city could still fascinate, but was curiously suspended in a time warp. Once a polyglot frontier to Europe, it was now a major recipient of Egypt's population boom as *fedayin* swept into the towns.

In Alexandria Mehmed, Nigel and Tony had their beards shaved off – on the boat from Bombay to Mombasa they had all given up shaving. They also caught up, here and in Cairo, with Mehmed's *Mamluk* cousins – an esoteric association harking back to the Ottoman past. The *Mamluk* were the old warrior caste in Muslim societies; although under nominal Ottoman suzerainty, they had dominated Egypt for centuries.

A visit through the dust to El Alamein – it means 'the two flags' – vividly recalled the Allies' decisive World War II victory over the Axis Forces. West from Alexandria the switchback road along the fringe of white sand dunes evoked images of the 'Desert Battle', and how touch-and-go it had been for both combatants. Now bright-eyed *bedu* children bounded out from among the fir-trees to wave handfuls of fruit or eggs at passing travellers. The coastal landscape was so brilliant; the intense blue of the sea – luminous at dusk as though lit from within – reflected in a sky that faded away inland to a misty grey and merged with scrub-covered desolation. Through the scene ran the Mersa Matruh railway, with the 'desert special' – only four carriages, with their paint peeling off – rumbling on in its own dust storm.

TASTING INDEPENDENCE

Import restrictions fostered the big black market flourishing in Cairo and Alexandria to satisfy the Egyptian townsman's desires: transistor radios, perfumes and cosmetics, cigarettes, car spares, even washing machines, refrigerators and electric cookers. It also helped the Expedition's finances, now almost at breaking point; Mehmed had to sell his cameras and photo accessories.

*

Egypt, for some observers, is one of the four countries throughout the Near and Middle East – together with Turkey, Israel and Iran – that in the last analysis weigh most heavily in the geopolitical scales of the region. If that is so, Egypt is deceptive. An economy with flourishing tourism, agriculture, manufacturing, construction, services and an attractive investment climate is let down by its political culture and ethos – or lack of them. Once seen as an intellectual magnet of the Arab World, Egypt has slipped down the scale of the developing world's success stories. Pent-up frustrations bubble away under this crucial theatre of the Arab Spring. A hard slog lies ahead towards a quality of governance with which Egypt can be a constructive force in this crucial hinge area of the Arab and African worlds – and between Jews and Palestinians.

*

On 3 May, a ship left Alexandria for Cyprus. Mehmed, Nigel, Tony and the Kombi said farewell to the African continent.

19
STAND-OFF
IN CYPRUS

Cyprus was then as now a bewitching island; and then as now an excruciating headache both for its own denizens and for Europe and the Near East.

A first call was on the Head of the Turkish Communal Chambers – Rauf Denktas – an extremely sharp barrister who was later to lead the Turkish community of Cyprus through turbulent years. He said the Constitution of the Cypriot Republic meant very little; the Greeks were striving openly after *Enosis*, and the Turks were in too much of a minority, both economically and commercially, to do much about it. *Enosis*, meaning 'union' in Greek, referred to the Greek Cypriots' aim to incorporate the island of Cyprus into Greece proper. Joint efforts at governing Cyprus were meant to be done on a 70–30 basis; in reality this rarely worked out.

The official residence of Dr Fazıl Küçük, the Vice-President, was thronged with uniformed policemen. Dr Küçük, in the course of a long conversation, explained why he didn't think that the Turks and Greeks would come together – in education or anything else. The gulf, he feared, would widen. 'What about the deal of Cypriotism?' 'Maybe after a century!' 'Shouldn't you have been trying more to spread the gospel of one Cypriot Republic however difficult it was in practice?' He shrugged his shoulders. The same applied to his views on the economy: 'Both the Greeks and Turks must work out their own economy.' Two equally strong nations should combine together; but if one was much stronger than the other, the weaker one would be suppressed. 'In Cyprus, only if the Turkish community became strong could the two come together. If not, there would be trouble.'

After this tuition in Cyprus politics Mehmed and Nigel toured Turkish schools on the western side of the island, while Tony stayed behind fixing up articles for newspapers. Their mentor on this trip was Fikri Direkoglu, who had been a teacher in Swansea. He struck them as quiet and modest; they found out later that he was a leading light in the TMT, the IRA-style resistance to Greek encroachment.

TASTING INDEPENDENCE

Before touring the Greek area, they profited from an introduction through Tony's cousin in the British Embassy in Beirut (met over lunch during the ship's brief stopover there) to his friend the High Commissioner in Nicosia, Ed Wynne. This visit was duly made in the Kombi – now chirpily back on the road with new pistons and cylinders for the third time in a few months. It was the chance for a long talk on Cyprus and the world in general. Ed was an ex-journalist and a sharp observer. His diagnosis for Cyprus was not encouraging.

It was dark by the time Mehmed, Nigel and Tony departed. They drove slowly across to Kyrenia. It was an ideal place for a painter or author, peaceful, with its beautiful little port and some great restaurants. Later they talked to another of the journalistic fraternity, John Osman, the *Daily Telegraph* correspondent for the Middle East, over a glass of wine at the Coeur de Lion Hotel. The English girl behind the bar had an unmistakable accent, and Tony for some obscure reason even pinpointed her home town – Colne in Lancashire. The lights of Nicosia from the hills on the return journey glittered away into the distance, illuminating the horizon in a seemingly never-ending line from east to west.

The next morning Tony rang up his journalist contact, John Osman, and invited himself down for a swim and more briefing. John and his wife Anne had a delightful house close by Kyrenia Castle. In the background, the hills rose up in wooded steepness. On the way back, Tony drove up to St Hilarion Castle – stretching several hundreds of feet up to the top of the mountain ridge looking down to Kyrenia. Swiss-blue skies hovered above, while white clouds were blown through the pine-clad valley below. Birds sang happily in the sunlight, and the only thing to mar the perfect setting was a Pepsi-Cola lorry bringing fresh supplies up for thirsty tourists. Tony just looked the other way and stared up at the thick, high walls surrounding the almost impregnable bastion above. This was normally a great country, away from the noise and bustle of the town, away from the stark reality of a mad, commercial world. Had it not been for the political cloud overhanging everything.

Education, however, mattered. At one school the headmaster told of his efforts to enlarge the school grounds. He persuaded a local farmer who owned the adjoining land to give some of it for free for a large playground for the children. Bulldozers flattened the ground out roughly, and then the parents voluntarily finished the job. 'They'd live on onions and olives for the sake of the education of their children – if necessary,' said the head. It was impressive how keen the parents and the children were on education, especially as it was not compulsory.

The parents played a very large part in the life of the schools, devoting much time and energy to them, as substitutes for the weak state.

Mehmed, meanwhile, had put up the flags on the Kombi – Turkish and British. He was only following the pattern followed hitherto throughout the Expedition. Nigel and Tony argued about whether this was the most sensible, or even 'diplomatic' thing to do in a place like Cyprus, especially with the Turkish holiday on. Maybe people would think this to be provocatively anti-Greek. Reason prevailed – down the flags came.

They were lucky enough to get an interview with the President of the Republic of Cyprus, Archbishop Makarios. He was off to Germany and America two days later, and so they were sandwiched in between ministers and ambassadors coming to pay their respects. They parked the battered Kombi proudly between highly polished Mercedes. Soon they were ushered into the presence of His Excellency or His Beatitude, depending on whether you came to see him in his capacity as President of the Republic or as Head of the Greek Orthodox Church Community. They made do with 'Your Excellency'. He was a distinguished-looking man, with the dark robes and long flowing beard of his religion. He looked odd without his hat, especially as it left a very distinct line around his head where the sun had not reached. But the overall picture was of a relaxed dignity. He was the acknowledged 'Father' and wholehearted supporter of the EOKA movement, whose aim was to rid Cyprus of British rule, partially achieved in August 1960 when Cyprus achieved independence. He poured sherry into his visitors' glasses and served himself. There was no one else in his book-lined study, and they talked for some time in English. They started off by asking him about education.

He claimed that the standard of education in Cyprus was rather high, though with many difficulties to overcome. The number of high school students had doubled. Attendance was becoming compulsory in elementary schools. Emphasis was mainly on the classical system – 'We must respect this, but understand that technical and agricultural students are much needed.' Emphasis on classical education reduced the number of people qualified for public administration, especially in agricultural and technical fields.

With the rise of education, said Makarios, will also rise the economy and the standard of living. Agriculture, small industry and tourism were priorities. If private people wanted to build hotels the government would put up to one-third of the cost. 'We also plan to build a Hilton Hotel ...'

TASTING INDEPENDENCE

Asked about Cyprus and the Common Market, he said, 'Cyprus has more advantages than Greece or Turkey and entry into the Common Market is under consideration,' adding paradoxically, 'If the UK joins the Common Market, it would be very difficult for Cyprus, a Commonwealth member.' No further explanation was forthcoming about what years later was to become a major European Union headache.

As for NATO, Makarios was emphatic. 'No – it's our intention not to enter any political or military block. It's much better to remain neutral! The question of the Common Market is closely connected with this question, and we have to look at it from two angles – the economic and the political.' Makarios was displaying his renowned political qualities as a master of imprecision.

Did he consider it beneficial to have a university on the island. Again 'no'. 'There are two difficulties; firstly we would have to use two languages, and secondly we can't attract students from abroad so would have to use English, therefore three languages.' 'Why was the Constitution not working fluently?' 'Because the Constitution is so complicated – it depends on mutual goodwill. There are provisions in our Constitution which are unworkable – for example, separate municipalities. Some people think this means we have to live in entirely separate areas. I say "yes", but I don't want Greeks in Greek property to be affected by this. The overlapping sectors will cause friction, especially in Nicosia.' They did indeed.

'Do you think Cyprus will manage to keep the idea of one Cypriot Nation?' A pause – 'Yes, but as a State, not as a nation.' At this point the British High Commissioner was announced, and the itinerant visitors shook hands, bowed and retired. It had been quite an experience – they wondered afterwards whether he knew he was talking to a Turk and a couple of Brits.

*

In 1962, Rauf Denktash said in an interview that the island was at near boiling-point. He was right. A year later President Makarios lunched with President Kennedy at the White House and said he wanted to amend the Cyprus constitution, especially about the separate municipalities and the veto powers of the Turkish vice-president. President Kennedy froze: 'Don't you touch that constitution, Your Beatitude,' he said, 'that constitution is the essence of your country!' President Kennedy was assassinated on 22 November 1963. Makarios started the amendment procedures almost immediately. Bitter fighting soon broke out between the two communities. In 1974, Greek nationalists, backed by the Athens military dictatorship, provoked intervention by the Turkish army. The north–south/Greek–Turkish divide festers. Glimpses of light have a habit of being swiftly doused. Europe is a collateral damage victim of the Cypriot impasse.

The Last Leg Home

From Cyprus on 18 May a two-day voyage across the Aegean brought the Expedition to Piraeus via Rhodes in the shadow of Turkey. Through Yugoslavia it was a fast drive to Graz, and Munich, and then up to Gartow, near Hamburg, where the companions reported to the Baron von Adelsheim – their patron with whom they had all stayed the previous year on what was actually his wife's estate not far from the East German border. Here Nigel celebrated his 24th birthday in some style. Then they drove to Bonn to sell the Kombi.

The dealer who had supplied the vehicles originally, the same nattily dressed 'executive' who had dealt with Peter months earlier over the other Kombi, spluttered. Not only was he amazed that the 'others' were back in one piece, but it was not part of VW policy to accept, as a trade in, 'such a piece of scrap'. Mehmed decided to keep it.

After a few days relaxing in Paris – what else do you do in Paris? – they embarked for home. Bureaucracy dealt its last swipe. For some obscure technicality connected with the Kombi and its *Zollnummer* licence plate, Mehmed had to take it all the way back to the original exit point at Waidhaus on the German-Czech border to get the correct stamp on the Kombi's *Kraftfahrzeugbrief* to say that it had not been 'exported' from Germany in the first place … yet it had. Try and work that one out.

Almost one year after the Expedition started, it eventually came in sight of the White Cliffs of Dover on 3 June.

EPILOGUE

What did we learn? It has not been a good half-century for ageing optimists, as we assuredly were in the 1960s, despite the Cold War and the threat of being blasted to eternity by nuclear weapons. Maybe here, too, are lessons about the evolution of geopolitics.

But let us first look at what this Expedition did to its members and how it impacted on their later careers. They were a heterogeneous bunch to start with – and their careers would be heterogeneous, too, but not unrepresentative of graduates of that time.

Tony and Mehmed kept close contact, travelled together subsequently, and talked about the Expedition all their lives. Their long-suffering spouses, Sheena and Gül, could surely have written a parallel book. Tony and Peter, too, kept in close touch over the years.

What Mehmed learned from the Expedition is 'bluntly told: almost all the countries we visited have been so mismanaged that one could not make a similar Expedition today in 2012, even with 50 times the budget and back-up.'

The only time Mehmed regretted the 'whole thing' was in Kunduz, north of Kabul, when 'the local police cum military person' beat him with a 'wooden something or another' whilst repeating the same question: 'Why did you go to Kizil Kale?' Mehmed was simply trying to convince him that all he had wanted to do was to see the Oxus.

Thirty years later, in 1991, Mehmed went to Moscow, which was in full post-Soviet upheaval, with two business colleagues. At the bar in the Hotel Metropole an Israeli asked for *Black Label* with a heavy accent. Mehmed chatted with him and was envious to learn that he had a ticket for the Bolshoi – that had not been so easy 30 years earlier. 'Very simple,' said the man, 'ten dollars on the black market.'

Mehmed turned to his friends and said, 'Leave your drinks, we are going to the opera'. They rushed to the Bolshoi, Mehmed with three $10 bills in his hands. A guy appeared out of nowhere, produced two tickets and took two of the $10 bills. 'Run,' said Mehmed to his friends, 'you have five minutes.' Mehmed stood alone with the remaining $10 bill in his hand. A huge policeman came towards him. Mehmed's mind went back 30 years to the many times they had got on the wrong side of the Soviet police. To Mehmed's surprise and delight, the copper took his 'greenback' and produced a Bolshoi ticket. The system had changed all right.

Tony recalls on returning to the UK his happiness to see family and friends again, and the time to reflect on the unique and fascinating experience – behind but still with him. Even then he was busy drafting the outline of a possible book – and trying to sell what remained of the Expedition's goods and chattels, whilst studying for his bar exams. There was a bit of a mental tug-of-war going on behind his ample mop of hair.

Tony acknowledges that now several of the countries visited would be unpleasant to go back to, 'putting it mildly'. The Expedition really did have few problems. Most people were kind, generous and helpful. They offered accommodation, provided contacts in places further down the road, and gave great warmth. It was all about a lot of interesting people in so many situations and occupations 'teaching us the realities about life in their countries, from the very poor through to the very rich'.

The Expedition further boosted Tony's existing love of travel. He has since been back to Russia, Iran, Pakistan, India, Nepal (five times), Ceylon and Ethiopia. Much of it was travel for pleasure. In Teheran he helped set up a language school in the late 1960s (the fate of which today is unknown) and went to Moscow to enrol students for his own language school in London.

For Nigel all Expedition members were 'marked' by the experience. This popped out from sporadic contacts with the others over the years. It certainly went beyond the now 'in' Gap Year experience favoured by students – in its depth, breadth and sheer wealth, the novelties thrown up day by day on the road, the unforgettable hospitality which one encountered everywhere. Return to the UK for Nigel was not all plain sailing. Settling down was hard and he had not much idea what he wanted to do. But it had to have an international dimension. Finally, the historian opted for accountancy – a profession which seemed to provide an entrée to working abroad. The experience was invaluable, too, later in his banking career and when he was a consultant in corporate finance. Geopolitical sensitivities help in those worlds. He was active in the GB-USSR Association and went back to Russia a few times, once leading a tour group which took him back to Tashkent, where he met up again with Kazim and his family, who had entertained him and Mehmed on their 'side-trip' to Central Asia.

For Tim the return to start full-time work was not made easier by turning up late, the Expedition having over-run its allotted time. Once with his nose to the grindstone in the grease and noise of the Ruston and Hornsby diesel engineering shops in Lincoln, he had so much to concentrate on that the recent travels were soon pushed into the background; but they were always hovering somewhere in his mind. The experience of the expedition was, however, invaluable in that it wrenched Tim further out of his familiar UK world and gave him a matrix of geography on which to pin anything that happened anywhere or was talked about in Europe and the Middle East. In particular, 'I also learnt from direct observation (and nearly disastrous consequences) that after two hours of driving the concentration required on difficult roads drops away.' Some months after returning, Bob and Tim nearly came a cropper in Tim's VW Beetle, sliding off the exit from a frozen *Autobahn* near Munich in the early hours of the morning on the way to visit a couple of girlfriends. With hindsight, Tim regrets that he did not keep up a network of contacts and that the group as such did not maintain their ties in general. Such were the demands of careers and everybody being scattered geographically.

Return to the UK for Peter meant that he now had to get on with it and qualify for the Bar. Meanwhile, for him there was a very special consequence in that it was through Mehmed and the Expedition that he first met his wife, Tahere, then an undergraduate at Girton College, Cambridge. Her family, the Alams, were a great help to the Expedition in Iran and from there the relationship blossomed. Peter and Tahere have been married for 48 years. For several years he gave talks about the Expedition to various audiences as his political career got going. 'The knowledge I got from it was irreplaceable.' Should anything have been done differently? 'That would be nit-picking. We got it about right which was the main thing.'

Elected subsequently to Parliament, Peter later went over to New Labour, rejecting the move of the Conservative Party to the Right in general and towards a limited, nationalistic approach to Europe in particular. The Expedition, with its broadening of his horizons, lurked and worked actively in the background of this decision.

The benefit in his later life was considerable. Peter felt stronger for having seen and done so much at that age. He held various offices in foreign affairs at Westminster and visited every country the Expedition had been to again and, in the case of some, many times. In Iran he could make use of continuing connections through his wife. He was Chairman of the USSR Parliamentary Group, Vice Chairman of the GB-USSR Association (he was the host to Mikhail Gorbachev when he came on his famous visit to the UK in 1984), and Chairman of the British Inter-Parliamentary Union. Without the inheritance from the Expedition his career could well have gone another way – the law. As it was, he was immeasurably strengthened by learning something of the Slav mentality at a young age and doing so without the cosseting VIP treatment his duties generated later on. 'Take out a Russian girl for an evening or two, by today's standards fairly innocently, and you learn more about Russia and the Slavs than in any number of seminars.' 'I have lived a full and fortunate life and the Expedition was for me as important as my University education in preparing and equipping me for that life.'

Roger, like Tim, on returning to the UK, started an engineering apprenticeship with GEC after barely a weekend at home to catch his breath and wits. It was again a busy period, tossed into the professional deep end, adjusting to living in Birmingham, making a completely new set of friends, and settling into an engineering environment – all a far cry from Kiev or Persepolis. Over the next two or three years he went to Tim and Peter's weddings, and found himself face to face, looking around the scrum, with Tony on the rugby field. Sadly, new demands and distances weighed against more consistent contact.

Maybe the effect on Roger's career was indirect – but real. Much of his working life was devoted to exporting engineering products. In that role he travelled extensively. Only on a few occasions did he go to the countries visited during the Expedition. Yet in dealing with 'foreign' clients he had that extra dimension of a greater instinctive openness which helps business people click. 'The attitudes and friendships that we experienced then have, I think, made for a more tolerant and inclusive approach in my character than many of my peers had.' How many of Britain's top export managers have that 'bit extra' today?

For Bob the Expedition's route would cover areas that featured large in his career. He started out as a journalist, writing on European and wider foreign economic and business affairs for *The Economist* in London. A chance introduction and a whim took him to anglophone Central Africa, running his own paper, reporting for the BBC and some German media and being declared 'prohibited immigrant', on separate occasions, by Malawi's Banda and Rhodesia's rebel Ian Smith. In Brussels, at the then EEC Commission, he served as a spokesman, as an adviser in a Commissioner's *cabinet* or private office, in the development department, followed by his posting as Head of Mission in Turkey, where he and Mehmed conferred over whisky and under the cloud of yet another military *coup d'état*. His Expedition Balkan odyssey came back to mind when he was assigned to the European Community Monitoring Mission (ECMM) at the outbreak of the Yugoslav civil war, and then in Albania after government collapsed in that now open country in 1996. The Expedition exposure was a constant asset in his responsibility for EU humanitarian aid. The Expedition 'taught me an enormous amount in practical, human and political terms to underpin my career – and perhaps make fewer mistakes than I otherwise would have done'.

Readers' curiosity will have sometimes been sharpened about the personality of Traicho. Only now, 50 years later, have some things become clearer, some thoughts of other Expedition members confirmed. Traicho, whose father was a die-hard Communist, high up in the Bulgarian security administration, was 'inserted' on an exchange scholarship into Cambridge on a badly defined 'intelligence' mission. His commitment would soon fade. He 'jumped' – the final act was probably in Istanbul. Not that British intelligence found that he had much to offer. In the meantime the Bulgarians sentenced Traicho to death in absentia. He married General Allenby's great-granddaughter – they split up several years later. Somehow he then ended up farming in Ireland, got an Irish passport, set up with an Irish lady – yet apparently preserved some Bulgarian connections. Word has it that he then benefited from a US scheme to offer a sort of asylum to IRA activists in the late 1980s. And in the USA he died.

*

A travel book owes somewhat more to its readers than providing entertaining, even educative, glimpses into societies. Harsh geopolitical realities of yesterday and today are part of the package – as of life. Particularly as much of that great swathe of land that the Expedition visited, from the eastern Mediterranean, via the Hindu Kush, to the Himalayas, is today a simmering world cauldron of insecurity and unpredictability with global implications.

The members started out on their Expedition in 1961 with the expectation and premise that the way to human and social salvation lay through education. That now looks, at first sight, to have been naive. Perhaps not. Not all but many of the countries visited have made little progress with education in nearly half a century. Nor have many of them got anywhere with political or economic development. But a wide consensus persists that education is the gateway to progress.

In the meantime, the power tables in the world have turned. In the early twentieth century, Europe represented some 20 per cent of the world's population. Now it is 7 per cent. Africa in the 1970s looked as if it were doomed to lose a whole generation killed by AIDS and plunge ever more deeply into poverty. Now Africa's demographics are picking up and many are starting to take positive bets on its future and as an investment option. Countries like Kenya and Uganda seem to be freeing themselves slowly from the grip of clan-based corruption and violence. Together with Tanzania, Rwanda and Burundi, they are bringing the institutions of East African regional co-operation back to life. Many tyrants are on the back foot. But Africa still faces the uphill task of educating and employing its burgeoning youth, and of harnessing its energies and raw materials for the benefit of its citizens.

The former Soviet Union and Yugoslavia, for example, had good educational systems, motivation and performance. Fortunately, much of that asset remains intact today despite those countries' subsequent tribulations.

Only two of the countries visited are in any way outright success stories – India and Turkey. In these important and dynamic countries, too, the fault lines of ethnic tensions, conservatism, radical temptations and social inequality are, among other things, constant threats to stability and progress. Their frontiers may be secure but their neighbourhoods are volatile. Turkey seeks a wider regional role. Mehmed, we have seen, was fascinated by the 'Turkic' world to the east. He is less bullish than Bob about the direction his country is taking.

Then there are countries like Jordan – keep your fingers crossed – and Tanzania which, despite obstacles, have weathered storms with some honour and progress. Cyprus, with once strong economic statistics but misjudged and premature EU and Eurozone membership, remains deeply undermined by the communal conflict, the presence of Russian mafia interests and often obscure financial practices. Egypt is in a state of upheaval about which there is only one safe prediction – the throes of change in that country will persist for some years yet, a factor of Middle East insecurity instead of being the bulwark against it. Ceylon – now Sri Lanka – struggles to emerge from a vicious, ethnicity-based civil war of which yesterday's promising democracy is a main victim. In the former Yugoslavia, Slovenia has 'left the Balkans' for the EU to quote founding President Milan Kučan (in a private conversation with an Expedition member). Croatia is in an uneasy anteroom of EU membership. Other Balkan countries, with their unfinished ethnic and boundary histories, nurture fragilities capable of bursting into more generalized disruption throughout the Balkans. Russia and its former Soviet satellites outside the European Union remain exposed to the whim of brutes and corruption. Their emergence from the old Soviet (if not Tsarist) authoritarian reflexes, along with their rulers' disdain of their citizens, and their demographic weakness, constrains progress. Pakistan and Ethiopia, despite occasional glimmers of hope in the latter, hover perilously on the brink of the category of failed states. Then there are others – Iran, Iraq, Afghanistan, Sudan – which have lapsed into their own versions of hell with associated capacities to destabilize their neighbours. Israel continues to be a paradox combining democracy, education and culture with attributes of a rogue state.

We started out on our journey as privileged, elite products of one of the world's best universities. Cambridge still is among the best. But Europe, which a century ago dominated the world, slides – worrisomely for some, indifferently for other Europeans – into less global relevance with its declining demographics, inability to resign itself to immigration and the evolving ethnic and cultural mix of its society, and refusal to draw the logical conclusions from the pooling of sovereignty. Confidence about the perpetuity of the Eurozone, and indeed of the EU itself, that prevailed a mere decade ago has been a major victim of the financial and economic crisis. Even the United States struggles to accept that it can no longer flick its powerful fingers for the world to jump to attention as self-doubt at home sets in.

The Expedition members' privilege as young 20-somethings in the early 1960s was to get first-hand experience of a key part of the world in transition – it still is. The journey provided extra perspectives on life and the world which have been invaluable companions in private and professional lives ever since. Fifty years later, with most of us still alive and kicking, we are doing stocktaking for our children and grandchildren. And, who knows, this unique exercise – for it was just that – might have something to say to a wider audience grappling with the challenges of change in a world community that is evolving ever faster.

The prospectus said: '*The future of Afro-Asia is as interesting as it is uncertain.*' Indeed.

Fifty years ago these companions of the 1960s saw themselves as the optimistic generation and carried that optimism through the countries they visited. Yet warning signs abounded. The tectonic plates of geopolitics, generation-breakdown and frustration, dynastic exhaustion, were already grinding together.

None of us foresaw the abrupt break-up of the Soviet empire in 1989–90.

Few can honestly say they foresaw the collapse of Lehman Brothers and the unstitching of the international financial system. Who foresaw in late 2010 the flood tide of desire to open up that would spread throughout the Arab world? Who can honestly pontificate about future stability in the Balkans, the perpetuity of the European Union, upheavals from water shortages, fuel, food and commodity supplies, climate change – to spotlight just some of the challenges faced by our planet in the twenty-first century? Yet that is the planet we are bequeathing to our children and grandchildren to whom this book is dedicated.

Could our grandchildren repeat our adventure, and would they want to? Probably not; why should they? Perhaps the modern version of our journey is to spend a gap year backpacking round the globe. A hundred years before, it would have been the Grand Tour of the differently privileged. Our grandchildren, with all the extraordinary instruments of information at their disposal, will do other things. What matters is that they have curiosity.

KOMBI Z1235

In Memoriam of a Faithful Chariot

Kombi Z1235 had a short but eventful life – certainly better than carting vegetables around grocery stores, builders' materials or school kids anywhere from Bremen to Barcelona as so many of her lowly sisters did. Her other (Expedition) sister had it easier. Like many true adventurers and frontiersmen Z1235 lived to the full. She saw several continents, had several engines, she exasperated mechanics – not because of the Kombi's fault but because of what she had to put up with from roads and weather and, above all, from people like her drivers.

Rumour has it that she met her end somewhere off London's North Circular Road – trying to navigate back to Cambridge – home of the churlish masters – rather than her natural Valhalla of VW Wolfsburg. Her heart was a mere 1,200 ccs – it had put up with much.

She was a great lady.

APPENDIX

Distances Travelled by Kombis Between Major Cities

Kombi Z1060

Cambridge to Moscow	1,800 miles
Moscow to Istanbul	1,700 miles
Istanbul to Teheran	1,700 miles
Teheran to Haifa	1,250 miles
Haifa to London	2,500 miles
Total	**8,950 miles**

Kombi Z1235

Cambridge to Moscow	1,800 miles
Moscow to Istanbul via Tbilisi	2,500 miles
Teheran to Isfahan and return	850 miles
Teheran to Kabul	1,250 miles
Kabul to Kathmandu	1,600 miles
Kathmandu to Bombay	2,000 miles
Bombay to Mombasa	3,100 miles
Mombasa to Addis Ababa	2,200 miles
Addis Ababa to Port Said	2,250 miles
Port Said to Cambridge	2,800 miles
Total	**20,350 miles**

Note: these figures include sea journeys with the Kombis, but exclude local journeys made in each country. If one included air flights and train journeys, the total distance covered by Mehmed, Nigel and Tony was about 28,000 miles.

INDEX

Adam's Peak   201

Addis Ababa   236, 239

Adelsheim, Baron Ernst von   xxiv, 6

Afghanistan   118–20, 132, 133–4, 158–9

Aga Khan   214

Agra   182

Akkoyunlu, Colonel   127

Alam, Amir Hosein Khozeime   70

Alami, Musa al   89

Al Azhar University   248

Albania   42–3

Alexandria   249

Ali, Professor Mohammed   132

Amritsar   176

Anatolia   52–5

Ankara   52, 97

Arnold-Lloyd, Professor W.   xxv

Arusha   217

Aswan High Dam   243, 246

Azerbaijan, Iranian   75

Azerbaijan, SSR   63

Ba'ath Party   86

Babur Shah, Gardens of   129

Baghdad   83, 86

Baku   63–4

Balkh   152

Bamiyan   139–40

Banda, Dr Hastings   xix–xx

Band-i-Amir, lakes   141

Belgrade   41

Benares (Varanasi)   186

Benler, Ambassador Talat   127, 133, 158

Birdwood, Lord   xxiv

Birgi, Muharrem Nuri   xxiv

black market   80

Blake, George   2

Brydon, Dr William   158

Bucharest   37

Bulgaria   37

bushkazi   116, 129, 152

Cairo   247

Caroe, Sir Olaf   166

caviar   97, 133

Ceylon (Sri Lanka)   200–10, 261

Chandigarh   179–81

Chandra, Dr Sorath   204

Colombo   200, 203

(Le) Corbusier, Charles-Edouard   179

Coşkun, Lütfi   127

Crawley, Aidan   xxv

Croatia   66, 261

Cry the Beloved Country   182

currency (and smuggling)   11, 35, 65, 123

Cyprus   25–5

Dar-es-Salaam   216

Daud Khan, Premier Mohammed   134

Dawn   175

Delhi   181

Demirer, Arif   xxiii, 51, 82, 215

Denktaş, Rauf   251

Dilla   229
Direkoglu, Fikri   251
Dupree, Dr   132
Durand Line   134, 164
Dürdü, Mehmed   103

East African Community   223, 261
Eastern Approaches   128
education   167, 168–9, 195, 221–3
    Afghanistan   131–2, 135, 152
    Ceylon (Sri Lanka)   203–4, 207–8
    comparative study   xviii, xxii–xxiii
    Cyprus   251–3, 260
    Ethiopia   238–9,
    Iran   81, 105–6
    Jordan   89
    Kenya   220
    Nepal   196–7
    Soviet Union   21–5
    Swat   171
    Tanganyika (Tanzania)   216–17
    Turkey   52
Egypt   244–50
Enosis   251
EOKA   253
Erzurum   58
Ethiopia   229–32, 239–40
Ethiopian armed forces   240
European Common Market   254
European Community (EU)   261–2
European Community Monitoring
    Mission (ECMM)   41

Falakser (Mount)   174
Fatehpur Sikri   183
Fazalullah, Maulana   175

Gailani, Lamia   83
Galle   204–6
Georgia   46

Georgian Military Highway   46
Gezira   240
gilded youth (of Moscow)   25
Golden Temple, Amritsar   176
Golestan   71
Gorbachev, Mikhail   66
Gromov, General Boris   158

Haile Selassi, Emperor   237
Haile Selassi University   238
Hamilton, Colonel   xxv
Hannay, David   128, 131
Hebrew University   92
Herat   118–19
Hikmet, Nazım   26
Hindu, The   209
Hindu Kush   137–8
Histadruth   92, 94

icons   25
India   210
Intourist   xxvii, 19, 27, 30, 46–7, 62,
    65
Iran   60, 70, 82, 102
Iranpour, Mr   102
Iraq   85–6
Isfahan   79–80
Israel   92–7
Istalif   137–8
Istanbul   38–9, 51–2

Jahanzeb College   168–9
Jalalabad   160
Jayasuriya, Professor   203
Jerusalem   90
Jordan   88, 261
Julfa   65–6

Kabaka (of Buganda)   219
Kabul   127–42

Kamal, Daud   166
Kampala   219–20
Kandahar   121–2
Kandy   201–2
Kardesh, Dr   130, 143
Kassa, the Dejazmatch   xxv, 236
Kassem, General   86
Kathmandu   188–90, 197
Kenya   221–3, 261
Khan, Abdul Ghaffar   166
Khan, Bahadur   162
Khan, Ghani   166
Khan, Mahmood   172
Khartoum   241
Khyber Pass   158, 165
Kibaki, Mwai   221
Kiev   31
Kilimanjaro (Mount)   217
Kiryat Gat (*Kibbutz*)   94
Kizil Kala   145, 147–8
Kombi   vii–viii, xvi, , xxiv, xxvi, 11, 19,
    50, 55, 67–9, 70, 80, 99, 109, 136, 168,
    186, 215, 229, 230, 235–6, 255, 264
Komsomol   19, 22
Kučan, President Milan   261
Kuchis   137, 159–60
Küçük, Dr Fazıl   251
Kunduz   143

Liel, Alon   97
Lumumba (Patrice) University   24–5
Luxor   244

MacLean, Sir Fitzroy   xxv, 128
Mclean, Colonel   128
Madras   199, 209
Makarios, Archbishop   253–4
Makerere College   219–20
Malakand   175
Malali Girls School   132

Mallaby, Christopher   17
Mamluks   249
Marghazar   171
Marsabit National Park   224
Mazar-i-Sharif   149
Mega   228
Mengistu Haile Mariam   240
Meshed   116
Mingora   168
Mombasa   214
Moscow   13–24, 30
Moscow University   20
Mosalla of Gandar Shah   121
Mossadegh, Mohammad   81

Nadir Shah's mausoleum   129
Nairobi   221
Naivasha   217
Najat German Lycée (Kabul)   131
naswar (narcotic)   126, 147
National Service   xxii
Nejjari, Mr   108–9
Nepal   188–205
Nesia, Mr   204
Newars   192
Ngorongoro   216
Nicosia   252
Nile   244–5
North from Kabul   143
Norwegian missionaries   228, 229–30

oba   104
Opersdorff, Mathias   125
Osman, John   262
Ostend   xxviii, 3–4
Oxus (Amu Darya)   143–4
Ozymandias   72

Pahlavi Foundation   70
Pakistan   164

Party Congress (22nd Soviet)   17, 136–7
Pashtun (Pathan)   134, 164
Pashtunistan   164
The Pathans   166
Paton, Alan   182
Penn, Colonel   xxi
Peradeniya (University of Ceylon)
    203–4
Persepolis   72–4
Peshawar   164–7
photography   34, 47, 63, 83
Pir Baba   168–9
prospectus (Expedition)   xxiv
Pul-i-Khumri   153–4
Punjab   179–80

Qissa Khwani ('story-tellers") Bazaar
    167
Qom   75–6

Rana, Field-Marshall Kaiser   188
Red Lion and Sun (Iranian)   70, 76, 79
religion   133, 182, 189, 213, 176–8
Reza Shah   106
Roberts, Ambassador Sir Frank   17
Romania   35–6
Royal Navy   xxii–xxiii
Russia   11, 22, 25, 28–30, 31–2, 65, 262
Russian aid   118, 135, 151, 157

Sa'di and Hafez (tombs)   72
Saidu-Sharif   168
Serendip   199
Shah, Mohammed Reza   82
Shehr-i-Nau   129
Shemiran   81
Shi'a Islam   214
Shiraz   72
Shomali, Murad   103
Sikhism   176–8

Skopje   42
Sochi   46
Soviet Union   10–11, 16, 22, 53
S.S. Achilleus   212
St Catharine's College   xxi
Stegall, Ron   137
Sudan   241
supplies and equipment   xxiii, xxviii,
    3–4, 9
Swat   168–72

Tabriz   61, 67
Taj Mahal   102–3
Tanganyika (Tanzania)   216, 261
Tashkent   62–3
Tbilisi   4–6, 65
Technion   96
Teheran   69–70, 81
Teheran University   71, 81–2
Tekle, Afewerk   237–8
Thurston College   207
Tibetan refugees   194–5
Tomach   105
Trevelyan, Sir Humphrey   86
Turkestan   154–7
Türkeş, Colonel Alparslan   181
Turkey   52–5, 261
Turkmen Sahra   102–10

Uganda   219, 261
US aid   122, 124, 134, 157, 195
Utrot   175

Vladimir (student friend)   34–5
VW (Volkswagen)   xxii, xxiv, xxvi,
    214, 255

Wali of Swat   171
water (Nile resources)   244
Weizmann Institute   92

Western aid   130, 134
Wilson, Andrew   143
Woldemariam, Wing Commander Abera
    235
World Youth Forum, Moscow   27
Wynne, Ed; High Commissioner   253

Yala (Ruhunu) National Park   206–7
Yirga Chefe   236
Yugoslavia   40–5, 261

Zagreb   40–1
Zanzibar   216
Zollnummer   xxvi, 133, 255
Zorlu, Fatin Rüştü   82, 181
Zulu, Father   182